LOVE AND EMPIRE

NATION OF NEWCOMERS:

IMMIGRANT HISTORY AS AMERICAN HISTORY

General Editors: Matthew Jacobson and Werner Sollors

Love and Empire

Cybermarriage and Citizenship across the Americas

Felicity Amaya Schaeffer

NEW YORK UNIVERSITY PRESS
New York and London

NEW YORK UNIVERSITY PRESS
New York and London
www.nyupress.org

References to Internet websites (URLs) were accurate at the time of writing.
Neither the author nor New York University Press is responsible for URLs that
may have expired or changed since the manuscript was prepared.

LIBRARY OF CONGRESS CATALOGING-IN-PUBLICATION DATA
Schaeffer, Felicity Amaya.
Love and empire : cybermarriage and citizenship across the Americas / Felicity Amaya
Schaeffer.
p. cm. — (Nation of newcomers)
ISBN 978-0-8147-8598-0 (cl : alk. paper)
ISBN 978-0-8147-5947-9 (pb : alk. paper)
ISBN 978-0-8147-2492-7 (ebook)
ISBN 978-0-8147-7049-8 (ebook)
1. Intermarriage—America. 2. Online dating—America. 3. Citizenship—America. I. Title.
HQ1031.S277 2012
306.84'5097—dc23   2012024881

New York University Press books are printed on acid-free paper,
and their binding materials are chosen for strength and durability.
We strive to use environmentally responsible suppliers and materials
to the greatest extent possible in publishing our books.

Manufactured in the United States of America

c 10 9 8 7 6 5 4 3 2 1
p 10 9 8 7 6 5 4 3 2 1

CONTENTS

ACKNOWLEDGMENTS

When I first encountered these international marriage broker websites on-line, I had no idea how entangled my life would become in the lives of so many people. I want to first thank all the women from Guadalajara, Mexico, and Cali, Colombia, as well as the men from the United States who shared their hopes and dreams with me in cyberspace, at the Vacation Romance Tours, in restaurants, and in their homes. And to the owners of the agencies, thank you for sharing your vision, welcoming me to attend the tours in Mexico and Colombia, and opening your doors to me at your agencies in Mexico.

The fleshing out of this project happened a long time ago, when I was a graduate student at the University of Minnesota in the American Studies Department. A warm thanks to Jennifer L. Pierce for always inspiring new ways of seeing and thinking. And to Catherine Ceniza Choy, whose book opened the door for many of us to imagine new kinds of academic inquiry. I thank the unconventional thinkers of the "Piercing Insights" group—Hoku Aikau, Karla Erickson, Amy Tyson, and Sara Dorow—and others who gave feedback during this early period of fleshing out my ideas: David W. Noble, David Roediger, Edén Torres, Amy Kaminsky, and Richa Nagar. I am infinitely grateful for the funding and community provided by the Interdisciplinary Center for the Study of Global Change (ICGC). Through this fellowship, I lived in Guadalajara, Mexico, for six months to attend the tours and conduct interviews. And of course, I could not have survived graduate school without the friendship, intellectual support, and distractions provided by many colleagues.

Support for the timely closure of my dissertation was possible because of the visionary leadership of Inés Hernández-Avila and a generous fellowship from the Chicana/Latina Research Center at the University of California, Davis. Without this fellowship I would not have met my *gran colega* and dear friend Miroslava Chávez-García, whose insight and humor allowed me to envision an academic path alongside her. A warm thanks to Carolyn de la Peña for her luminous editing support and belief in me, as well as to Sergio de la Mora and Lorena Oropeza for their friendship.

The continued support for this book renewed my inspiration to turn the dissertation into a book. For this, I am deeply indebted to the UC President's Postdoctoral Fellowship program for providing me the financial support to write among a stellar community of scholars who have sustained me intellectually and personally. With this fellowship, housed by the Latin American and Latino Studies Department at the University of California, Santa Cruz, I was able to conduct new field research in Colombia and to reframe the manuscript. My sincerest thanks to Rosa-Linda Fregoso for being such an enchanting presence in my life and for her fierce mentorship. Rosa-Linda's intellectual guidance and friendship grounded me and reminded me of the humor and passion for change that guide our academic endeavors. My colleagues at UC Santa Cruz deserve extra mention. I have shared ideas and writing with an inspiring and supportive group of *colegas*: Patricia Zavella, Aida Hurtado, Olga Nájera-Ramírez, Beth Haas, Catherine Ramírez, Gabriela Arredondo, Jennifer González, Norma Klahn, Marcia Ochoa, and Cecilia Rivas. I am deeply endeared to some of the most stimulating and provocative colleagues, in particular Anjali Arrondekar, Gina Dent, and Neda Atanasaski: to Anjali for her tireless reading and engagement with the manuscript and to Neda for being the only one to read my entire manuscript (!) and pushing me on when I hit a wall. Thanks to Cat for your friendship and savvy in charting the paths ahead of me and to Marcia for those long nights of watching *Sin tetas no hay paraíso*.

A special thanks to all the *mujeres* I think and write alongside, and who make this work worthwhile: Lucy Mae San Pablo Burns, Dolores Inés

Casillas, Deb Vargas, Amalia Cabezas, Deb Paredes, Maylei Blackwell, Anne M. Martínez, and Sandy Soto. A special thanks to Rhacel Parreñas for her mentorship and spirited conversations. There are so many who have generously supported my work: Eileen Borris, George Lipsitz, Radha S. Hegde, Eithne Luibhéid, Beth Haas, Josie Saldaña-Portillo, Nancy Raquel Mirabal, Chela Sandoval, and Sandra Alvarez for her early help editing the manuscript.

I received invaluable support as I was finishing this book from the Ford Foundation for Diversity Fellowship and various grants from UC Santa Cruz, including faculty grants from the Chicana/o Latina/o Research Center, an Institute for Humanities Research (IHR) faculty grant, and the generous support form the Committee of Research. Thanks to the Transnational Popular Cultures Cluster, now the Bodies, Borders, and Violence Cluster. And a special thanks to the *mujeres* of MALCS, whose political vision and community have shaped this book.

Thanks to the editors from NYU Press who believed in the project, Eric Zinner and Ciara McLaughlin, as well as the series editors, Matthew Frye Jacobson and Werner Sollors. Thank you Anitra Gonzales for your sharp editing, and my warmest thanks to the anonymous readers who so generously dedicated great insight and feedback that helped me stretch and refine my ideas in the book.

And lastly, I could absolutely not have sustained such a long project without the support of Eric Grabiel. Even during a time when everything has fallen apart, I have not forgotten the ways you tried to hold things together to make space for me to write this book. Thanks to Amaya and Diego for reminding me to slow down and enjoy every moment. To my parents, Henry and Christina Schaeffer, and my spirited brother, for their unwavering love, faith, and support throughout my life in ways too numerous to enumerate. And finally my heartfelt thanks to Susie and Pablo Grabiel for their tireless energy, love, and guidance during the ups and downs of this journey.

* * *

Significantly revised sections of this book, including part of chapter 3, appear in my article "Planet-Love.com: Cyberbrides in the Americas and the Transnational Routes of U.S. Masculinity," in *Signs: Journal of Women in Culture and Society*. An early version of chapter 1 can be found in my article "Cyberbrides and Global Imaginaries: Mexican Women's Turn from the National to the Foreign," in the *Space and Culture Journal*, which was republished in

Women and Migration in the U.S.-Mexico Borderlands: A Reader. I also sketch out the broader contours of this book in dialogue with feminist debates on technology in "Flexible Technologies of Subjectivity and Mobility across the Americas," *American Quarterly*, special issue, "Rewiring the 'Nation': The Place of Technology in American Studies."

Introduction

Intimate Investments

Latinas are famous for their natural beauty, warm personality and family loyalty. Only in Latin America can you find a woman who is more tolerant, understanding, faithful, and true to the idea that marriages are forever.
—international marriage broker web page

Without a doubt, passion is our citizens best raw material.
—Colombian Tourism Ministry ad campaign, "Colombia Is Passion"

[Cosmetic] surgery is a way to invest in myself, invest in my future.
—Colombian participant at the Vacation Romance Tour

Latin America's association with abundant love and sexual passion continues to structure gendered opportunities, mobility, and citizenship. Over 200 international marriage broker (IMB) websites, advertising romance and marriage between U.S. men and Latin American women, lure in male viewers with pictures of young women in skimpy swimsuits, bracketed by luscious tropical settings, casting salacious glances at the Internet viewer. Women's bodies have long figured as the seductive force of regional and national trade, enticing investors and travelers from colonial times to current tourism brochures and, more recently, Internet marriage websites. In particular, the global marketing of women on cybermarriage websites borrows from Latin American tourism and investment campaigns, especially the most recent branding of one country's best resources, titled "Colombia Is Passion." With the goal of uplifting its global image, Colombia exports a respectable middle-class image of the nation's gendered labor force through a video campaign depicting giddy shots of light-skinned married couples, alluring beauty queens, a sharply dressed woman speaking into a company headset, and the passionate swing of pop singer Shakira's hips around the world. The Colombian state's marketing of its citizens' passion to court foreign commerce naturalizes heterosexual romantic exchanges, rendering patriotic the turn to foreign marriage as a viable route to happiness, while also opening up new avenues for women to invest in themselves and their futures. In fact, various women I met at a Vacation Romance Tour in Cali, Colombia, explained their desire to upgrade and beautify their bodies through cosmetic surgery. These images and acts of (passionate) conversion transform the body and nation into a moral but also productive surface, even as the body becomes a pliable tool for women to remake themselves; a natural resource that with the proper capitalist investment will yield the possibility of foreign marriage, mobility, and/or better opportunities in their everyday lives.

My inquiry into the cybermarriage industry underscores the deepening of free market capitalism into intimate desires. For example, participants' descriptions of love and marriage are told through the language of reciprocal exchange, investment, and risk. The commercialization of intimacy here, I argue, does not support the widespread association of this industry with sex trafficking. In fact, I aim to dislocate government scrutiny of foreign marriage and instead to elucidate the very practices of the state that espouse normative understandings of love and marriage as a technique of governing foreign marriage migration. Passion binds citizens to moral and gendered opportunities in Latin America, while romantic love and marriage ensures migrants mobility and citizenship in the United States. In the first chapter, I examine the United States' regulation of marriage laws to argue that marriage serves state interests in scrutinizing and adjudicating proper practices of intimacy and love in relations between citizens and noncitizens. It is love's democratic appeal that immigration laws and policies rely on to differentiate whether foreign marriages are chosen based on free choice or coercion and subsequently whether they are bona fide or fraudulent. My critical perspective of the cybermarriage industry (as a market that obliges women to particular kinds of sexual and intimate arrangements) also sees marriage as one that may transport participants into new lives. While there are constraints on women's mobility, the ties that tether bodies and emotions to particular intimacies and forms of governance should not always be thought of as conditions of force or enslavement but also as demarcations of what some women express as the desire for more equitable and enduring relationships characterized by mutual obligations between husband and wife. Thus, I contend that U.S. and Latin American states play a critical role—via the global governance of populations and trade—in shaping how foreign marriage migrants express intimacy and move across borders as middle-class, modern citizens versus undocumented (or exploited) subjects. These constraints do not, how-ever, foreclose other desires for foreign marriage, such as the hope for more authentic intimacies and upward mobility. In sum, *Love and Empire* looks at how the squeeze of modern life directs intimacy into the virtual marketplace, rearranging notions of freedom and obligation across national borders.

Cybermarriage industries took root in Mexico and Colombia, as in Russia and Asia, in the mid to late 1990s, during a time of considerable global economic and social transformations.[1] The economic crisis in Mexico and other Latin American countries in the late 1980s, leading to the liberalization of "free trade" with the passage of NAFTA in Mexico in 1994 and increased trade between the United States and Colombia,[2] further entrenched these nations' dependency on foreign loans, businesses, and tourism as the route to solve their economic woes. Furthermore, the opening of Latin America to foreign trade and commerce occurred at the time when the United States passed draconian legislation, erecting walls and entrenching border person-nel and surveillance cameras to shut down migrant crossings at the busiest sites of entry into the United States.[3] U.S. cybermarriage industries launched their web encounters in Latin America starting in 1996, when Internet technologies transformed communication, information sharing, and inti-macy across otherwise difficult-to-cross borders. Of course, Internet-based romances are not entirely new. Newspaper ads assisted elite Mexican women in their pursuit of U.S. businessmen and diplomats living in Mexico City since at least the late 1930s and early '40s, when President Roosevelt fostered good feelings, tourism, and business relations between the United States and Latin America through a series of cultural exchanges meant to promote his "Good Neighbor Policy." Even as the Internet now stretches its reach to a more diverse clientele and mediates contact through a variety of interactive menus, Internet marriage brokers (IMBs) continue to market international goodwill across borders through the liberal logic of free trade and equitable exchange, redirecting personal strategies from the state to the marketplace, from the national to the foreign. These tactics of self-governance and par-ticipants' expression of themselves as free-market actors warrant a critical inquiry of the neoliberal contours guiding these virtual intimacies. Accom-panying Latin American countries' swing to (rogue) capitalism and the feminization of labor, many women, from the lower and middle classes, find themselves responsible for the financial support of their families when tradi-tional labor structures have fallen apart. Given the charge of women as head of their household during a time of great economic decline, an astounding number migrate into feminized labor markets—as service workers, *maquila* workers, nannies, and domestics—in urban centers in Latin America, the

United States, and around the world. Feminist accounts of these changes have forcefully challenged traditional understandings of migration, family, and the global economy, but the desires and experiences of aspiring and/ or middle-class women who turn to foreign marriage, and the state's governance of intimacy more broadly, have been understudied.[4]

Although the process and participants have changed since the pre-Internet era of "mail-order bride" industries developed in Asia and Russia in the 1980s, stereotypes of exploitation in the cybermarriage industry have endured. During one chat-room debate, U.S. men married to Latin American women swapped stories detailing the difficulty of overcoming the stigma of foreign marriage among friends and family. Especially poignant was one anonymous Latin American woman's response: "I have stopped speaking to some American friends who have implied that the only reason AM [American men] date latinas or any foreign woman is because they can control us. As though there is no other reason an AM would want us. . . . AM usually make more solid, less controlling, modern husbands" (Latin-Women-List, June 6, 2002). Her description of U.S. men as "modern husbands" complicates the popular perception that international cybermarriages are unilaterally exploitative, part of the trafficking-of-women trade, and entrenched in power relations between the victimizer and the victim. Equating foreign marriage with abuse negates the value and positive contributions of Latinas, while obscuring from view women's own interest in U.S. men. The chat-room post just quoted is critical of the emphasis on exploitation or "control," which reduces women to malleable pawns of male desire (e.g., prostitutes), thereby dismissing Latin American women's status as modern subjects with their own hopes and desires. Yet what exactly did she mean by a "modern husband"? Do women's aspirations for a modern relationship contradict men's desires, advertised on hundreds of marriage websites, for a more traditional and family-oriented Latin American woman, rather than a U.S. (feminist) woman?

For more than ten years, I conducted a virtual ethnography that traces the *mutual* desires of Latin American women and U.S. men who turn to the foreign cybermarriage industry. To do this, I followed the intimate iterations of foreign marriage in chat rooms and interviewed participants who attended the Vacation Romance Tours in Guadalajara, Mexico, and Cali, Colombia. I call my ethnography "virtual" not only to refer to my use of the Internet to conduct research and communicate but also to foreground my analytic lens for understanding how mediated fantasies assist in the proliferation of the global political economy of desire and mobility in cybermarriage. Virtual imaginaries, then, encompass the spectrum of past and present fantasies that penetrate men's and women's everyday lives through technologies of foreign exchange produced via Internet and face-to-face exchanges, as well as media images, especially when language difficulties stunt the ease of verbal communication. The sometimes colliding fantasies between women seeking modern husbands and the men interested in more traditional-minded women flared up at the face-to-face encounters at the Romance Tours. In 2001, I attended my first Guadalajara Vacation Romance Tour, located in an upscale tourist zone.[5] After several hours, the men were prompted to line up on stage and introduce themselves to the more than two hundred women clapping in encouragement. The most enthusiastic applause from women followed the Anglo-American men with sincere demeanors, those who made some attempt to speak Spanish, and especially those who were professionals such as doctors, lawyers, or pilots. The mood shifted, however, when a Latino from Texas in his late forties took the microphone.[6] George, after describing his profession, announced proudly, in broken Spanish, that he was looking for a woman who would make handmade tortillas.[7] The festive atmosphere suddenly went cold as women's claps and cheers froze into waves of silence, erupting into a few scattered boos.

The tortilla comment and ensuing silence signal a rupture of desired gender roles that align Latin American women with tradition and domesticity and U.S. men with modern perspectives. These gendered expectations are complicated further as Mexican women's transnational alliances with U.S. men result in their projection of difference and excessive tradition onto local Latin American masculinity and governance (see chapter 2). Despite cracks in this eroticized imaginary at the tours, Latin America and its women are staunchly upheld as an erotic alternative to the crumbling of family traditions in the United States, whereas for these women, the United States and its men continue to hold the potential for upward mobility and a just legal system. For many middle-class, professional women from Guadalajara, this incident confirmed their association of white, corporate manhood with modern intimacy, or what some see as more equitable or even complementary gender roles. Various women I spoke with from Guadalajara and Cali explained their desire for a professionally minded suitor, one who was *más detallista*, or more thoughtful and considerate than local Latin men. The emphasis on modernity and a professional husband attendant to women's needs and desires raises questions about how corporate modernity and intimacy intersect at the height of an era of global capitalism. What do these costly and highly mediated courtship rituals say about gender, nation, love, and intimacy in the twenty-first century? The emergence of intimate markets during a time when goods move more freely than people conveys not only the importance of women's eroticized bodies in their access to global circuits of trade. At the same time, the channeling of erotic sentiments—love and passion—into marriage and U.S. citizenship stimulate feelings of patriotic nationalism as love translates modern values of choice and equality in contrast to marital contracts procured out of necessity, economic exchange, or coercion.

This book is as much about understanding the desires that fuel foreign intimacies, marriage, and middle-class migration as it is about how local and global discourses and technologies shape transnationally directed desires. *Love and Empire* places the eroticized body and sentiments of love at the center of subjectivity, mobility, citizenship, and future possibilities, especially during a time when new technologies, state economic strategies, and media imaginaries promise virtual transcendence, to shuttle people into exciting futures that seem untenable within their local contexts. As my research in Guadalajara, Cali, and on-line uncovered, for some women and men, the Internet and the marketplace foster new connections between the interiority of feelings and one's relation to the body, especially the idea that national borders, and even the body, are virtual and thus pliable terrains. To imagine oneself as pliable counters the various regimes of femininity enforced and stabilized by familial codes of female respectability, dominant definitions of beauty and attractiveness, feminized labor regimes, state immigration policies, academic scholarship and activism, popular media representations, and international marriage broker websites. Thus, throughout the book, I trace the tension between the forces of globalization, and especially the neoliberal marketplace—such as the idea that everyone has equal access to mobility— as they grate against regimes of governmentality. I analyze the political economy of desire in relation to technological and neoliberal discourses, state governance, and media images that disseminate romantic representations of the good life.[8] When one privileges an understanding of the global through virtual intimacies, the foreign and the nation are experienced as prosthetics that extend the body in ways and places that confound the lines between here and there, the virtual and the real, the self and the other, and the traditional and modern.

Through virtual romance, participants find confirmation in a sense of belonging that unmoors them from identities and opportunities tied to geographic, racial, social, and cultural locations. The aspiration to upward mobility depends on and reconfigures three technologies for transcending one's subjectivity: sentiments of love, virtuality, and entrepreneurialism. Each of these facets of self-making are predicated on the rewiring of mobility and citizenship in a global era. *Romantic love* invokes the religious and secular in its promise to transcend the specificity and locality of bodies and borders, including social, legal, and economic barriers, and to dissolve differences into universal, or even divine, notions of the human. *The virtual terrain of the Internet* similarly promises utopian futures in which bodies are pliable (infinitely changeable and upwardly mobile) while rendering national borders and geographies meaningless. And lastly, neoliberal policies and *entrepreneurialism* promise to accelerate nations and individuals into the future of global capital and American ingenuity, into class strata otherwise unattainable.

Intimate contact with the foreign relies on the myth of remaking the self and national body, of purification, rejuvenation, and new beginnings. Latin American women describe their search for intimacy and marriage with foreign men on-line as a critical avenue for self-realization, of positioning oneself as modern and emotionally human and thus as deserving of love and devotion by men who travel a great distance. Not coincidentally, U.S. immigration laws force couples to demonstrate "true" love as an indicator of their innocence, or unselfish distinction from the potential economic benefits of immigration and citizenship. Furthermore, as Latin American countries restructure their economies toward "capitalist democracies," states must "clean up" the image of the nation. More specifically, the Colombian state projects itself as productive—through images of enterprising workers alongside fertile raw materials—by wiping out dissenting, or merely poor, populations; displacing people from their farms, trade, and land; and projecting an alluring image of the nation as a pure, innocent, and eroticized woman. In a similar vein, some Colombian women turn to cosmetic surgery to project their enterprising spirit, while rendering invisible the compulsory nature of femininity and beauty permeating their everyday lives.

These forms of emotional innocence are central to the forging of what I call *pliable citizenship*, or the grounded ways Latinas become part of the most intimate structures of the family, the nation-state, and the global economy. Women's placement within transnational labor markets and entrance into U.S. citizenship rely on their role as raw materials and pliable subjects that can be remade by development and molded into U.S. citizens. Their perceived malleability, youth, and innocence assures they will not be a threat to the U.S. family or nation and that their eroticized sexuality will be productive rather than destructive of the moral boundaries of the nation. Gendered emotions are naturalized into the fibers of the body as the productive sphere of the market meets the reproductive capacities of women's association with domesticity and family. Women's mobilization of passion situates the Latin American nation in both the secular time of production, futurity, and profit and the sacred time of reproduction and eternal rejuvenation. Thus, rather than construe women's erotic placement in the Western imaginary as simply the exploitation of gendered labor traded for the economic perks of marriage migration, I use the term *pliable citizenship* to underscore the ways women's virtual remakings of their bodies and affective trajectories augment their local value but also reinforce how states authorize moral migration and national inclusion, while justifying the surveillance and exclusion of illicit and dangerous bodies. By moral migration, I refer to the state's adjudicating of migrant inclusion based on an individual's positive contributions to the economic and ideological order of the nation. Codes of morality here rely on proof of love as the criterion for individual (or exceptional) accounts of free choice versus the masses of migrants who are, in contrast, encumbered by economic necessity and thus a lack of freedom.[9] There are intersecting dynamics at play between my conception of pliable citizenship and Aihwa Ong's use of "flexible citizenship," a term that highlights the dispersed connections that elite Chinese actors have to multiple passports and national belonging. For these actors, argues Ong (1999), national citizenship is less important for the feelings attached to a place and its forms of governance than for the desire to flexibly take advantage of uneven currencies and privileges offered by each nation. In the case of foreign intimacies, pliability stresses strategies of advancement and personal fulfillment whereby some women resculpt their bodies to emphasize emotions and practices that align them with entrepreneurial strategies, as well as with global and national citizenship. For many, their body is a surface that translates femininity and eroticized beauty when language differences compromise verbal communication, but it is also a raw material that women themselves cultivate as they adapt to changing global economic conditions and access to rights.

In addition, Elizabeth Povinelli's approach to the relational binds between carnality and corporality clarify my approach to the entanglements of flesh and discourse, or the embodied consequences that contour how people are imagined.[10] Rather than argue that power structures how men and women act, or presume a cause-and-effect relation between the discursive and material expressions and enactments of the body, I am similarly interested in their interconnectedness, how they "mutually oblige."[11] By examining the language used by participants in their desires for foreign marriage, this book seeks to understand how ideologies of American democracy, marketplace freedoms, and benevolent law are reinforced, repurposed, and sometimes broken down in the most intimate expressions governing desire. I am interested here in how the distribution of opportunities obligate, but does not fully contain, certain forms of embodiment and intimacy for Latin American women.

My focus on intimacy—heterosexual love, sexuality, and desire—is an analytic, drawn from women's accounts, to demarcate proximity or closeness to foreign nationalism, the human, and citizenship. When viewed from women's perspectives, foreign marriage translates as protest, or the refusal to abide by traditional gender roles and opportunities at home. Traditional roles—enforced by a middle-class structure of respectability, Catholicism, and a national economic strategy reliant on (devalued) feminized labor—feel out of touch but also restrict women's ability to fulfill everyday hopes and dreams. In contrast, foreign intimacy offers a coded political language for privileging marketplace values of equality, democracy, and an entrepreneurial spirit as well as entrance into global dramas of belonging. Women's turn away from Catholicism to Protestantism reflects the aspirational pull of the American dream in satisfying women's longing for hard work, rather than faith, to materialize goals and dreams. In this context, sentiments of love, then, necessitate a more expansive understanding of the political in relation to forms of belonging and citizenship. Ideologies of heterosexual love for migrant women enforce their compliance to traditional gender roles, as love translates patriotism but also offers a coded language to differentiate women's robust humanity and thus distance from a U.S. culture that some characterize through the symbolic of alienation. The last chapter of the book explores women's declarations of love to claim patriotic inclusion, while others come to understand the heavy cost of U.S. citizenship in their everyday lives. Women's turn to U.S. marriage through a marketplace that emphasizes their family-oriented tradition (as distinct from U.S. women) does not explain women's feelings of intimate proximity to modern U.S. culture. This shift in perception renders visible new transnational middle- to upper-class alliances and migration patterns across borders.[12]

Throughout the book, I find seemingly innocuous forms of love at the heart of struggles over empire. Women negotiate Western structures of recognition through the state's governance of "bona fide" foreign marriages and moral migration that rely on women's erotic adherence to femininity. At the height of the global economy, women's hyperfeminized bodies communicate pliability and an erotic passion calibrated toward the service of man and country, yet they also provide the inroads to fulfill women's own intimate and economic goals. Given these complex entanglements between private strategies and the state, I am wary of overprivileging women's agency as this may perpetuate neoliberal capitalist notions of individualism and pliable subjectivity.

How, then, do we reconcile women's own desires for a virtual sense of themselves unencumbered by their social location, local opportunities, and their bodies in relation to an industry that markets their value through familiar feminized scripts? How is it that Latin American women enter into marriage commerce as superior wives than U.S. women, even during a time of heightened militarization in Mexico and Colombia and across the U.S.-Mexico border and growing nativist sentiment against Latino/a migrants? Eroticized borders and the violence of state surveillance continue to shape intimacies, even as participants desire to cross, to transcend, and to become someone new.

Heterosexual marriage is a relatively safe avenue for crossing the border unmarked by economic need during a time when many Latino/a migrants are dying in the desert and when women migrants in particular are targets of violence, such as detention, rape, and murder, by state and corporate structures complicit in the devaluing of their bodies and labor.[13] Thus, marriage appeals to (and is compulsory for) women who yearn not only for a more intimate and equitable relationship but also for social respect, the ability to move across borders, and class mobility that is unavailable to nonwealthy and nonheterosexual people of color throughout the Americas. At the same time, the utter dehumanization of women on websites, in state tourism ads, and in the fantasies of some men who traffic images of their bodies as erotic objects of pleasure competes with men's and women's turn to cyber-romance for heightened intimacy, value, and exchange. In sum, sentiments of love express an analytic of feeling difficult to disentangle from the global economy and state governance. Emotions communicate desire and become an exceptional strategy for some women to transcend moral codes of respectability, national boundaries, and state surveillance.

Transnationality across the Américas

This book engages in an analysis of the cybermarriage industry across the United States and two cities in Latin America: Guadalajara, Mexico, and Cali, Colombia. I had not initially intended this book to be comparative. Yet my initial interest in Mexico could not answer why Colombia soon replaced Mexico as one of the most popular Latin American countries for cybermarriage.[14] As I write this introduction, one of the marriage agencies I have followed for over ten years no longer offers Vacation Romance Tours to Mexico. GlobalLatinas recently dropped Mexico, expanded service into more regions of Colombia, and added tours to Peru and Panama.[15] The proximity of Mexico and the excitement of intensified commerce in the late 1990s proved ideal in the beginning of the industry, but interest in Mexico has waned greatly as the surge of corruption and violence, coupled with heightened fears over smuggling and sex trafficking, has hindered the ease and legitimacy of commerce, marriage, and travel. Increased trade relations with Colombia and the remaking of the country as a land of "passion" brought even more beautiful and "untouched" women into the Western imaginary. Equally important, but unremarked on websites, is the political and economic context that contributes to some Colombian women's motivation to leave the country, especially at a time when migration is on the rise for the Colombian middle class as a national solution toward a better life. Similar to U.S. corporate empire, this industry works through its ever-expanding reach into more "untouched" or virgin territories. Both countries' popularity, however, reflects the continued relevance of imperial legacies animating the global circuits that bind Latin America with the United States. Both Mexico and Colombia have been drastically transformed (albeit unevenly) by economic and social crises, histories of migration to the United States, commerce, and trade, including trade policies and tourist markets that shape trajectories for a more prosperous future to be found elsewhere. Perhaps cybermarriage is more feasible today due to the feminization of labor, migration, and the normalization of an entrepreneurial ethos of self-help that makes contact with U.S. business culture and men attractive, rewarding, and desirable. And that both countries figure centrally as threatening sites for drug and human trafficking ensures that the United States plays a significant role in mandating how goods and people (especially women) cross borders, on the basis of moral categories of licit versus illicit, moral versus immoral.[16]

In comparing two regions with such disparate colonial histories and their attendant formations of race, class, and sexuality, a complex story emerges, even as I followed couples through the same U.S. web-based company offering tours to Mexico and Colombia. Women's representation through traditional femininity and/or an erotic imaginary affected where men traveled and how women navigated their relationship to these stereotyped categories. Women from Guadalajara, the majority professional and middle class—known for their *ojos tapatías* (dark, Moorish eyes) and light skin, reflecting colonial contact with the Spanish and French—maneuvered U.S. men's perception of them as mysterious yet familiar and compatible because of their family traditions. On the other hand, mostly working-class women in Cali (who aspired to upward class mobility)—an Afro-Colombian region known for salsa and exotic *mulatas*—flaunted their sexual and entrepreneurial prowess, oftentimes through cosmetic alterations. In both countries, yet through distinct articulations, women emphasized their desires for foreign romance and marriage through a sense of themselves as entrepreneurial and modern. Once again, women turned to U.S. men hoping for a more modern and equitable marriage than those found at home.

Intimacies across great geographic and cultural differences, such as between Latin American women and Anglo cowboys or even Spanish colonizers, remind us that contemporary cybermarriages are not new. The violence and death caused by colonization, war, industrialization, and global capitalism cannot be underestimated. But alongside these brutal contact zones arise unexpected alliances, intimacies, opportunities, and migrations.[17] Colonial encounters and U.S. empire produce violent borders of inequality and categories of difference, but these territories have also been the locations where the exotic "other" excited the Western imagination.[18] In a similar fashion, the theorization of the borderlands in Chicana/o scholarship documents the physical and psychic violence of U.S. empire but also the complicated negotiations with power that enabled the colonized, including women, to challenge Spanish rule and Catholic dictates through shifting alliances with U.S. culture and religion.[19] These transnational intimacies capture the longings of aspiring Latin American women, many who have taken flight from Spanish Catholic dictates of duty and fate as the means for securing their spiritual and economic destiny. Instead, women turn to homegrown informal economies, local strategies that collide with Protestant and American corporate values of ingenuity, flexibility, and inventiveness. Similar to colonial studies that theorize hybrid processes through the lens of syncretism, this book bridges the ways contemporary entrepreneurial erotics merge local Latin American informal economic strategies with the U.S. drive toward global ascendancy.

It is the legacy of these paradigms that inform feminist transnational approaches to cross-border phenomena, extending my analysis from the erotics of borders to the erotics of capital. The eroticization of difference not only relies on territorial borders and power imbalances between nations but follows the discrepant flows of capital. It is perhaps the figurative occupation that cyber-romance gestures to—the psychological, even productive, presence of the United States in the Mexican and Colombian imagination and vice versa, however conflicted and contradictory these sentiments may be.[20] Border conflicts, produced during moments of empire and struggles over land and sovereignty, have been culturally resolved in the United States via representations of intimate affinities between the sexy *señorita* and the benevolent U.S. cowboy, a marriage that legalized U.S. men's ownership of key trade industries and property.[21] Cybermarriages persist in espousing the ideological belief that love can solve personal and global woes and usher in a world order characterized by free trade, choice, and individual freedom.

New corporate cultures and the rapid infusion of capital into Latin America, Russia, and Asia follow a celebratory logic of the inevitability of globalization, new markets, sexual cultures, and desires across global zones. Yet, as I discuss in chapter 3, interviews with U.S. men reveal other outcomes of global capitalism, as some express a sense of alienation and fear of being replaced in the home and workforce. They blame these feelings on intimate rearrangements and, in particular, former U.S. wives who fled the home for a seat in corporate America, rather than seeing their woes as connected to global profit and labor restructuring. It becomes necessary to understand social and cultural processes from a U.S. and Latin American perspective but also, in the context of virtual imaginaries carved at the borders of these fields and territories, to assess the flexibility of meanings and power relations across time and space.

Postrace Multiculturalism and the Virtual Imaginary

Given the heightened security of national borders and state sovereignty, virtual worlds and imaginaries offer a viable medium to transcend the limitation of bodies and borders. These imaginaries may prove fertile engagements with U.S. nationalism, itself a virtual space for generating dreams of a futurity beyond difference, race, pain, and suffering. The rise of the Internet in the early 1990s shuttled information and fantasies of elsewhere into one's everyday life, akin to other advances such as the railroad, ships, the telegraph, the postal service, the newspaper, photography, radio, and television. The spread of the Internet into Latin America accompanied the march of Hollywood and local *telenovelas* offering melodramatic solutions to economic and political problems—where chivalrous Western (or light-skinned local) men promise to transform any downtrodden situation into a glamorous romance. The romance of marriage also appeals to U.S. men, who, in chat rooms, discuss which countries and regions they should travel to in order to find a foreign wife.[22]

Men's perception of difference is not expressed racially but instead through fantasies of global multiculturalism that celebrate individualized difference as a marketable trait that promises to rejuvenate the self and nation. The paradigm of individualism negates the possibility of pointing to structural inequalities informing racial and sexual categories inherited from colonization and U.S. empire. In cyber-studies on race, the rise of the Internet alongside the neoliberal marketplace discursively shapes the idea that identities are flexible and the stability of race, gender, and the body obsolete.[23] Virtuality symbolizes a democratic palimpsest where all is possible for those who connect, offering a tool for the subversive spread of information and the intermixing of bodies across otherwise closed borders.[24] Nevertheless, the idea that everyone has equal access to transcending nation-state borders (or the social consequences of race, class, gender, and sexuality) and to becoming someone new merges dangerously close to neoliberal dreams in which all who connect are promised new beginnings, unfettered mobility, and democracy.[25] It is in the virtual multicultural imaginary that a romantic ethic of individualism and an entrepreneurial, do-it-yourself romantic spirit comes to life. Through virtual romance, participants find confirmation in a sense of belonging that unmoors them from identities and opportunities traditionally tied to geographic, racial, social, and cultural locations.

To analyze global processes through affect foregrounds an individual's craving to become someone special in the face of a culture of insignificance and alienation affecting broader sectors of the population at the margins of modernity and society. To focus one's energies on romance, and especially foreign marriage, is to express one's desire to be noticed and to arrest the attention of another across great distance. Similarly, becoming someone is inextricable from the desire to become valuable in a culture increasingly predicated on visibility. In culture industries *and* the state imaginary, romance and marriage offer respectable forms of female empowerment, placing intimacy and foreign love at the center of global dramas. In addition, desire is an act of becoming, of movement, of enacting oneself in the world through the image of how one is valued on a global stage.[26] While media is a powerful venue for fostering collective desires and possible worlds, the Internet is a unique place where those who have access can play a leading role in these broader social dramas. The Internet fosters what Henrietta Moore calls "fantasies of identity," which are "ideas about the kind of person one would like to be and the sort of person one would like to be seen to be by others."[27] While the colonial contours of Internet fantasies have material consequences, I am also interested in how women and men themselves occupy and destabilize what Lisa Nakamura calls "cybertyped" identities. Despite utopian claims that technologies such as the Internet will usher in a "post-body" era in which the stigma of race, gender, and class no longer matter, race continues to matter, albeit in forms that continually morph and restabilize.[28] The present national narrative of arriving at a postracial moment reflects the ideology of nation building. Individual migrants continue to be lured in with the ideology, "you can craft yourself anew on these shores!" Americanization is itself a virtual fantasy emptied of racial and class strife, a temporal present in which the violence of indigenous conquest and slavery reside outside national borders and in the past. This story of marriage migration complicates where the lines of exploitation reside and how Latin American women who aspire to class mobility negotiate representations of their sexualized bodies in creative and meaningful ways, while also reproducing exceptional paradigms of the successful individual.

These virtual quests are just as much about the magnetic draw of romance with the glamorous life of visibility as they are about the desire to become normal and to live a life full of love, respect, safety, and comfort. Furthermore, while some Latin American women feel devalued by Latin men and a culture they feel takes them for granted, they take pleasure and find fulfillment in being sought after by U.S. men who travel a great distance to meet them. They also see opportunities for a better life for themselves and their families in these international romances. For men and women, being valued from afar confirms a sense of respect that positively shapes their sense of themselves at home and around the world but may also reproduce gendered power differences.

It is not simply women's (or even men's) bodies that are eroticized through desire, but nationality and citizenship itself. I listened to many U.S. men explain how empowering it felt to capture the attention of so many Latin American women (and vice versa), and both expressed a lack of value and general invisibility in their local contexts. Despite the fact that the majority of male participants were Anglo men, Latino and African American men also expressed a sense of displacement from the promise of national inclusion and empowerment, even when they achieved economic success in the United States. Most men experienced themselves as more valuable—via their heightened attractiveness and access to more rights as tourists with greater spending power—during their love quests in Latin America. Ironically, men use the advanced technology of the Internet to mediate their travel abroad in the hopes of finding a more caring, loving, and feminine woman, fantasized as unscathed by the spread of capitalism and modernity.

When Mexican and Colombian women describe *feeling* like an American even before they reach the United States, this says something about the need to reconceptualize the time and space of the foreign and the nation.[29] What it *feels* like to be an American, however, changes once they marry and move to the United States. Affinity with the West (which differs depending on women's class and regional location) follows women's familiarity with U.S. culture, which can include years of schooling in private international education; the consumption of Western products and ways of life (such as watching U.S. films, news, and media programs); work with American corporations; or contact with U.S. tourists, migrants, or family and friends living in the United States. The range of Western intrusions instills deeply held desires for living the American dream. When I was living in Guadalajara, some Mexican comrades and I experienced the collective shock of 9/11, which reminded us how strangely close we felt to a moment that came to affect all of us and our loved ones in unforeseen ways. The transnational reach of Mexican media caters to the majority of Mexican nationals whose daily lives involve entangled relationships and sentiments with the United States.

Other women I interviewed felt more American through their shared values of Protestantism or a culture of meritocracy based on hard work and the idea that one should live one's life according not simply to custom, or through a religious cosmology preset by destiny and the afterlife, but a spiritual orientation tailored to one's individual needs. To feel American, then, is expressed as potential, as a future. U.S. men's chat-room discussions about traveling to Latin America and finding a wife there often included the pleasure of being treated "like a king" outside the United States, a virtual sense of self that may or may not translate when one returns home with a Latin American wife. Men feel that their "natural" role as head of the family, idealized during the 1950s, has changed dramatically, compromising their present moral placement in relation to the law, citizenship, and the national imaginary.[30] Their desire to reclaim this dominant position flies in the face of some women's desire for an equitable relationship, although men in these discussions often qualified their role as head of the family as involving great care, economic support, and attention to their wives. To "feel like a king" and to feel like an American go hand in hand. Perhaps this desire explains why men spend many hours of their day, and in fact years, lurking and/or communicating with other men who share similar romantic desires in on-line chat rooms, whether they marry or remain single. For both Latin American women and U.S. men, feeling like an American is invented, deeply felt, performed, and enacted across virtual and face-to-face contact with others.

Despite the range of experiences with foreign marriage—some end up happy in a long-term marriage; others leave home full of hope only to be disappointed and forced to return; some use the system to attain citizenship; and a few were even killed—foreign cybermarriage fantasies flicker in the minds and hearts of many women as *the* route to happy futures and better lives. Heterosexual love within foreign marriage—as proof of one's capacity for choice, modernity, and the ability to enter into contracts out of emotional attachments rather than economic (or selfish) rationales—translates as the moral place for equitable governance and value, in contrast to women's potential as exploited objects, the most inhuman abuse of a subject disassociated from affect or value.

True Love: A Modern Value

My conception and use of the term *cybermarriage* refuses the genealogy of "mail-order brides" as merely exploited bodies of transit. Given the association of cybermarriage with trafficking, these industries must morally differentiate intimacies procured through the market (i.e., prostitution) from marriage, a domain historically tied to privacy, or authentic love and emotion-based sexuality.[31] Current cybermarriage legislation—provoked by state rumors over trafficking "epidemics," sensational media accounts, and a few feminist activists[32]—demands better protection of women and acute surveillance of a potentially exploitative industry.[33] Similar to the smuggling trade, international marriage brokers (and marriage migrants) are viewed as dangerous because they operate as an agent of migration, brokering the movement of female bodies across national borders and operating within the vast frontier of the Internet, at the margins of state control and scrutiny. State surveillance over foreign intimacies and marriage gains moral traction through the need to "protect" women, rendering invisible the complicity of state immigration policies in mandating foreign marriage commerce for the purposes of migration and citizenship.

My intent in the book, however, is not to prove whether or not cybermarriage is part of the sex-trafficking trade (a goal other scholars have persuasively argued against)[34] but to question why foreign marriage intimacies symbolize such an important barometer of modernity and national inclusion but also a threat to freedom, feminism, and the U.S. state, thereby justifying more state surveillance and regulation. In getting to this question, it is useful to take seriously why many Latin American women view foreign marriages as more equitable, modern, and associated with freedom, while policy and immigration debates, influenced by some feminists concerned with women's exploitation, characterize cybermarriage as a coercive industry that takes advantage of women who lack other choices. Part of the discrepancy between exploitation and choice can be explained through differing definitions and demands required of citizenship as an obligation that must be entered into freely by participants across the United States and Latin America.

Trafficking discourses project such a potent language of exploitation because they demarcate women's "lack of choice" or bondage to patriarchal power in marriage and their forced mobility through a sexual labor contract. Cybermarriage industries, similar to sex trafficking, have attracted the attention of feminist scholars, activists, the media, and policymakers as a key arena for negotiating the lines between freedom and enslavement. Many dredge fears that foreign marriage may serve as a venue for transporting women into enslaved conditions of forced sex in marriage. These debates pivot on differentiating choice from obligation or coercion, resurrecting older feminist concerns about universal gender exploitation and the idea of marriage as a patriarchal institution that exploits women's labor.[35] This return to a preindustrial separation of authentic intimacy from capitalist relations of exchange dovetails with state discourses on trafficking and contradicts the new direction of transnational feminist scholarship attendant to the complexity of structural power and agency across and within national borders, with which this book more closely aligns.[36] The resurgence of U.S. feminist debates prompted me to consider not only how foreign romantic fantasies influence the everyday lives and choices made by U.S. men and Latin American female participants but also how this imaginary continues to inspire state immigration policies as well as some mainstream feminist theories and activism meant to protect women.

The separation of Latin American women from the spread of global capital, entangled in most relationships today via capitalism's squeeze into our everyday lives, also informs U.S. men's fantasies of Latin American women, whom they associate with spirituality, innocence, and tradition. And while these various contingencies cast doubt and suspicion on relationships that traverse national boundaries, U.S. Internet dating practices are normalized, thereby motivating me to ask, what investments in love—as it intersects with race, class, nationality, and gender—are threatened by foreign marriage migration? In turn, what consequences do struggles over foreign marriage migration have on who counts as a patriot, a citizen, and a human? In addition, how do we make sure critical portrayals and perceptions of foreign marriage do not collude with regimes of governmentality and citizenship that determine who should have access to life (value, respectability, futurity, migration, and the good life) versus death (evacuation of economic resources and opportunities, invisibility, and undocumented migration and possible death)?

The uniting of exploitation with the lack of choice are taken up and naturalized in immigration policies that determine authentic marriages and citizenship through the proof of "true love." The separation of intimacies based on choice from those procured through family contacts or economic need relegates other intimate formations—such as the marriage of convenience, in which intimacies develop over time and through mutual obligation and support—as backward and exploitative. Today, state immigration debates classify the marriage of convenience (also known as the "arranged marriage") as a "sham marriage." Marriages orchestrated for personal gain or other strategic purposes raise suspicion and define the limits of national borders and bodies. For mainstream society, from Hollywood to Immigration Customs Enforcement (ICE), the marriage of convenience typifies a social contract that is not only outmoded but a threat to modern societies based on love, or the freedom of choice, individualism, and democratic governance based on equality (see chapter 1).

The state's curious protection of love as the criterion for citizenship actually guards the virtual ideology of the nation as freely chosen, equitable, and democratic. Marital contracts procured out of need or gross inequalities, rather than altruistic love, continue to determine difference and the exteriority of U.S. national boundaries and kinship. Forced contracts depict conditions of enslavement and forms of governance that contrast with those that are freely chosen in the United States. It is the patriotic bonds of love and mutual gain that prop up ideologies of national equality and freedom in marriage, labor, and citizenship contracts. Thus, modern U.S. definitions of freedom, as constituted through free choice and equality, are intelligible as the *freedom from* obligation, while I argue that for Latin American women, the marketplace of foreign marriage symbolizes the *freedom to* enter into contractual relations based on mutual obligations. I contend that it is the West's stubborn sense of negative freedom, the freedom *from* obligation that continues to define authentic intimacies, sociality, and even citizenship. For this reason, love encapsulates the ideal Western sentiment to express an obligation that is freely chosen and unconstrained by social obligation (family or oligarchy) or economic restraints.

My argument here is influenced by Elizabeth Povinelli's book *The Empire of Love* (2006), in which she locates structures of governance—embedded in medicine, law, and rights—through what she calls the "intimate event." Western ideologies of normative love, typified by liberal values of individual freedom in settler colonial societies, solidify in opposition to social constraint (or the genealogical society, traced through the Aboriginal community that Povinelli knows deeply). It is the interdependence of these imagined social worlds today that restimulate one's adherence to the myth of national belonging.

I label these structures of obligation as they converge with citizenship *liberal citizenship*. U.S.-style liberal citizenship—the heightened focus on individual freedom through liberal notions of a nonbinding relationship to others (what some Latin American women define as a cold or alienating culture), or one's entrance into contracts through free choice (unencumbered by economic desperation, family, or selfish factors)—coincides with the shift in governance from the welfare state to the neoliberal state, where individuals are encouraged to free themselves from an unhealthy dependency on the state, instead being encouraged toward self-sufficiency and independence. Yet idealizing modern sentiments of freedom as the departure from obligation bolster neoliberal state governance at a time when the state has increasingly withdrawn, even pathologized, its obligation to citizens (evident in the demonizing of welfare recipients, the criminalizing and sexualizing of migrants, etc.).

Mexican and Colombian women express an alienated relation to citizenship not because of their exclusion or alien status (foreignness) from U.S. citizenship but because of feelings of abandonment in Latin America, especially their decreased value and disposability in the home, in the labor market, and in relation to state power and national belonging. During a time of great global changes, women's value and earning capacity has the potential to increase through their global marketability and access to foreign capital and markets. The foreign serves as a viable strategy during a time when economic and political conditions at home have made it difficult to earn a middle-class wage, have stressed familial and social ties, and have increased violent conditions for women. It is thus no coincidence that in interviews, Mexican and Colombian women blame Latin men and excessive state power for the breakdown of the family, law, and order (see chapter 2). In other words, women blame the failed contract with men in marriage and with the state, institutions that fail to provide economic security or personal safety in protecting women from violence inside and outside the home. Access to more equitable intimate and legal structures promise women closer ties to others and the state, a notion of reciprocity, rather than freedom, that eschews the alienation of a culture of individualism in the United States. Thus, women's willing entrance into the foreign marriage marketplace as erotic objects of exchange not only demarcates how women's sexualized bodies provide the conduit to labor exchange and citizenship status but also explains their subjective desires for more affective contracts that bind people together intimately and economically offering more legally binding obligations between citizens and the state. Relations with U.S. men and the nation-state are valuable for women who seek a more equitable exchange than local marriage, labor, and citizenship contracts.

These desires for mutual exchange challenge U.S. perspectives that attribute the increasing encroachment of Western modernity and technologies (i.e., capitalism) into human relations to heightened exploitation and alienation. Even within sociological studies that uncover globalization through a gendered analysis of emotions, scholars lament the rationalization of emotion and intimacies that collapse utilitarian values endemic to capitalism and business culture with nonmarket, private-sphere exchanges.[37] Examples of this collusion of affect and capitalism can be found in new studies in which corporate life is generating more emotional-style management to project democratic work relations; marriage is identified by companionate models based on friendships and the "team spirit" of the corporate shop floor;[38] romance and sexuality are entangled in the culture of consumption, bought and sold on-line; and on-line sexuality and intimacy proliferate with others with whom one may never have face-to-face contact. Anthony Giddens' influential theorization of the pure relationship, an intimate exchange of pure pleasure unencumbered by obligation (and most ideally found, he argues, in gay couplings), reinforces the divide between emotionally based relationships and the transactional relationship, marriage, or commercial sex.[39] The collusion of love and sexuality alongside liberal ideals of democratic equality perpetuates the idea that sexual intimacy based on consent is more modern than "traditional" intimacies contracted by families and based on social obligations, differentiating certain social relations as the basis for a modern democracy.

Against the dehumanizing thrust of modern technologies and its potential alienation, participants in the cybermarriage industry emphasize sentiments of love to counter feeling devalued, deviant, or alienated from social norms. During my interviews with U.S. men, Mexican and Colombian women, and agency owners, sentiments of love differentiated moral business and personal practices from illicit avenues for profit or sexualized economies of trade. For most women, marriages based on love set them apart from traditional marriages based on uneven obligations; for married couples and immigration officials, true marriage founded on romantic love distinguished authentic from fraudulent couplings; romantic love assured middle-class moral status in contrast to the sex trade; and lastly, love determined authentic (and patriotic) citizenry.

Newly emergent desires and intimacies warrant more nuanced theories for the expression of modern subjectivities by the middle class in Latin America that go beyond one's access to consumption and participation in the global culture of taste.[40] In addition to consumption, *sentiments* increasingly translate, and bring into proximity, modern transnational affinities.[41] In privileging sentiments, scholars argue that transformations in intimacy across the globe—due to changes in economic, political, and social structures—demonstrate a shift in marriage from an institution based on tradition, kinship obligations, social reproduction, and survival to one that privileges individuals and their desire for intimacy, pleasure, and individual expression.[42] As Mark B. Padilla et al. argue, expressions of love are more often articulated alongside the lure of modernity, as individually chosen, deeply felt, and "authentic."[43] It is through romance that modern values of individual choice, democracy, development, and utopian futures of abundance are enunciated.[44]

A sense of oneself as modern, when examined from a transborder perspective, also confounds these divides as they may include inequalities, kin obligations, exchanges of services, and discrepant meanings of love. For marriage migrants, rights and citizenship status no longer rely solely on visual categories of race and birthright but also on affective claims to innocence (as another expression of whiteness).[45] In the cybermarriage industry, both men and women describe themselves as marginal actors in their native regions but as more valuable subjects to people outside their respective nation. Through claims to an affective disposition with the West, some Latin American women reconfigure their bodies not through difference but through sameness. While websites and tourist zones rely on difference to sell the "other," global citizenship depends on universal structures of recognition or sameness. Women, and even men, are caught in the middle of having to attract the other through niche marketing while also translating their worth as equitable, democratic partners through the language of romantic love. Western middle-class values of "choice" are also smuggled into intimate paradigms, such as Anthony Giddens's assertion that the promise of democracy is evident in intimate relationships.[46] The language of affect, or love, proves an appropriate technology for claiming individuality and innocence, or moral and proper engagement with the nation and citizenship. At the same time, women's declarations of love confine them to certain speech acts and normative structures of desire. Their expressions of love also go beyond the state, gesturing toward the sacred and divine and thus transcending the governance and ideology of the West and that of the family as they touch a notion of the human that extends to all, challenging the binary position of self/other that plagues U.S.–Latin American relations.[47]

Love and Empire's analysis of the politics of intimacy draws from queer and transnational feminist scholarship that theorizes the political sphere as inseparable from and, in fact, produced through affective cultures and investments.[48] As argued by Lauren Berlant and Michael Warner, intimacy has increasingly expressed the normative place of heterosexual politics and citizenship, especially as private sentiments including ethics, responsibility, and values replace state mandates for social justice and thus enforce the boundaries between moral persons and economic ones. They argue,

> Ideologies and institutions of intimacy are increasingly offered as a vision of the good life for the destabilized and struggling citizenry of the United

States, the only (fantasy) zone in which a future might be thought and willed, the only (imaginary) place where good citizens might be produced away from the confusing and unsettling distractions and contradictions of capitalism and politics.[49]

In this book, eroticized emotions exceed personal and social fantasies;[50] become the productive force driving Colombia's and Mexico's labor, tourism, and marriage markets;[51] and delineate moral and immoral migratory movements and rights. Women's eroticized emotions, virtualized onto their bodies, are national goods to be exported, critical symbols of the nation's hospitality and safety, and abundant natural resources waiting to be developed by international investment. Thus, foreign marriage—while an institution idealized as providing access to privacy and a life protected from intrusion by the state—renders natural (or unnatural) middle-class affections, making it difficult to ascertain how emotions function as a moral passport facilitating passage across borders.

Gender, Sexuality, and Migration

Feminist scholarship on gendered migration gained momentum in the early 1990s, challenging traditional push/pull models of migration that privileged masculine actors and economic triggers. These approaches examined global restructuring and its effects on the feminization of labor and migration, while others reached back farther to question how colonial institutions shape gendered labor markets today, including feminized service industries such as domestics, nurses, wives, and sex workers.[52] This seminal scholarship contributes to the broader context of eroticized femininity whereby Latin American marriage migrants are idealized for their sensuality, care, sexuality, and traditional family values. Much of this work has generated new understandings as to how impoverished women participate in gendered migration circuits as an economic survival strategy. Less examined, however, is this book's focus on middle-class or aspiring marriage migrants whose rationale transcends strictly economic reasons or survival strategies to include affective claims to citizenship and belonging.

Other feminist scholars, refuting the inherited economic measurements of migration, have turned to the emotional repercussions of border crossing for individuals and families left behind when parents, and especially mothers, transfer their care from their own families to those of their employers.[53] Rhacel Parreñas charts the intimate ties binding migrants in the Global South with their Western employers through what she calls the "chain of love."[54] Building on this, Arlie Hochschild similarly argues that love and care are the new natural resources, the "new gold" excavated from the Global South, a form of labor rendered invisible by its naturalization onto bodies in the Global South.[55] Drawing from a Marxist framework in which modern capitalism increasingly alienates subjects from the process and product of their labor, Hochschild asks, what happens when the labor produced is not a commodity but a feeling? What kinds of alienation and trauma do women from the Global South suffer when feelings are transferred from their own family in the Global South to another's in the Global North?[56] While marriage websites and company owners pitch the benefits of plundering Latin America for its natural resources of passion, abundant in images of available women, women's own descriptions of love as a claim to belonging move the discussion beyond their alienation as usable commodities for U.S. profit and pleasure.

In the vein of rethinking the unintended consequences of global restructuring on intimacy, other scholars follow the recent surge in international marriages that cross uneven geographies and labor migrations among Asia and Pacific Island regions. The use of ethnographic methods here affords greater insight into the relevance of borders and difference on the ground as well as the complicated meanings of class, race, and power in cross-national marriages.[57] These studies open space to assess the flexibility of meanings that permeate these encounters and the possibility for agency and press us to rethink dominant imaginaries and cultural norms. It is with these scholars, and those who look to the entanglements of sexual and economic relations in the Caribbean, including Jacqui Alexander, Kamala Kempadoo, Amalia Cabezas, and many others, that my work converses. Alexander argues that states of the Bahamas and Trinidad reanimate colonial laws through contemporary economic restructuring that legislates against certain deviant sexualities while profiting from a political economy of desire that relies on women's hypersexuality.[58] In an attempt to carve a space for alternative desires and economies, to deconstruct the macro depictions of global inequalities that reproduce the Global South as a mecca for hypersexuality, Kempadoo argues that Caribbean women accentuate their sexualized bodies as a decolonial tool toward their own economic uplift.[59] If governments and pimps can exploit women's global cachet as authentic sites for eroticized sensuality, then some women may also enact this stereotype for their own personal gain. Other scholars, similarly concerned with agency, acknowledge the complexities of sex work within specific countries, regions, and spaces as inseparable from economic pressures but also open up the possibility for mutual responsibility, intimacy, and sometimes even pleasure.[60] Alongside these studies, this

book understands the importance of microstructures of power through pleasure but warns that the paradigm of agency may reinforce neoliberal models
that privilege the individual.

In my analysis of eroticized sentiments, I am not interested in excavat-
ing an inner "truth" of sex (or of the subject).[61] Queer scholarship, heavily
influenced by Foucault's theorization of sex as a technology of governance,
foregrounds sexuality as a discursive construct (with material consequences)
that is historically managed and produced through a variety of state institutions. Burgeoning studies on the intersection of sexuality and migration
trouble the coupling of sexuality with the private or intimate sphere, leading some scholars, such as Eithne Luibhéid, to question the role of the state
in making heterosexuality compulsory when crossing borders or through
the marketing of bodies to attract foreign capital for sex tourism.[62] It is here
that my analysis of transnational intimacies concerns not only individual
structures of desire but an understanding of how desire is inextricable from
an engagement with power *and* its demise. These intimate stories dislocate
obvious iterations of modernity and citizenship and are quiet cries for divine
placement within universal understandings of the human premised not on
sameness but on reciprocal relations of care, love, and respect.

Methodology: Virtual Ethnography

In order to follow U.S. men and Latin American women across time and
space—from before and during their romantic encounters to after some of
them marry—I conducted virtual ethnographies with men and women in
chat rooms, sometimes as a participant in the discussion and other times
as a "lurker," or unidentified voyeur. In addition to interviewing couples at
the Vacation Romance Tours in Guadalajara, Mexico, and Cali, Colombia, I
translated for couples during their dates (and followed one man's search for a
bride for over a year by translating e-mail love letters) and then interviewed
couples when they married and moved to the United States. In order to
conduct longer interviews with women before and after the tours, I bought
e-mail addresses from the marriage agency GlobalLatinas.

During the tours in Mexico and Colombia and within chat-room debates,
I was struck by the fact that men and women rehearsed the same stories.
Rather than assume that the repetition of these stories confirmed a "truth"
about Latin American women and U.S. men, I found myself more interested
in questioning why certain representations of Latin American women and
U.S. men remained stable, even when men and women confronted each
other face-to-face. How and why do these representational frames of Latin

American women in the U.S. imaginary and of the modern, feminist U.S. man in the Latin American imaginary—fantasies begun on-line, flickering on one's monitor screen—continue even in face-to-face contact and despite the endless proliferation of experiences shared on men's chat rooms? How might experience, and ethnographic evidence more generally, confound more than it reveals?

Alongside feminist debates about the radical possibilities and problems of documenting "experience,"[63] women and men are caught within particular paradigms of knowledge and representational frames across transnational exchanges.[64] I am hopeful that this book's critical ethnographic approach will open up new ways of understanding the constraints and possibilities of transnational exchanges, such as how gendered forms of respectability and power interface, shaping what is possible for participants to say and what is possible for readers and myself to see and hear. Patricia Zavella's analysis of the cultural poetics of silence opened up a space to discuss how Latinas indirectly maneuver various structures of power. It is this deconstructive approach to ethnography that generates a literary discussion about what is said against what cannot be said in the context of sexualized control.[65] Feminist ethnography does not achieve a higher truth about the "other."[66] Instead, ethnography belies its fictional origins, and thus a feminist approach that explores the impossible moments of its trajectories may teach us more about the inherent betrayal and impossibility but also the need to engage in cross-cultural exchanges.

Keeping in mind the mediated fantasies, as well as the silences and limits of ethnography, this book turns to *telenovelas*, U.S. romance films, beauty pageants, cosmetic surgery, and state-sponsored advertisements in Latin America to provide a broader social context that contributes to the dialectic between virtual intimacies and everyday subject-making. In fact, I discovered that virtual mediations ingrain so deeply into women's and men's daily lives that the virtual feels more satisfying and real to participants, and the real more fictionalized and at odds with their expectations. Taking seriously the blurred nature of what is understood as virtual versus real enables an understanding of how and why eroticized representations of Latinas persist and morph in the U.S. imaginary from colonization to our current era of neoliberal capitalism, decontextualized from the specificity of the interaction, location, and temporality. Participants in the cybermarriage industry seek each other over e-mail exchanges, in short encounters on the Romance Tours, and during sporadic vacations. To be sure, these bounded encounters—the majority facilitated by some form of translation, whether language devices or actual bilingual translators—necessitate the virtual to stretch meaning into the places that language and cultural meanings of difference falter.

Language deficiencies challenged communication between couples and abetted the persistence of fantasies in face-to-face encounters. Most men I encountered did not speak Spanish, and women varied greatly in their ability to speak English. Female translators, hand-held digital dictionaries (and now voice-generated translations available on cell phone applications), and a romantic cultural imaginary mediated the fluency and intensity of transnational romance and marriage. For the nonbilingual, other aspects of the body—beauty, the eyes, gestures, and dress (professional attire for men and feminine clothes for women)—communicated gendered expectations and desires. Women often shouldered the burden of crossing language divides, while men absorbed the costs of this linguistic conversion as they paid translators to accompany them on dates and to translate e-mail exchanges and paid for women's English classes in Latin America (and for fiancées in the United States). Though some women found this gap frustrating and typical of the uneven exchange endemic to Latin American–U.S. relations, many were also motivated to learn English as they were well aware of the global dominance of English and the opportunities it could lead to at home and abroad. Language discrepancies were hardly a barrier for men excited by the challenge to induce women into the American dream.

Structure of the Book

Because of my interest in the book in foregrounding the role of the state and citizenship in practices of intimacy, chapter 1 draws from immigration-hearing debates, interviews with married couples, and recent films dramatizing green-card marriages, to question why foreign heterosexual intimacy has, since the 1980s, been so heavily scrutinized. In other words, what do these forms of marriage and intimacy threaten? I argue that it is women's erotic citizenship—their moral standing, family values, superior reproductive qualities—that works to distance them from bodies in need—bodies of welfare, criminality, and trade—and to turn them into pliable bodies that produce and accrue value across borders. In chapter 2, I contextualize women's stories of shifting desire from local to foreign men alongside broader transformations in Mexico that shape professional women's conversion from the Catholic Church to Protestantism. They express this shift through from the sense that their lives are spiritually predetermined to an entrepreneurial ethic that values hard work and individuals' ability to alter themselves and their futures. Chapter 3 analyzes men's chat-room exchanges alongside the emergence of a self-help culture and the formation of global masculinity wedded to U.S. expansion, free trade, and empire. In line with website images and narratives, for U.S. men, Latin American women's bodies figure centrally as the final frontier, as pure bodies and superior genes that are highly valued within a capitalist culture that men describe as devoid of domestic care, affection, and intimacy. U.S. men's access to foreign markets and bodies promises to patriotically rejuvenate not only their identities (across race, class, and regional differences) but also the national stock and to provide an alternative to lonely and alienating lifestyles.

Chapter 4 situates interviews with women who attended the Cali tour alongside media representations of beauty and desire in *telenovelas*, advertisements, beauty pageants, and films, as well as in the current state campaign "Colombia Is Passion." I analyze how working-class Afro-Caribbean women in Cali, Colombia, described their bodies as "pliable" in relation to the beautification process (and for many, this includes plastic surgery) in order to alter their class status, to move safely across space, as a form of pleasure, and as the compulsory reconfiguring of the body that is necessary to participate in local and global markets. Rather than understand women's erotic bodies only through male clients and agency perspectives—as a natural resource to be exchanged and extracted from Latin America—for some Colombian women, the body can be remade as highly valuable within transnational romance, especially in the context of a local society where women describe high degrees of uncertainty, lawlessness, and stagnation.

Chapter 5 extends my inquiry into the role of love as a state-sponsored project of surveillance to a questioning of our own investment in scrutinizing particular embodiments of foreign love and marriage. In this chapter, I contend that Latin American women's assertions of love and care for their husbands manage the lines between the "foreign" and the "native." Influenced by Chicana, feminist, and queer scholarship, I argue that marriage migrants toe the line between their status, on the one hand, as erotic citizens, or as exceptional patriots through proper marital femininity and thus bodies deserving of rights and life, and, on the other hand, as alien or "antipatriotic immigrants" who threaten normative structures of the nation and thus must be deported or left with few rights and/or death.[67]

The journey some women take to the United States via foreign marriage takes many turns, as do the journeys of U.S. men. Rather than engage in a moral debate over how to determine authentic marriages versus those based on the exploitative exchange of marriage for a host of other perks, I find the tensions between increased state surveillance over mobility and individual desires to transcend local meanings, norms, and possibilities key to understanding the constrained desires for those who see a renewed interest in marriage on a global stage. Unfortunately, the critical role the state plays in shaping these desires is rendered invisible in these debates. Addressing the state head-on ensures that we understand this industry through individual or personal desires as they are shaped by unequal access to rights, migration, and citizenship.

1

Enforcing Romantic Love through Immigration Law

After September 11th, the existential question of "Why do they [for-eigners] hate us?" was hotly debated in the American media with-out any real conclusion ever being reached. This [article] seeks to answer the opposite question: "Why do they love us?"
—David Seminara, former consular officer

Huddled together at a party that gathered a growing community of Colom-bian women married to U.S. men, various women admitted to each other in Spanish that they did not love their U.S. husbands when they decided to marry and migrate to the United States.[1] I discovered during my interviews with some of these women two years later that three of the women ended up falling in love with their husbands over time. One woman fell in love even after agreeing to pay a man $6,000 to marry her until she received her permanent residency. A couple of the other women's relationships ended in divorce just a few years later (after they were granted permanent residency). One returned home soon after arriving because her husband realized he was not ready to share his life with someone. And another continues to be mar-ried despite not being in love. Women must guard their hushed exchanges about love (and its absence) closely, lest they be perceived as calculating and manipulative, prostitutes, lesbians, or even criminals of the state, if it were discovered that they took a chance on marriage, hoping that love or at least a mutually satisfying relationship would develop.

Even though transborder relationships and marriages might better resemble the kind of love that evolves from building trust and intimacy over time, spouses are required to profess romantic love in route, as they pass through the scrutinizing gaze of the U.S. Immigration and Customs Enforcement (ICE). Disclosing their lack of love is dangerous. Women could face steep fines (up to $250,000) and jail for five years, or ICE may choose to deport them if it found out they used marriage to gain state benefits. According to self-help books, love continues to be "at large" in a U.S. culture characterized by heightened modernity and alienation,[2] a sentiment that in part shapes U.S. men's expectations for heightened love, care, and sexual passion in Latin American women.[3] At the same time, a white woman who attended the same party described this group of Colombian women as incapable of love because their harsh lives demand economic savvy, as opposed to the luxury of choice that being in love assumes.[4]

Part of the challenge of interviewing women about their private lives and desires at the tours and after migrating to the United States undoubtedly reflects their surveillance by family codes of respectability, but it also reveals their close monitoring by ICE when crossing the border. It is riskier for women to speak out than for men, complicating the ethnographic and feminist project of "giving voice" to Latin American women seeking a foreign marriage partner.[5] For this reason, I tell this piece of the story through and beyond the accounts shared with me by women who migrate with their husbands to the United States. In Patricia Zavella's articles on the construction of Chicana/Latina sexuality, she analyzes women's cultural poetics, the ways women discuss their sexuality through discourses of *juego y fuego* (play and fire), to link local speech patterns with broader forms of gendered power relations as well as women's resistance to control through sexual comportment.[6] Even when it appears as though some Latinas may not directly contest power, it is through the poetics of silence that anthropologists bridge what is said with what cannot be expressed. Zavella argues, "Women's cultural poetics, the social meaning of sexuality, entails struggling with the contradictions of repressive discourses and social practices that are often violent toward women and their desires."[7] In a similar vein, women's silence—or even their attesting to being in love with their husbands—alerts us to the forms of surveillance and repression by immigration laws that determine eligibility for and the right to citizenship. By invoking "poetics," I hope to shift the weight of women's speech from willing deception and to crack open the possibility of other meanings to permeate. In addition, women's reticence during interviews to voicing alternative understandings of marriage point to the cultural and social norms in both the United States and Latin America that yoke marriage and sexuality to love and reproduction, in opposition to the consumption of love in the marketplace. The irony of solidifying this moral separation by social dictates is that in popular culture, Western-style "romantic love" defies this separation between intimacy and marketplace exchange, as romance is fully intertwined with leisure and consumption.[8] Yet here, even the bureaucratic functioning of the state is invested in the poetics of nation-building founded on the patriotic bonds of love.

The separation of innocent migrant marriages based on love versus fraudulent couplings entered into for self-gain took on an especially high tenor post-9/11, as immigration debates swerved back to the question stated earlier—not simply "Why do immigrants hate (attack) us?" but "Why do they love (marry) us?" The space between hate and love collapses through fears that terrorists and other unwanted migrants drag as newlyweds to enter the country. Other figures have similarly raised ire in the public when "imposters" attempt to take over an institution that is distinctly, or should I say exceptionally, American. While today these figures are gays, migrants, smugglers, and terrorists, historically the profile has changed depending on what body politic threatened to take hostage of love-based marriages and normative kin relations within the nation. In particular, some immigration advocates interpret the sharp rise in visa petitions for a foreign spouse as a potential national security threat and lobby for more rigorous investigation of these marriages. For example, David Seminara, a former consular officer, draws from ICE statistics to lobby for more stringent scrutiny of the alarming number of cases of immigrant marriage fraud. His article, written for the Center for Immigration Studies,[9] equates an increase in foreign marriage with higher rates of fraud:

> More than 25 percent of all green cards issued in 2007 were to the spouses of American citizens. In 2006 and 2007 there were nearly twice as many green cards issued to the spouses of American citizens than were issued for all employment-based immigration categories combined. The number of foreign nationals obtaining green cards based on marriage to an American has more than doubled since 1985, and has quintupled since 1970.[10]

Rather than scrutinize migrants for "fraudulent" love, I argue that there is a more complex story to understanding why marriages have quickly surpassed the numbers of employment visas, why love must accompany these marriages, and why foreign marriages have, since the 1980s, raised fears of fraud and the need for more stringent immigration surveillance. Immigration policies, since the inception of the Immigration and Naturalization Service (INS) in 1891, have screened migrants as excludable based on an array of

Fig. 1.1. *L.A. Weekly*, cover page, "Make a Run for the Altar" (July 8, 2010).

threats to the normative white family. And since the 1952 Immigration and Nationality Act (amended in 1965), family reunification served as *the* route to legal migration.[11] With the decline in alternative channels for "legal" migration, marriage becomes a desirable avenue for migrants who seek legitimate entry into the United States, the right to labor, mobility, and for some, the possibility of eventual legalization.

A recent article in the *L.A. Weekly* called "Make a Run for the Altar" describes how some citizen Latinas/os living in the United States exercise their right to marry an undocumented migrant to protest the lack of other options for legalization for migrants who live and work in the United States. Figure 1.1 plays off of signs posted close to border-crossing areas in San Diego that caution drivers to watch out for people running across the highway. Here one is to be on the lookout for migrants involved in sham marriages who are running not across the border but to the altar to gain citizenship. In response to public fears that mass numbers of migrants are infiltrating the border through "sham marriages," Gustavo Arrellano's article debunks the criminality of migrant marriages through uncovering the deep political sentiments and affinities between Latino/a citizens and those without documents that motivate some to take great risks in marrying an undocumented friend or fellow Latino/a migrant.[12] The article finds that the penalties for marriage fraud do not stop some who see marriage as their only route to remain in the United States legally.[13]

Raging debates over what constitutes an "authentic" foreign marriage are curious given a lengthy 2010 study by the Pew Research Center that reports the finding that one in four Americans say marriage is obsolete.[14] As traditional marriages continue to decline from the 1980s until today as the structure for intimacy, raising children, and family formation, the ideology of heterosexual marriage has surged rather than waned in political and immigration debates in the United States. Some questions that emerge from this contradiction between practices of intimacy and the intent of the law are: What norms are embedded within immigration policies that have, since the inception of the INS in 1891, focused on reproduction and the family? How do these historical debates inform why foreign cybermarriages, and foreign women's migration from developing to first-world nations more broadly, are so closely monitored and debated? What foundational fears and beliefs do foreign marriage migrants threaten?

My desire to contest official depictions of foreign marriages as a potential threat by generating countervoices of Latin American women who are "truly in love" would only reproduce neoliberal state policies. Consular and ICE inspections of "authentic" foreign marriage justifies the state's authority and power to ramp up border scrutiny in the name of protecting the rights and citizenship of the exceptional few. Instead, in this chapter, I argue that the U.S. state plays a critical role—via immigration law, politics, and procedures—in shaping how foreign marriage migrants express intimacy and move across borders as potential citizens rather than second-class subjects. I am not interested in proving whether love is true or not in these arrangements. Instead, I contend that romantic love is a compulsory sentiment for migrants to prove their potential for modern citizenship. Women's practices of citizenship and self-making as subjects in love, and thus as innocent and pliable, are far from natural but instead are necessary to projecting their sexual labor as moral and their bodies as productive rather than a risk to the nation. Immigration policies perpetuate deeply engrained values of neoliberalism through laws that scrutinize "risky" foreign marriage migrants or those thought to fraudulently enter marriage for the economic perks.

In the chapter, then, I begin with an analysis of immigration and naturalization laws that have historically protected rights and citizenship obligations through marriage. This history is crucial to understanding how the scrutiny of foreign marriages, and the cybermarriage industry in particular, emerges in immigration debates beginning during the turn of the twentieth century and continuing into the 1980s and into the present. The 1980s signify a key moment for interrogating the tense ties between political debates on protecting family values and the rise of a backlash against those who threaten the nation via fraudulent marriages. Scholars have made important contributions in examining the role of the law in policing "foreign" bodies that are deemed (sexually) excessive and thus a threat to the normative state—such as in the case of lesbians, gays, polygamists, sex workers, and terrorists who attempt to migrate across borders.[15] There has been little discussion, however, about the way women's *seemingly* normative migration through marriage poses a similar perceived threat to the nation and thus is subject to constant scrutiny and surveillance.[16]

ICE's use of love as a barometer for determining migrant citizenship sets up a strict binary between intimacy, agency, and democracy, on the one hand, and relationships based on trade, exploitation, and anachronistic governance, on the other. Marriages agreed on outside the love bond smack of a forced contract that shadows the dark past of slavery thought to threaten the boundaries of the nation. Thus, by interrogating the foundational values of love and intimacy through the law's scrutinizing gaze, the supposed naturalness of heterosexual love and marriage comes into question. Instead, these sentiments prove foundational to national ideologies, shaping the state's odd role as an arbiter of love arrangements and rights.

The Making of (Sexual) Subjects via Immigration Laws

Marriage as a political institution has long defined women's rights and obligations, especially since the nineteenth century, when, as argued by Linda Kerber, marriage law relied on a system of coverture that "transferred a woman's civic identity to her husband at marriage, giving him the use and direction of her property throughout the marriage."[17] Marriage was an institution that entrenched gender roles into law, delineating rights and obligations, with the husband serving as the economic provider and family head, communicating his wife's voting, jury, and contractual rights to the state.[18] *Coverture*, a French term defining the system in which women's rights were covered by their husbands, originated from a longer legacy of coverture defining unequal relations between parents and children as well as masters and slaves.[19] The exchange of citizenship rights and obligations within marriage is often obscured, especially today through the ideology of equality embedded in romantic love. As we will see later in the chapter, changes to immigration policies after a 1985 Senate debate on fraudulent marriage resurrected a temporary system of coverture, as migrant women were forced to rely on their U.S. spouses for financial and legal support the first two years or so until their husbands petitioned for their permanent residency.

Furthermore, as argued by Peggy Pascoe, because marriage stretches seamlessly from romance to respectability to responsibility, it has extraordinary power to naturalize some social relationships and to stigmatize others as unnatural.[20] The power of marriage to stigmatize, but also to distribute rights, has ignited some gay and lesbian activists to demand the right to marriage. Yet while some activists argue for inclusion based on mutual love and highlight the unequal distribution of political perks, rights, and benefits conferred through marriage, foreign marriage migrants must prove the marriage is based on love solely rather than economic benefits.[21]

The preoccupation with marriage in immigration law from the 1980s to the present builds on previous exclusion acts in which the state's concern with national inclusion/exclusion and citizenship rights reproduced racialized norms concerning marriage and sexuality. More contemporary laws base exclusion on the potential for a migrant's threat to national security. This is especially the case as media accounts have associated women's migration and mobility with unruly and hypersexualized behavior.[22] Immigration laws have long excluded women whose sexuality (determined through one's race and class) outside marriage was associated with immorality, prostitution, or criminal deviance. As Eithne Luibhéid argues, family preference in U.S. immigration law has historically served a host of purposes including to maintain the heterosexual family unit and to construct women as dependent wives following pioneering migrant husbands; to protect whiteness; to prevent intermixing; to exclude women, especially prostitutes, who violated or threatened to dismantle the family structure; to bar married women whose childbearing was feared to result in the birth of "too many" poor children; and to generate explicit racial, ethnic, and class exclusions that helped to

consolidate the "immigrant family" as necessarily of European (prefer-
ably Northern or Western) origin, heteropatriarchal, and of some financial
means.[23]

In fact, the national preoccupation with marriage and the family as the
conduit for regenerating the nation coincided with the formation of the
Immigration Naturalization Service (INS) in 1891 during a period of heated
eugenics debates, in which the racial makeup of those who would reproduce
and populate the nation fixated the attention of many Euro-Americans.[24]
Poor people as well as "licentious" women were barred entrance through
popular medical discourse during a time when female prostitutes' bodies
were labeled as diseased and thus a threat to the nation.[25] Family reunification
laws were debated and enforced in the late 1800s, even before the creation of
the INS, to prevent intermixing between mostly Chinese, Japanese, and Filipino laborers and white women. Bans against interracial unions privileged
white families and prevented "ethnic" migrants from inheriting property.
Curiously, Chinese women were excluded from family reunification laws
on the basis of their hypersexuality, but they were later admitted because of
the fear that male laborers would sexually "degrade" white women. Women's
experiences of discrimination depended on class biases, as wives of Chinese
merchants had an easier time migrating than those of Chinese "coolie" laborers.[26] In fact, both prostitutes and Chinese laborers represented "slavery-like"
status and threatened to import un-American forms of governance, such as
authoritative hierarchy and deference that signified their coercion by, rather
than consent to, absolute conditions of power.[27]

Between 1907 and 1908, the United States negotiated the Gentlemen's
Agreement with Japan and halted the immigration of all Japanese migrant
laborers, except Japanese brides, in the hope of deterring male immigrants
already in the country from interracial sex with white women or from seeking sex with prostitutes. Given the crackdown against prostitutes tucked into
the 1907 immigration law, many foreign women married U.S. men in the
hope of evading deportation. The surge in numbers of women attempting
to marry, coupled with the manufacturing of public fear and attention to the
"White Slave trade," set in motion legislation and scrutiny by immigration
officials to make invalid any marriage procured for the purposes of evading immigration laws. By 1914, the INS Department of Labor recommended
a ban on the entry of "alien immoral women" who tried to marry citizens.
These policies led immigration officials to scrutinize foreign marriages, such
as Japanese "picture brides" (or proxy brides),[28] European war brides (1917),[29]
arranged marriages (sought out in Jewish "brokered" couplings and Asian
relationships aided by families), and polygamy—all relationships thought

to collapse the lines between individually chosen intimacy and "brokered" arrangements. Demarcations of licit and illicit intimacies hardened national boundaries into the fibers of everyday desire. The governance of marriage proved forceful for differentiating between the old world and the new, tradition and modernity, falsity and truth, and tyranny and freedom.[30]

Laws proscribing marriage and sexuality shaped how the state distributed rights to labor, land, and citizenship. During a period of great xenophobia against Chinese and Japanese migrants, a 1907 law also stipulated that a U.S. woman who married a foreign man lost her citizenship, even if she remained in U.S. territory. Later amended in 1922, under the Cable Act, a female U.S. citizen could only keep her citizenship if she married a foreign man who was eligible for citizenship (which excluded men from China or Japan).[31] It is worth remembering that U.S. male citizens, in contrast, automatically passed their citizenship rights to their wives, including foreign wives (except Asian women). During the mid to late 1800s, however, marriages between Anglo men and Mexican American women oftentimes were not scrutinized by antimiscegenation laws because the law understood Mexicans—or *mestizos* of a mixed racial background including Spanish, indigenous, and African roots—to be white.[32] This was especially the case during the nineteenth century, when Anglos married fair-skinned, upper-class Mexican women in order to gain access to the women's wealthy California ranchos.[33] This particular coupling was considered a legitimate and even advantageous marriage, especially for land but also due to the dearth of Anglo women in the colonial United States at that time.[34]

Family Values versus Marriage Fraud (1980s to the Present)

It is hardly a coincidence that during the 1980s, Reagan's rhetoric of protecting family values accompanied state surveillance and public fears over figures that threatened the normative family. The onslaught of AIDS and the demonizing of gays, the pathologizing of the black welfare mother, and draconian immigration policies excluding people with AIDS (such as homosexuals and Haitians) accompanied the rise in surveillance of foreign marriages. Heightened awareness and visibility of the "mail-order bride" industry and other "marriage scams" in the 1980s led the INS to focus its energy on creating more barriers and technologies to monitor foreign marriage migrants. In 1986, President Reagan signed the IMFA (Immigration Marriage Fraud Amendment) in order to prevent fraudulent marriages for the purpose of migration.[35] The IMFA imposed a two-year waiting period for women to obtain permanent residency status[36] and required parties to meet in person before marrying.[37] Family-based migration accounts for approximately three-quarters of all legal immigration to the United States each year. Within this category, U.S. citizens bringing opposite-sex spouses have, for many years, accounted for the largest category of family immigrants.[38] In 2001, 95.06 percent of Mexico's total immigration was enabled through family reunification, and for Colombia, the figure was 88.97 percent.[39]

Neoliberal policies gained momentum in the 1980s, during Reagan's presidency, especially as the state not only slashed public services but also privatized federal aid. With the Family Reunification Act, originally passed in 1986, the federal government began relocating the burden of financial responsibility from the state to the petitioning migrant families themselves. Through family reunification policies and, more specifically, the foreign marriage amendment, the government minimized financial risk and cut down the numbers of lower-class migrants, while also protecting its image as the protector of family values.[40] This was accomplished by requiring migrant petitioners residing in the United States to show proof that they could provide support to maintain the sponsored alien at an annual income that is not less than 125 percent of the federal poverty level.[41] Not only did the state minimize its role in the financial welfare of migrants, but the focus on family migration has "increased immigrants' exposure and structural dependence on heteropatriarchal relations and regulatory structures" such as the family.[42]

One decade after the Family Reunification Act, Eithne Luibhéid found striking similarities between the 1996 Defense of Marriage Act (DOMA) and the Personal Responsibility and Work Opportunity Reconciliation Act (PRWORA). Both acts distribute privileges (rather than rights) such as residency and citizenship through encouraging "responsible" sexuality from migrants and sponsors, who must bear the brunt of financial responsibility for bringing over immigrant spouses and family members.[43] The PRWORA, signed by President Clinton in 1996, inadvertently blames poverty on sexually irresponsible women who are required to take personal responsibility over their lives by seeking work and/or marriage as an avenue for economic reform and security.[44] In the case of foreign marriages, the state has also shifted the burden of economic responsibility to the petitioning U.S. spouse so that if the marriage should fail, the foreign spouse would not become a drain on the nation as a potential welfare recipient. U.S. spouses must sign paperwork assuring they will financially support their sponsored spouse for ten years, even in the case of divorce. The class implications here are significant, as only those U.S. citizens who can afford to sponsor spouses or family members are administered visas.

In the mid 1980s (even before 9/11), immigration policy debates warned of the need to better regulate marriage migration. Those who used marriage to enter the country were in dire need of detection as potential welfare abusers, prostitutes, terrorists, smugglers, and/or criminals of the state. In an interrogation of the naturalness of heterosexual marriage, David Bell and Jon Binnie state, "The fact that some use marriage for visas, or for self-enhancement . . . without having to bear the responsibilities, opens up the institution of marriage for scrutiny . . . as an institution that is not natural but centered in various benefits and opportunities.[45] Even as the family is idealized as a site for privacy, a domain outside of state scrutiny, immigration policy debates must turn it into a question of national security in order to authorize the state's intrusion into the private sphere of its citizens. In a 1985 Senate subcommittee immigration policy hearing, the threat that the marriage migrant posed to the moral boundaries of the nation aligned the migrant with criminality. A subcommittee report states,

> Most aliens are ineligible for visas because they have flaunted the law: through illegal entry, as a visa abuser, as an illegal worker, as a prostitute, criminal, narcotics violator, or terrorist. (A recent joint FBI-INS investigation of Sikhs suspected of involvement in terrorist and subversive activities disclosed that two of the five individuals arrested were involved in sham marriages. One had already acquired immigrant status, and the other was in the process of seeking permanent residence through a marriage contracted immediately after he was arrested as an illegal alien.)[46]

In 1985, newspapers covering areas such as Miami ran articles aggrandizing the scope of marriage fraud. In fact, the front page of the *Miami Herald* ran an article characterizing marriage fraud as an "epidemic," with droves of "subversive types" (typified by the marriage ring discovered by the INS of a Miami group with ties to Little Havana).[47] The release of the transcript of the subcommittee hearing by the U.S. Senate two days after the release of this newspaper article focused not only on the heightened security threat of "subversive" or "terrorist" activity through sham marriages but also on the probability that perpetrators would usurp precious U.S. resources:

> In Kansas City, Kansas, seven Nigerians were recently indicted for their involvement in sham marriages. They married United States citizens not only to acquire INS benefits, but also to qualify for guaranteed student loans and grants, food stamps, federally subsidized housing, and the lower

tuition fees available only to United States citizens, legal permanent resident aliens, and state residents.[48]

Another case detailed fraudulent marriages between Pakistanis and welfare mothers in Chicago. The selection of cases, resting on race- and class-based threats to national security, targeted welfare mothers, immigrant "profiteers," smugglers, and "terrorists"—popular figures in the 1980s (and today) who have been used to justify social services cutbacks, the 1990–1991 Gulf War, and immigration reform bent on curbing the entrance of lower-class migrants.[49] The Senate subcommittee hearing debate also justified more stringent surveillance of marriage visas for fear that these marriages enabled unskilled laborers to enter the marketplace. Within the hearing notes, thousands of fraudulent marriages were uncovered in Mexico, the Philippines, the Middle East, and Haiti, as well as in border towns such as El Paso.[50]

Though the state works to move immigrants from "dependent" welfare recipients into "responsible" citizens, foreign marriage spouses, through the discourse of true love, must carefully negotiate their identification as desperate, poor, hypersexualized, or criminal, versus innocent and moral subjects in love. One of the questions that remain is, Despite these prolific risks, how and why do officials rely on love to discern the fraudulent versus the bona fide?

Love and Democracy

I contend that romantic love and heterosexual marriage perpetuate foundational myths of U.S.-style democracy, citizenship, and freedom of choice. Western ideologies of romantic love symbolize the universal right to self-expression and support popular beliefs that love is deeply embedded in values of democratic freedom and equality. Citizenship, as a legal and cultural structure of self-making in relation to blood ties and land (property), rests not only on the fact of marriage and kinship ties to the nation but on the act of "choosing" a heterosexual partner in marriage—the place for normative expressions of emotional and economic modernity. As a structure for dispersing rights and creating obligations between people and the state, U.S. citizenship can be thought of as a practice that in part structures who we are in relation to others. In other words, choosing a marriage based on love proves one's status as innocent (i.e., unselfish and devoid of economic motivations), modern, and possessing the ability to be self-governing and to display equality.

In the infamous interracial marriage case between a white and black couple, *Loving v. Virginia*, Chief Justice Earl Warren argued that the right to marry could not be tied to the accident of ancestry without shattering the doctrine of equality, a doctrine foundational, and fundamental, to the American notion of freedom.[51] This case broke from race segregation to uphold a more important ideal. The right to choose one's spouse represented a fundamental entitlement of those who live in democratic societies, where individuals' fate is popularly held in their own hands. This version of democratic freedom is posited against economies where class hierarchies are thought less permeable, societies where families or the church play a more central role in determining the fate of individuals.

In fact, as Elizabeth Povinelli argues, normative understandings of love as foundational to "freedom" go back even further, to the justification of secular government. Love as an act of choice—free from social or familial constraints—reinvigorates the founding moment of self-government for U.S. colonial settlers, who prided themselves in having the capacity to detach from Europe because of a philosophical opposition to the constraints of familial, aristocratic, and religious power.[52] Self-government represented human freedom and universal equality under the law. The importation of pioneer brides by new colonists hoping to make a new life on the frontier coincided with the notion that subjects could make themselves anew, that they could be freed from their past. In the formation of the "self-made man," as Povinelli states, "the course of a man's life should be determined by *his* life, the life *he* made, rather than from his placement before his birth in a genealogical, or any other socially defined, grid."[53] Contemporary marriage migration strengthens this foundational fiction through women's opportunity to remake themselves across borders and to uplift families left behind through remittances. Returning home with U.S. stories and consumer goods proves one's participation in the "American Dream" that mythically offers a stage to enact a pliable sense of self that defies race, class, and economic hierarchies. At the same time, women's reliance on marriage, and the emphasis on romantic love, cloaks inequalities.

The institution and culture of marriage continues to offer the promise of futurity, of dreams of becoming, social recognition, and belonging and rights. For migrants, marriage to a U.S. spouse offers an avenue for respectable mobility, and although some women are from a higher social, although not necessarily economic, class than the men they marry, they hope to preserve or increase their socioeconomic position through marriage, both in the United States and back home.[54] For example, after migrating from Colombia to Miami to stay with a cousin on a tourist visa, Mariana described being close to marrying a Cuban American who spoke broken English. But he was not exactly what she expected: "He was Cuban. I wanted American—I wanted the real thing, the real American. My Cuban boyfriend was . . . very tall, very dark skin, a little old. I wanted blue eyes, like white, . . . someone who spoke perfect English. . . . I grew up in a bilingual school. I know English. I consider myself American. Why can't I have American?"[55]

Mariana's desire for the "real" American reveals the class and race bias in marriage selection repeated to me by many other women who preferred an American man with light skin and blue eyes. Her dilemma over marriage reflects how she wants to craft herself, as a migrant who expects to be treated not as a foreigner but as an American. Many women refuse to migrate as second-class citizens or to be mistaken as racially and/or ideologically "foreign" or "illegal."[56] In contrast to "illegal" migration, cross-border marriages offer men and women "a measure of value, self-worth, and citizenship" or "becoming a fully realized subject."[57] In fact, Mariana's and other women's resistance to migrating to the United States as a "foreigner" also speaks to their self-definition as already Americanized and as racially white, even before they arrive in the United States. Mariana, light-skinned with brown eyes and hair, described herself as fortunate enough to attend a private bilingual school in Colombia on scholarships. In school, she learned English and about American culture (they even celebrated Thanksgiving and Valentine's Day), which ideally would translate into opportunities for becoming part of the transnational dominant white class in Bogotá or in the United States, alongside some of her cousins living in the United States. Foreign marriage provides a route to migrate as middle class for women such as Mariana, rendered a challenge by the direction of her move across borders. This is especially the case for many migrants who come from professional backgrounds and, when they arrive in the United States, are forced to start at the bottom rung of the social and economic ladder because their skills and education are not recognized by a biased U.S. credential system. Her aspirations do not diminish the way she characterizes herself—similar to many other Latinas I interviewed across ethnic and class backgrounds—as someone who is *cariñosa* (caring and affectionate) and who desires to share these feelings with someone who will understand and respect her. While it might seem contradictory, she expressed "feeling" like an American and white while also feeling affectionate, a national and gendered trait that distinguishes her from U.S. white women, whom company websites and men I interviewed characterized as cold, selfish, and materialistic. Being caring and affectionate for these women translates into deep feelings of affinity with other Latin Americans, despite their sense of alignment with a U.S. culture that supports individual aspirations. These complex ties to national territories reinforce the messiness of power relations across borders that defy binary frameworks of the Global

North versus the Global South. Additionally, Mariana's desire for a particularly racialized U.S. man and state laws and opportunities go hand in hand. In other words, while the state demands migrant marriages to be founded on love, it is clear that personal desires and the political economy of rights and mobility cannot be disentangled.

Also at stake is the role of the state in admitting an increasingly narrow contingency of migrants who can prove they enter as equal citizens and choose the United States out of patriotic love rather than economic need. To perpetuate the myth of the nation as a homogeneous, upwardly mobile class means that the state targets working-class migrants, all the while deflecting this bias by drawing on the deracinated language of love to project inequalities onto racialized bodies outside the nation. Sentiments of love project a patriotic spirit that strips one of economic motivation, fraud, and the attending racialized and sexualized meanings attached to the body-as-threat biometric. Not only does whiteness represent a vehicle for safe mobility across borders, but it also marks the space of invisibility, the right to privacy outside state and social surveillance.[58] That some Latin American women turn to foreign marriage migration as a moral, safe, and middle-class avenue to move across borders takes on even more urgency in the context of media campaigns and laws that equate working-class Latino/as who cross "illegally" with immorality and crime.[59] Even more significant are the images and stories of violent beatings, killings, and rape of undocumented female border crossers by Border Patrol and immigration agents.[60] Marriage with U.S. (white) men is in some ways more secure because these men's legal and social status guarantees their petitioning wives a longer stay than contract work and may potentially become a permanent form of relocation that affords them the ability to periodically return home. But, as stated earlier, women must remain in the marriage for at least two years, when, with the consent of their husbands, they become eligible for permanent residency.

In Colombia, explains Mariana, U.S. marriages are popularly associated with a glamorous lifestyle in which women have successful careers and a romantic relationship. This expectation failed to materialize for Mariana, as she described first boredom and then depression during her marriage. She spent a long time without working once the couple found a remote, safe, and self-sufficient house (equipped with solar panels and a water well) before Y2K was predicted to hit in 2000, when her husband, Jason, feared the onslaught of a computer-related economic disaster. After marrying Jason, Mariana explained a discrepancy between the status she enjoyed back home and her experiences as a new migrant and spouse: "Even if I am depressed, if you are married to a gringo, you have high status."[61] As a newlywed yet ineligible for a work permit, Mariana relayed the difficulty and pleasure of hustling illicit work, such as erotic dancing. When she finally obtained a work permit, she began looking for a job related to her education as a journalist. Again she struggled, driving over two hours to volunteer for a radio station, then moved her way up slowly to work for a major Spanish-language station as a writer and then later as a news anchor.[62] It is through meaningful work that Mariana describes regaining confidence as a productive member of her new home. She told me that she has always worked, mostly with foreign and U.S. companies back home. This goal proved incompatible with her goal of having a successful marriage, however. The more hours she worked and the more successful she became, the longer stretched the distance between her and her husband. Jason described feeling as though he failed to get what he signed up for with Mariana. He wanted kids, while Mariana thought her burgeoning career as a journalist on a major Spanish television network would be impossible to juggle with a pregnancy or having to care for small children. Despite an amicable divorce, both Mariana and Jason realized that they wanted different things and that marriage was not a priority for Mariana, as it was for Jason. Jason said, "In effect, she looked at marriage as a stepping stone to developing herself as an individual rather than two people developing a marriage. . . . I don't think she really wants to be married, . . . and if there's no children, two people don't have to be married."[63] Mariana concurred that she is less invested in marriage but more so in a relationship. As a now prominent reporter for a Spanish-language news station, she transposes sentiments of affection to political action by bringing attention to the economic, legal, and racial struggles facing Latinos living in United States. Mariana's turn to marriage, through the individual passion she has for following her dreams, is difficult to separate from her political desire to make a difference for others who are less fortunate.

Hollywood has long projected the romantic love plot as the idealized route to U.S.-style democracy and the belief that access to class mobility is available to all. Most films about cross-cultural love that are targeted to a Western audience entail some kind of crossing of tabooed boundaries—whether racial, class, gender, religious, or national. Films such as *A Walk in the Clouds* (1995), *Lone Star* (1996), *Fools Rush In* (1997), and *Bend It like Beckham* (2002) associate romantic love across national and cultural boundaries with youthful rebellion against familial control. In these films, freedom symbolizes the move from tradition, culture, and the past to the future of individual choice as proof that modern democracy—as an economic, social, cultural, and intimate expression—reign supreme. For viewers, the films satisfy youthful longings to rebel against family and social norms and expectations, even as the happy Hollywood endings consolidate liberal individualism as the collective avenue to access middle- and upper-class dreams of modern subjectivity and belonging. The framework of romantic love reinforces the national fantasy of multicultural tolerance and equality—that the United States, unlike other ethnic nations, supports kin relations based on individual choice rather than on family oligarchies premised on enriching the family's blood line, land, and financial status. Even though scholars have contested the placement of arranged marriages at the far end of modernity and romantic love, marriages contracted through families rather than based on "free choice" continue to provide a contrast to U.S. democracy.[64] Curiously, immigration law reinforces Hollywood fantasies that romantic love must be freely chosen, selfless, innocent, and naturally binding through chemistry or the irrational attraction between a man and a woman. The irony is that ICE officials demand proof of "love" as part of its governing apparatus against potential marriage cheats and other "security" threats.

The nation, like the body, is itself a virtual space, imagined and experienced as flexible and inclusive, hyperlinked not by "elite" blood alliances but by the potential for transformation, a continually changing space capable of assimilating difference into common goals and ideals. The nation's potential for individual transformation—as a virgin and unpopulated terrain—projects itself as rejuvenating and therapeutic, as magically erasing conditions for structural inequalities. This multicultural ethic, reinforced by some participants in the cybermarriage industry, mediates the nation's self-projection as inclusive—a projection that must be guarded and protected from immigrant hackers who threaten to infiltrate the nation's supposed "openness." The critical factor here is that the desire for transformation must come from the individual, rather than be forced by family, "culture," or other social criteria.

Love, like affect more broadly, is imagined as pure action, as the site of true subjectivity before language, social dictates, or reason, and is thus seen as representative of the authentic self.[65] "Falling in love" has been mythologized in the West as the purest form of intimacy that happens spontaneously, outside one's control. Thus, love, and raw passion, occupies the place of the transcendent, outside quotidian time and place; love defies social orders and perhaps, as argued by Eva Illouz, symbolizes an avenue to enter a utopian moment unconstrained by social, legal, or economic constraints.[66] It is this association of love as being outside societal constraints and the idea of marriage as a contract based on consent rather than force that binds Western-style love and marriage with liberal notions of democracy as the ultimate expression of individual freedom.[67]

Freedom to Choose, Freedom to Date: Repeal
the International Marriage Broker Law

While the right to individual choice and privacy presumably extends to all
(a premise used by some gay and lesbian advocates who demand the right to
marry), this argument has been recently used by marriage agencies to advocate against encroaching state surveillance of the cybermarriage industry.[68]
For instance, the International Marriage Broker Regulation Act (IMBRA),
passed in 2005 as part of the Violence Against Women Act (VAWA),[69]
sought to curb abuse against "mail-order brides" by requiring international
marriage agencies to provide agency participants any man's criminal and
marriage records before they communicate via e-mail or in person at the
Romance Tours. Many agencies have been forced to restructure their business approach, as IMBRA legislation makes it almost impossible to continue
selling women's e-mail addresses to men. This act also limits U.S. sponsors
to two visa petitions.[70] Several international marriage brokers filed a lawsuit
against IMBRA, arguing that it is unconstitutional. Although the suit was
dismissed in court, an immigration law attorney began a petition against
IMBRA, arguing that it was an assault against the right to free speech, privacy, and choice: "Freedom to Choose, Freedom to Date: Repeal the International Marriage Broker Law."[71]

Legislation against the international marriage industry gained traction
after media accounts recycled two horrific incidents of abuse against two
Internet brides, which led to their deaths. Newspaper attention on the most
egregious cases, such as the terrible death of an Asian woman in a Seattle
courthouse in 1995 and the trial of Indle G. King Jr., a man convicted in 2000
of killing Anastasia King (his second "mail-order bride" from the former
Soviet Union), opened debates about the need to control an unwieldy global
industry, popularly positioned as part of the underground trafficking trade.
Media attention to abuse and the swing in immigration legislation against
the trafficking of women has sex trafficking and marriage colliding in academic scholarship, newspaper articles, film, and policy debates. Senator
Maria Cantwell, a Democrat from Washington State claimed, "The advent
of for-profit international marriage brokers—companies that bring together
men and women of different nations solely for the purpose of marriage—
has become closely interlinked with the problem of human trafficking and
abuse."[72]

Stereotypes of international marriages have led to policies such as IMBRA
that demand more surveillance of international web agencies. One of the
curious inconsistencies of IMBRA is that domestic-based matchmaking

companies, such as Match.com, are not part of this legislation and thus are not required to provide female clients with men's criminal records. The Tahirih Justice Center, one of the most vocal feminist organizations cited in defense of IMBRA, has responded to questions about why domestic-based matchmaking companies are exempt from the need to provide background checks. Based on its own in-house research, it concludes that foreign women are abused at a rate three times that of the national average found in domestic Internet dating. Unlike U.S.-based Internet dating sites such as Match. com, where only 3 percent of women come from lower income brackets, the Tahirih Justice Center states that virtually no women who use international marriage brokers come from higher income *countries*, ignoring the fact that many middle-class and professional women living in developing countries also use marriage brokers.[73] In subsequent chapters, I document the high percentages of women from Guadalajara, Mexico, and to a lesser extent Cali, Colombia, who are more educated and of a higher (albeit local) social class than the men they marry. What is significant here, then, is that poverty is used as the basis for exploitation rather than as an analysis of how immigration laws, economic imbalances, and imperial histories contribute to the kinds of choices men and women make in decisions about marriage, love, and migration.[74] The most valuable aspect of IMBRA is that it requires companies to arm women who decide to migrate to the United States to be with their fiancés with information on their rights in this country. The inclusion of extra protections for women in this law, meant to prevent possible abuse (such as allowing abused women who divorce their husbands to petition for citizenship on their own), highlights the uneven terrain in which women enter as "conditional residents" until their husbands help them petition for permanent residency.

The utopian promise of foreign intimacies coexists with an alternate view that these marriages are destined for failure because of the assumed unequal commercial exchange between participants. A closer analysis of immigration law shows that poverty, and too many differences between partners in foreign marriage, threatens the equal and democratic veneer of national belonging. As expressed by an immigration lawyer attending an annual immigration conference in 2004 (and confirmed by the USCIS Fraud Referral Sheet released in January 2010),[75] the kinds of red flags that alert immigration officials and consulates in the review of spousal and fiancée visa cases, include the following:

Wide difference in age between the partners; lack of a common language, wide differences in socio-economic, cultural or religious backgrounds;

initial contact via Internet or E-mail; use of a marriage agency; a short time span during which the partners have known each other or only a brief time shared together; a previous "immigration-procured" spouse or fiancée by the petitioner; four or more divorces by one or both partners; past arrest record or criminal history involving fraud or serious offense; sloppy presentation and dress at interview with missed, inaccurate or inconsistent answers to basic questions.[76]

This immigration lawyer (and active cybermarriage chat-room participant and consultant) confirmed the uneven surveillance of foreign marriage globally, as certain consulates with higher fraud ratios—such as Bogotá, conducting over fifteen hundred interviews daily—have bolstered their antifraud unit. This concentration of attention on the most politically volatile countries, coupled with the gendered association of Colombian women with trafficking and transit (films such as *Maria Full of Grace* only exacerbated this U.S. perception) were reflected in my interviews with women and men as well as in experiences they shared in chat rooms. Various Colombian women shared stories of having to undergo invasive medical inspections and of warding off the onslaught of suspicion by immigration officials' questioning. Monica, who agreed to marry John after their first meeting at a Cali tour, was outraged after an immigration official asked her if she had ever been a prostitute and whether she was trafficking any drugs. Other couples passed immigration screenings with little delay, no doubt telling of the lack of consistency and clarity over such fraught terrain.

Another standard convention driving immigration interrogations is the documented presence of romantic love, confirmed by photos of couples engaged in leisure activities and evidence of love letters. Evidence of a bona fide marriage includes factors such as the length of time couples are together before marriage (the longer the courtship, the better) and various questions that prove cohabitation (such as what side of the bed one sleeps on, preferred meals, cleansing habits, etc.). Couples must also prove legitimacy through shared financial practices, often accomplished via proof of bank statements (those with consistently high bank balances fair much better). John, in the process of petitioning to bring his fiancée from Cali over on a fiancée visa, had to provide not only bank statements but documents of all his assets, including paperwork showing he owned a car and a home.[77] Thus, the relation of immigration policy with neoliberal policies of self-sufficiency, in the context of diminishing public investment, fits well with the criterion of romantic love as the basis for supporting self-sufficient and enduring heterosexual units. In a similar vein, Susan Coutin followed immigrant "suspension of deportation" cases to identify what criteria would help immigrants successfully evade deportation. Immigration court cases, she found, rewarded immigrants who could prove cultural values of self-sufficiency. Only those migrants who were working toward assimilation (such as demonstrating good English skills), who exhibited an entrepreneurial spirit and desire to be upwardly mobile (who sought better-paying jobs), and who could show proof of stability through family values such as heterosexual marriage (or relationships with the future promise of marriage) were considered fit for citizenship and eligible to stay in the country.[78] These cases and examples demonstrate how the state and national politics fashion immigration policies through intimate practices of uplift and choice.

As discussed earlier, marriage enables privileged avenues for movement across borders and protects a woman's moral standing through a veil of innocent love defined against criminality, or those who intentionally break the law. Love and money, or intimacy and economic concerns, while completely entangled in Internet romance culture, continue to be relegated by law to binary subject positions. The innocent, loving citizen-migrant stands in opposition to the conniving, opportunist illegal migrant. This dissonance between innocence and opportunism based on rational criteria is reflected in recent legislation such as the Trafficking of Women Act that protects only those women who can prove their innocence, women who do not knowingly break the law.[79] Thus, the gendered association of women with selflessness, innocence, and an inability to speak back are far from natural but are compulsory by law. It is no surprise, then, that women's claims to citizenship are filtered through an emphasis on love and domestic morality rather than economic self-interest. Foreign marriage migrants must prove that their love is divorced from the financial and personal rewards of U.S. citizenship (including the ability to work, bypassing restrictions, etc.).

Conclusion

The focus on sex trafficking further entrenches an affinity between women's mobility outside heteronormative spaces and social anxieties and fears of sexual and social disorder. More importantly, the attention to sex trafficking normalizes women's migration through heteronormative channels such as care industries and marriage.[80] Other neoconservative agendas behind trafficking legislation include moralizing U.S. intervention around the world and justifying the need for stronger border control, which then further pushes migrants into more dangerous underground economies.[81] Finally, antitrafficking legislation blames trafficking on individuals (mostly by demonizing the smugglers) rather than larger structures of power between wealthy countries and their poorer neighbors, and it showcases the moral character of the United States around the world.[82] Binary categories of innocent/criminal and citizen/alien leave no room for the complicated reasons and forces that contribute to women's migration in marriage or sex industries. As I argue throughout the book, women are neither smuggled nor simply agents of their own choosing. More importantly, confining our understanding within this binary structure elides the deeper intrusion and compulsion of U.S. national fantasies of liberal individualism, tolerance, and the promise of democracy and equality for all.

In the context of marriage industries in Latin America, and more broadly of falling in love, the intentionality of women's desire for middle-class mobility is difficult to separate from intimacy.[83] L. A. Rebhun argues that in the United States, "we tend to believe that sentiment is genuine only if it is spontaneous; conventional, required, manipulated sentiment seems false . . . and its falseness morally reprehensible." But, she continues, "deliberation and requirement are as much a part of emotion as spontaneity."[84] This Western philosophy on love frequently rears its head in chat discussions in which men debate how to tell if a woman is truly in love with you rather than your wealth.[85] Rather than to separate emotions from rationality or to argue that women's agency is mediated by their "strategic display of emotion," or as an expression of "deep acting,"[86] I argue that claiming to be in love is compulsory but also part of women's self-conception as passionate, moral, and self-autonomous subjects hoping to alter the pattern of their lives, to become someone new.[87]

This chapter addresses the difficulties of discussing that which cannot be seen (the interiority of love) or even expressed by the very methodologies we use, such as ethnography and interviews. For this reason, I have premised this chapter on the tensions between women's turn to foreign marriage out of love and the legal construction of them as innocent and thus moral subjects of U.S. nationality. State immigration procedures use these women's status as the innocent and loving migrant to determine whether they are equitable subjects and thus migrants who deserve rights and citizenship. Rather than inquire into women's genuine love for their husbands, I argue that it is impossible to separate the state's demand for women to migrate through love marriages from women's own intimate desires. State investments with regard to migrant love in great part structure and discipline women's mobility and subjectivity within heterosexual marriage, given the lack of other legal channels for migration.

Foreign marriage illustrates the fine line between intimacy and relations of exchange. While the interventions of immigration laws are justified based on their adjudication of the potential risks to migrants, the risks and gains are not as easy to assess. Assumed stereotypes of inequality between the first world and the third world obscure how benefits and risks are distributed. There is no way to calculate the risk of a woman who takes a chance on love in a marriage, in the hope that it may develop over time.

So much emphasis on love—whether the relationship is "real"—contributes to an entire assemblage of chat-room debates, guidebooks, and self-help practices aimed at guiding men in their search for a Latin American bride. In addition, the silencing of women's complicated needs and desires in marrying and migrating with foreign men may cause multiple misunderstandings and thwart forms of intimacy based on knowing how to satisfy each other's material and emotional needs (see chapter 5). In any discussion of foreign marriage, whether or not couples enter into a relationship and form nurturing lives together, one must examine how immigration law and national myth work together to enforce women's mobility through romantic love and "innocence," as well as how they violently discipline movement and incriminate others who fall out of this moral category. The fact that immigration enforces middle-class migration through the moral lens of "respectable" forms of love and the family becomes the basis for further criminalizing all of those who veer from heterosexual normative behavior. Thus, heterosexuality, marriage, and the family have become compulsory for one's moral placement within a transnational cultural economy. It is this transnational perspective I turn to next to expand the scope of how and why Mexican women seek marriage with U.S. men. The state's scrutinizing gaze on foreign marriages fails to consider the seduction of the West via the influx of U.S. businesses, tourists, films, and the Internet in shaping the shift in Latin American women's intimate affinity away from the Mexican nation and local Latin men and toward Western values, men, rights, and ways of life.

2

Conversions of the Self

Mexican Women's Turn from the National to the Foreign

> With Mexican men, . . . they don't like that the woman improves
> herself.
> —Jessica, in the documentary *Cowboy del Amor* (2006)

As I approached the glitzy Presidente hotel where I was to interview men
and women at the International Singles party—otherwise known as the
"Romance Vacation Tour"—the bus veered into Plaza del Sol, one of the
wealthiest and most well manicured and touristy areas of Guadalajara,
Mexico. As women began to arrive, it was quite apparent that these were
not your typical "mail-order brides" popularly thought to marry men
from the United States out of poverty and desperation. On the contrary,
the majority of women were well educated and from a small, burgeoning,
professional Mexican middle class. They were confident, savvy, and cosmopolitan in their familiarity with U.S. culture through film, television,
the Internet, encounters with tourists, and stories from family living in the
United States, as well as through their own travel abroad. The owner of
GlobalLatinas gave me permission to attend the tour for research because
my bicultural identity set me apart from the "feminist type," the white,
female journalists from the United States who, after attending his tours,
wrote a scathing report on his "exploitative" business. I, on the other hand,

spoke Spanish and was part Mexican, the offspring of a mixed Anglo-Mexican union.

Many of the Mexican women I interviewed turned to foreign men and lifestyles as a way to escape "traditional" value systems in the family, a corrupt and unstable government, and confining definitions of gender, sexuality, and womanhood. As the epigraph to this chapter reflects, many women from Mexico and Colombia, including Jessica, depict Latin men—as well as the economic, social, and political situation in their countries more broadly— as stunting their personal and economic growth. As women articulate their hope to leave what some consider is "oppressive" about Mexican men (and Mexico) for a seemingly more open and liberating journey with foreign men (and the United States), they demonstrate how powerful such a shift in their imaginary—from national to transnational citizenship—can be. The space of the foreign promises greater prospects for self-improvement and growth through a more intimate and equitable marriage partner, opportunities to travel, better education, and sometimes, careers.[1] The rise of this industry, and some women's turn to the foreign, also tells us how gendered claims to rights percolate here not through social changes demanded by Latin American feminist scholars and activists but through the more personal sphere of intimacy within one's immediate reach.[2] Foreign intimacies, however, do not always detach women from their association with Mexican "traditions" and gender roles.

Aware of the national and cultural differences between themselves and women in the United States, these Mexican women accentuate their feminine and loving nature on marriage profile pages. These virtues translate into a marketable trait, especially since many U.S. men perceive U.S. women as cold, materialistic, and self-centered. Though traditional motherhood in Mexico is a trait that many women feel constrains their options, a trait that is taken for granted there, in the context of the United States, these same roles become highly valued and better compensated. Mexican women appreciate being highly valued by U.S. men. This is especially the case when women face collective decline in value in the eyes of local men and labor markets as the state devalues local currency and wages to maintain a competitive edge in the global market. Not only do local men, and the state institutions that support male power, shirk their responsibility to women, but many women also experience gendered violence (or the potential for violence) in their everyday lives. Despite the material consequences of these shifting value structures, women's turn to the foreign to trade up their embodied value also works to discipline their speech, movements, and desires within the parameters of the neoliberal marketplace.

In line with the Mexican state's turn to the foreign to uplift the economy, some women similarly direct their hopes to the foreign for personal and economic uplift.[3] It is no coincidence that those who seek out U.S. romance and potentially a husband work in the professional sector or for multinational corporations and tourism industries, making higher wages than local positions provide. In addition, the global reach of the Internet, which constantly brings new people, ideas, and fantasies into the intimate spheres of men's and women's lives, makes it a key medium to try out, and sometimes achieve, personal fantasies.

Just before my trip to Guadalajara, I bought a comprehensive package of women's mail and e-mail addresses directly from the GlobalLatinas website. I used a male name to purchase a full-color magazine that included photos of all 654 of GlobalLatinas' women; a short description of each woman's interests, including the kind of man she sought; and detailed measurements of each woman's body. When the magazine arrived, it was difficult, flipping through page after page of women's photos, not to feel what some men might experience as a consumer shopping for the best buy. In addition to contacting women via e-mail, I interviewed couples and documented participants' data through two marriage organizations with full website services. Mexican Wives, a small agency owned by a North American man in his early forties, was tucked inconspicuously in one of most affluent neighborhoods of Guadalajara.[4] GlobalLatinas, based in Houston, Texas, offered tours to Mexico, usually two to three times a year.[5] These companies attract hundreds of women through radio announcements, ads in the back of *Cosmopolitan* magazine, and by word of mouth.[6] In exchange for the women's posting their profiles and photos on the GlobalLatinas website, they attend the Vacation Romance Tours for free, while men pay from $500 to $1,200 (not including airfare, hotel, and other incidentals).[7]

I spent several weeks interviewing couples at Mexican Wives, often arriving early so I could spend a few extra hours compiling data from 307 women's profile pages in agency folders, stacked by women's age (to assist men as they select prospective dates during their stay at the agency). Women varied from eighteen to fifty-five years old, and almost half had a university education (49 percent). They held a range of professional jobs, most in business but also as doctors, accountants, teachers, business owners, secretaries, bankers, models, and beauticians. Of these 307 women, 31 percent marked their status as divorced, and only 4 percent claimed to be *"una ama de casa,"* or a woman who stayed at home—a small number given that just over 50 percent of the women had at least one child. On women's profile pages, the majority stated that they were Catholic or Christian or that they believed in God. Only 5 percent reported that they did not have a religion. Some attended the tours out of curiosity, to practice their English, or to enjoy a night out on the town with a foreigner. Most hoped they might get lucky and find true love and, eventually, a husband.

The majority of women I interviewed came from a small but privileged middle or upper-middle class. In Mexico, middle-class status denotes more than merely one's economic level. Other factors that distinguish class status include family name, higher levels of education, English competency, owning a car or home, one's neighborhood, access to private schooling, technological access, being light-skinned, and exhibiting the desire for self-improvement. The acquisition of a tourist visa is also telling of class status, as this document brokers (legitimate) travel across the U.S.-Mexico border. From women's profile pages, I found that just less than half of the women who signed up with the agency had visas, while another one-fifth who did not hold a current visa had had one in the past.[8]

There are plenty of reasons why Mexican women want to marry a man from the United States, yet these desires sometimes conflict with the types of men the agencies attract. Women in their late twenties and older hope to escape the stigma of being "older" and single in Mexican society, which generally assumes they are past their prime. Just as marriage symbolizes positive qualities such as happiness, opportunity, and advancement, the state of being single is stigmatized as the exact opposite: lack of achievement, solitude, stagnation, and failure.[9] Websites tell men they can expect to date and/or marry women up to twenty to thirty years younger than themselves—accentuating the market for younger women. When I questioned women about what kind of man they found attractive at the tour, many agreed that men's age and appearance were less relevant than their upstanding character and attentiveness to women.

Social Changes in Class and Gender Roles:
Guadalajara in the Global Economy

As middle-class Mexican women enter the job market and earn their own money, more women question the utility of traditional gender roles in Mexico that position men as head of the family. During the twentieth century, various changes took place in Guadalajara, including the rapid influx of people from rural to urban areas, industrialization, the global expansion of commerce and services, an increase in mass communications, and the spread of Protestantism. As this city transformed from a rural to an urban economy, women enjoyed better employment, education, and health care.[10] The peso crisis of the 1980s especially affected single and middle-class women. Because this widespread economic crisis resulted in the loss of jobs, large numbers of men migrated to the United States, creating both opportunities and responsibilities for women left behind.[11] When this newly found independence was coupled with higher levels of education, women began to want more equitable gender roles; they waited longer to marry, divorce rates increased, and a greater use of contraception resulted in fewer children.[12]

The peso crisis also shook the nation's faith (as well as that of the international community) in a stable and moral governmental body in Mexico. In 1987, the minimum wage in urban areas fell to 58 percent of levels found in 1980, while the cost of living and food continued to rise.[13] The repercussions of the economic decline continue to be felt today as professional women—professors, psychologists, bank executives, lawyers, and so on—find it increasingly difficult to live off one salary.[14] Many women I interviewed described the urgency of augmenting their salary by working extra hours on the weekends or adding a second job in the evenings. Their exhaustion was palpable as they shared having to work long days, often six a week, deflating the promise of women's liberation from domestic drudgery into professional careers.

Guadalajara is a fascinating location because, while not a regional border zone, the city throbs in liminality between the modern and traditional, rural and urban. Tourism ads have long mythologized the city as cosmopolitan yet steeped in traditional femininity (where religious and family-oriented Mexican women can be found) and traditional masculinity (idealized in ranch traditions such as rodeos, mariachi, tequila production, and artisan crafts). The city, located in the state of Jalisco, retains a particularly strong grip on the national imaginary as the bastion of tradition, with its iconic image of rural gendered traditions, even as dramatic changes have obliterated many rural ways of living and thinking. Ironically, the conservatism that accompanies the middle and upper classes in particular resides alongside the largest gay community in Mexico.[15] In addition, the city is experiencing rapid transformations due to migrant cultures that bring ideas and remittances back home, boosting their local economy, family income, and status, as well as accelerating the city's transition to high-tech industries.

Once you leave the airport, a large sign on the road to the city reminds tourists and business travelers that Guadalajara is the Mexican "Silicon Valley." The city attracts Mexican students and workers, as well as international corporations, into its burgeoning technological industries. While I conducted research in Guadalajara during 2000–2001, Internet providers such as AOL heavily invested in glitzy advertising campaigns featuring Latina/o actors such as Salma Hayek and Ricky Martin in order to showcase Mexico's potential entrance into modernity and the limelight, as a central player in the global information highway. With more than twenty-three million users in 2008 (21.6 percent of the total population), Mexico has the second-largest Internet market in Latin America, a privilege enjoyed mostly by the middle and elite classes.[16] Now it is home to Google, Microsoft, and other high-tech industries. Guadalajara embodies what Saskia Sassen calls a "global city" that is connected to cities in the United States through a high-tech infrastructure, professional jobs, and migration networks.[17]

As Mexico liberalized its economy by turning to foreign markets and trade agreements such as NAFTA in 1994 to stimulate its economy, Mexicans also turned to the consumption of foreign goods to mark their status as cosmopolitan and privileged members of society. Legacies of Spanish and French invasion linger prominently in Guadalajara's colonial architecture and reside in the attitude of some of its residents. In other words, for the middle and upper class in Guadalajara, the foreign is a familiar presence of everyday life, transferring sentiments of grandeur from the past to expectations for the future. Today, the influence of the United States seeps into the economic strategies of the professional classes, while also reorienting intimate affinities. Similar to what Maureen O'Dougherty has documented among the middle class in Brazil, Mexicans turned to symbolic markers of class standing, such as foreign products and lifestyles, education, and careers, as well as cultural and moral standing, to distinguish themselves from the lower classes as well as to claim an affinity with a global cosmopolitan class.[18] For some Mexican women, it is not simply a desire for proximity to consumption and participation in the global culture of taste that they desire.[19] In addition to consumption, *sentiments* increasingly translate modern transnational affinities.[20] For the privileged, intimacy with U.S. men communicates attachments to a cosmopolitan nationalism in which foreignness is constantly woven into the fabric of the nation, rather than a neocolonial presence that threatens to obliterate other ways of life.

Intimate Defections

As women I interviewed described why they wanted to marry a man from the United States, it became difficult to distinguish their accounts of Mexican men from the body of the Mexican nation. They looked to men from the United States to embody utopic, egalitarian relationships and lifestyles with partners who would share in household chores, offer a better way of life, and provide more economic stability and opportunities—qualities that various women argued Mexican men lack. During interviews and in written accounts from agency books, women continually stated they wanted a man who was loyal, understanding of and responsive to their needs, and hardworking. When I asked women at the tours why they could not find a man like that in Guadalajara, they shook their heads and repeatedly voiced their dislike for "macho men."

Anna, a thirty-four-year-old widowed mother who works as a part-time accountant, responded enthusiastically to my e-mail and agreed to meet me at Sanbornes, a well-known chain restaurant.[21] She told me she juggles working and taking care of her three children, who attend private school, with the support of her family. According to Anna, men in Mexico are more *machista* than U.S. men because they are threatened by the fact that women earn more than they do.

> Economically, they [Mexican women] are more stable than the men. . . . They already have their own house, car, and luxuries that many men cannot give them. And, even more curious, what angers men here in Mexico—and for this reason they are more macho—is that women are more successful than them. But the good thing about people from other countries is that they admire this kind of woman.[22]

While Anna believes Mexican men's machismo stems from threats to their power in the home and workplace, she interprets foreign men from first-world countries as the opposite, the kind of men who respect strong and successful women. Anna keenly asserted that men in Mexico need to subordinate women in order to feel like a man. Machismo, according to Anna, is a defensive state against women's elevated social and economic positions. Interestingly, during our later correspondence, after Anna had more experience meeting men at the Vacation Romance Tours, she noted that many U.S. men arrived with the assumption that women were underdeveloped, that they lived in ranches or little *pueblos*. They could not believe that she had bought her own apartment in Puerto Vallarta. She smiled at me and said, "*Somos una buena opcíon, eh?*" (We're a good catch, huh?). After about five distressing months of not hearing back from the man she had corresponded with for over a year, she reluctantly returned to the next tour. She feared that his sudden military transfer to Iraq was the cause of his silence.

When I asked women why they thought men from the United States differ from those in Mexico, they attributed it to the fact that Mexican men are irresponsible, "*como niños*" (like kids), and inattentive to their emotional and intellectual needs. Men, they argued, were coddled in the home by their mothers and moved out only to expect the same from their wives. On the other hand, Anna explained,

> I have noticed that men from over there [the United States] are willing to share in the chores. . . . I've seen something that almost never occurs here. . . . Over there they have told me, "I will cook for you," not like what they say here: "What do you mean I'm going to cook for you?" [*laughing hard*]. Over there men are more independent from a younger age. I think that they learn to value all of these aspects, you know, . . . and this gives them a little more maturity. It's liberating that they themselves feel this way and that they have fewer prejudices than men here.[23]

For Anna, U.S. men's willingness to participate in "women's work" is liberating, as it opens relationships up to negotiation, flexibility, and communication. While processes such as urbanization and increases in education and employment for women contribute to changing gender roles, it appears women are changing faster than men.[24] Guadalajara is a city in motion, as many men cross into the United States to find work. Josephina, a fifty-two-year-old divorced doctor with two grown children, expressed her frustration with the lack of eligible men left in Mexico, specifically in the state of Jalisco, who "*no valieron la pena*" (were not worth the effort). Of those who do remain, she described three types: men affected by macho culture (especially those from the lower classes with little education, although she noted that even men from the higher classes try to downplay or control their machismo); homosexuals (who in Jalisco, she said, are abundant); and *mojados* (migrant farmworkers, many who have migrated to California). And of those men who have not married, "many want sex without commitment or sex in exchange for going out to eat or for going with him to the movies." Josefina does not see a fair exchange between men whose earnings, lifestyles, and cosmopolitan outlook do not match her own. Again, she characterizes machismo as a juvenile or childlike state when compared to the paternal father/husband to the north. A couple of other women looked at me sideways and complained under their breath that many men in Guadalajara are gay, thus limiting women's options for available partners. The various comments I heard from women about the proliferation of macho and gay men in Guadalajara reinforced women's typecasting of both groups as childlike and selfish in their search for pleasure since, presumably, they have no interest in long-term, monogamous relations leading to marriage. Although it is important to challenge popular sentiment that women's abandonment of their domestic responsibilities causes social decline, women's remarks about men's sexual immaturity (such as their failure to effectively lead the family and nation) disciplines men's pleasure back to their role in the family as providers and as better leaders of the home and nation.

The overwhelming consistency of women's complaints about machismo reveals the broader context of the Vacation Romance Tour as a ritualistic site for romance and a transnational space that mediates how stories are told.[25] In other words, there are scripts that operate within these spaces, through which women translate their desire to seek out men from the United States. Women's statements are less important for being "true" or "false" than for alerting us to the figurative weight these stories carry as being easily digestible by a Western audience that is familiar with the trope of Latin men as hypermacho womanizers.

There are, however, both salient and problematic critiques here that are embedded within women's characterizations of Mexican men. First, women reveal class biases in associating Mexican men with negative macho qualities. In particular, intimacy with local men thwarts equitable structures of capitalist exchange (what Josephina says is an unfair exchange), as Mexican men are economically unable to reciprocate women's affection with marriage, gifts, and leisure activities. Women's complaints of machismo are connected to their critique of men and the Mexican nation, as a structure of feeling characterized with excessive sexualized (homoerotic) emotion, as unproductive, inequitable, and violent, binding women's love and marriage to a subordinate position in the family and nation. The personal betrayals and sexualized traumas expressed by divorced and single women are connected to women's relationship to patriarchal and national structures of power. Negative characterizations of Mexican men are also a critique of an irresponsible, abusive, and overly patriarchal government and nation-state. Josephina said it best:

> The Mexican woman of the year 2001 is waking up from her cruel reality. She has and is being given more options to live a rich life, full of work and personal accomplishments, to improve her per capita income. She is being taken into account within the workforce of the working class and not only as a baby-making machine, nor as a housewife who is more like a servant without a salary and without any recognition from her own family or those around her. The Mexican woman has for many years been awakening to better opportunities in her life in all aspects, and with this outlook, she wants her day-to-day labor to be recognized as having the same skill and intellectual capacity as that of the man. Women from our country, "The Bronze-Skinned Race," are waking up from a long slumber that has lasted centuries and are now accepting their proper value (even though this is

causing her to be badly treated, humiliated, tortured even until death. I am not exaggerating, Felicity. It is true). The most important, I think, [for a woman] is to recognize her proper value before herself and before others, and that she be respected as a valuable human being.[26]

Josephina verbalizes not only women's dissatisfaction with their subordinate gender position in the patriarchal family, culture, and society in general but, more insidiously, the gendered violence and backlash against women's assertions of value and equality with men. As many Latin American and U.S. feminists acknowledge, it is impossible to separate women's devaluation vis-à-vis men in the domestic sphere and labor market from women's subordinate access to the political sphere—most grotesquely evident in the violence and unresolved killings of women in Juárez, Mexico, as well as in other Latin American countries. As Marcela Lagarde y de los Ríos argues, feminicide, or the genocide of women, "is produced by the patriarchal, hierarchical, and social organization of gender, based on supremacy and inferiority, that creates gender inequality between women and men."[27] While most women did not bring up these horrific acts of gendered violence in my interviews, women's turn from local to foreign men resonates with the broader context of women's fragile relation to social and legal rights that makes them vulnerable to everyday forms of gendered violence, especially for those who refuse to abide by traditional gender roles. I want to be clear that Mexico has long enjoyed an advanced legal system altered by revolution, French conquest (the Napoleonic Code), and independence, as well as by liberalism and Enlightenment thought. More recently, in August 2010, Mexico's Supreme Court ruled that every state must recognize gay marriages performed in the capital city of D.F., where adoption rights have been extended to gay couples. It is not the law but the culture of lawlessness that women refer to, that men do not comply with divorce laws (or that they do not earn enough to pay alimony) and that there is little legal redress or social support to make sure men comply with the law. Even for the middle class, there is little national support of women's new professional careers or equitable gender roles in the family.

Mexican feminists have recently brought attention to a backlash against women's advancement, appearing in popular TV shows, newspapers, and even a popular radio talk show in Monterrey, Mexico. The host of the talk show, Oscar Muzquiz, solicits men to call in with stories of neglectful wives, in search of the "Female Slob of the Year," or wives who are channeling their energy into careers rather than their families. Muzquiz attributes this shift to the "Americanization" of family values and is quoted in an interview as saying that too many Mexican women are confusing "liberty with licentiousness," and too many Mexican men are becoming "mandelones"—Mexican slang for browbeaten wimps or overly feminized men.[28] These popular discourses and images of women out of control are meant to morally pressure or discipline women's bodies back into the home and traditional gender roles. Josephina and several other women also pointed the finger toward mothers who they claimed perpetuate machismo in their preferential treatment of boys. In addition, class tensions were apparent at the tours. Some middle-class women disapproved of the behavior of the *morenas*, or dark-skinned women, who they claimed took their desire for American men too far by sleeping with those they met at the tour. As I explain in more detail in chapter 5, women themselves governed other women's sexual behavior by differentiating Mexican sexual practices from the sexual licentiousness of U.S. women.

Historically, women garnered social status for their reproductive role in populating the nation as well as serving as the cultural force in educating the nation's future generations in how to be good citizens.[29] Thus, women's role in the heterosexual family, as wives and mothers, was mythically narrated to guard women's placement within the home. Women who stepped out of these roles were marked as outcasts, prostitutes, whores, or *malas mujeres* (bad women).[30] Well documented are the ways national projects target women's bodies as the focus of disciplinary control,[31] though few accounts take seriously how women themselves disrupt the moral body of the nation through negative characterizations of men. Conversant with global scripts of family behaviors and structures, women pollute their own national boundaries by characterizing the nation as an overly "macho" male body. Women naturalize their defection from their own nation and highlight their affinity to another. They reverse the gender hierarchy by polluting the body of Mexico as a "spectacle of men out of control."[32] As we will see, women view themselves as having to abscond from Mexico, a nation they equate with immature, selfish, violent, and backward men.

Las Malinchistas: Betraying the Nation

By characterizing Mexico as a *machista* or macho nation, women are responding to negative reactions from mainstream Mexican society to their (sexualized) involvement with foreign men. For this reason, many women keep their interactions with the tours, e-mail exchanges, and dates a secret from friends and family. Lacking other outlets, many of the women I approached eagerly spoke with me as someone they assumed would validate their modern sentiments. Alicia, a single thirty-three-year-old, owns her own photography studio and has traveled to the United States through a previous career with American Airlines. She has green eyes and light skin and asked that we meet in one of the new hot spots in Guadalajara, El Centro Magno. This is a hip, cosmopolitan, and expensive mall with a Hard Rock Café, a Chili's (with higher prices than in the States), Italian restaurants and cafés, clothing stores with trendy styles from around the world, and a multi-plex cinema that features mostly films from the United States.[33] Alicia mentioned that most of her friends call her a *"Malinchista."* When I asked her why, she said, "'Cause I only date foreign men: Europeans, Canadians, and Americans. . . . I just don't like the men here: short, fat, and dark-skinned . . . no-o. . . . I like them tall, slender, and well dressed."

The term *Malinchista* has deep historical roots in Mexico. The union between the Spanish conquistador Hernán Cortés and his indigenous con-cubine, Malintzin or La Malinche, has been mythologized as the birth of the first *mestizo*, or mixed-race Mexicano. La Malinche has been narrated through Mexican and Chicano literature as the one who was literally sold by her mother into slavery but also the one who metaphorically "sold out" her people to the colonizer, the enemy.[34] This historical narrative of the origins of Mexico and Mexico's mixed racial heritage continues to infiltrate popu-lar memory through colloquial language today.[35] A *Malinchista* is popularly known as a traitor, or *la chingada*, literally, the one who has been "fucked over," sexually or figuratively, by the penetration of foreign imperialism and policies.[36] Thus, the consumption of "foreignness" is particularly intertwined with gender, sexuality, race, and class, setting nationalism and Mexico's turn to modernity in constant conflict. The lighter one's skin color, the more one is associated with the upper class, the conqueror, modernity, wealth, and cul-ture. While middle-class women associate freedoms and opportunities with foreign culture, those who benefit less—especially poor men and the indig-enous—internalize this "phallic" intrusion of imperialist, global capital as an emasculating and neocolonial process. For the elite of Mexico, the United States and "things foreign" connote culture, professionalization, and status. This idea of boosting the economy of Mexico through foreign culture is fur-ther complicated by contemporary popular Mexican filmmakers, musicians, and artists who speak for the voiceless and condemn elite culture for selling out the country to foreign companies and buying into foreign taste cultures. The contestation over the national image varies depending on one's gender, race, sexuality, class, and vision for the future.

Alicia characterized men from Mexico as short, balding, dark-skinned, and overweight (and thus lazy); this translates to the lower class, the unedu-cated, and those with more indigenous roots. Conversely, she associated for-eign men—the tall, slender, well dressed, and light skinned—with education,

culture, and professionals who wear suits. Alicia internalizes this very dichotomy between first- and third-world countries, between the United States
and Mexico, as a modern versus a traditional nation, and she aligns herself
with a more cosmopolitan class that extends national borders. My focus here
on Alicia's personification of foreign intimacy, what I see as the corporate
makeover of the image of the United States with benevolent patriarchy (and
differentiated from local forms of violent patriarchy), resonated with many
other women at the tour. I remember sitting with Blanca, a fifty-two-year-old
woman I discuss in more depth later, in her gated home in a beautiful neighborhood of Guadalajara, as we pored over the sixty or so e-mails and letters
she received, many accompanied with photos. She laughed as she handed me
photos of men covered in dirt tending to their farms, pictures of surprisingly
young men, others clearly unkempt, and still others who sent in dated photos from the heyday of their youth during the 1970s. She shook her head in
disgust because of the low quality of men. And then she handed me a photo
of an African American man in his midthirties wearing a track suit. "Oh,
no," she repeated over and over, and her face turned sour while she shook
her head. It was not immediately clear whether it was his age or his race that
caused such revulsion, but when she pointed out another black man's picture, with the same horrified look, her point clarified. Then her face suddenly
erupted into a smile as she found the only one who interested her. A photo
emerged of a tall and confident Anglo man in a suit, about her age, maybe in
his midfifties. Her face drooped again as she explained his lack of interest in
her once he learned her age. He confessed that he was looking for a woman
in her late twenties or early thirties.

Women's enthusiasm for a successful, light-skinned, and tall man
extended beyond the tour and could be heard over the airwaves of Guadalajara's Radio Mujer. Women called in inspired by the prospect of snatching
an eligible date. One of the station's programs, *Al fin te encuentro!* (At last
I've found you!), brought women to the station who would, similar to the
visual photos of women on marriage websites, announce their personal data
to listeners in Guadalajara: "I have green eyes, long brown hair," and so on.
Many sought similar traits in the man they hoped to meet: "*que tengan posi-
bilidades económicas*" (that they have money) and that the men "*sea alto y
delgado*" (are tall and thin). Whereas the women I interviewed meet men in
person via marriage agency tours or men's personal travel, these women met
up with their potential suitor at the radio station, which brokered and paid
for a blind date for those who successfully found a match. The lack of eligible
local professional men caused some of these same women to visit foreign
agencies and to attend the vacation tours.

When describing men in Mexico as macho, women turn the moralizing discourse away from their own bodies and from the accusation that they are the *Malinchistas*. Instead they degrade the national body with images of poor, uneducated, and/or abusive men. They conflate their individual experiences—with abusive, insensitive, immature, and adulterous men—with popular images of the Mexican nation. Men who make money in the professional economy signify a moral economy and the most upright citizens. While women turn this discourse onto Mexican men as unfit fathers, husbands, providers, and role models, they do not discuss the lack of economic opportunities for men in Mexico that limit their ability to be as economically stable, well traveled, and experienced as men from the United States.[37]

Historically, scholarship and popular films trafficking stereotypes of macho Mexican men proliferated during periods of conflict between Mexico and the United States, especially during Mexico's struggle to assert itself as an independent nation against the pull of the "modern" West. These struggles have long materialized in the U.S. imaginary via a heterosexual romance between a sexy señorita and the Anglo who must save her from the backward and violent macho.[38] As argued by Héctor Domínguez-Ruvalcaba, within critical discourses of machismo after the Mexican Revolution, "the masculine image appears . . . as an allegory of domination, the colonial condition, and the obstacle for modernization."[39] In a similar vein, that the majority of women I interviewed justified their turn to foreign men out of their distain for "machos" operates as another form of modernizing a nation they see as lapsing into another state of disorder.

Women's expressions of intimacy resonate not simply with nationalism but also with conquest. When I pressed women about their e-mail exchanges or dates with men, some who lacked conviction in the man or the relationship used the expression "*ya no me conquistó*" (I haven't been conquered yet). To be colonized by love invokes a personal conquest that happens not by force but by a man's ability to shower a woman with attention that can only come from one's ability to intimately know the other. Thus, colloquial expressions of intimacy and love reframe conquest from a violent takeover to the benevolent and mutual conversion of the heart.[40] In fact, Anna narrates her quest for a U.S. husband through the success of a close friend's marriage to an Anglo-American she met at the Romance Tour. At first the friend was not interested in him; he was unattractively simple, tall, pale, and thin, while she was short and more full-bodied. Despite her friend's personal preference for an older and more handsome man, Anna explains how during the three days of the tour he conquered her with his thoughtfulness and won her heart through his persistence and attention to her, despite her initial dislike for him.[41] Regardless of great differences in their language, body type, and culture, and even though she knew her life would be challenging given the racism against Latinos/as in Michigan, his consideration of her needs and fears won her over. He even invited her to visit him in Michigan so she could step into his life and decide if she wanted to share it with him.

Narratives of love have long enabled the United States to project itself not as a violent empire based on usurping territory but as a more benevolent force pitched as mutually beneficial and desirable. While women have been cast as beautiful maidens who wait for the chivalrous Yankee to save them, Mexican men have often emerged as lazy, violent, backward, and incompetent. Women's recirculation of these gendered stereotypes—lodged in the cultural imaginary during conquest, U.S. empire, the U.S.-Mexico War, and in film narratives during Franklin Roosevelt's "Good Neighbor Policy"—speaks to their discursive authority and legibility within a transnational context. Women also turn to the foreign to reimagine their placement within U.S. national narratives, to catapult them forward into the modern future. Many women conflate U.S. men and the West with a notion of capitalism premised on hard work and high rewards, a democratic system that reciprocates.

Conversions of Self: Love, Work, and Protestantism

These transnational marriages offer women the prospect of dual citizenship, the flexibility to combine Mexican traditions of the importance of the family and a strong work ethic with heightened mobility. By distinguishing their difference from norms of Mexican culture and society, women demarcate their symbolic move away from the Mexican nation-state to that of a transnational family, citizen, and consumer. Through consumption, argues Nestor García Canclini, most Latin Americans experience sentiments of belonging and citizenship by forging similar taste cultures across national, rather than regional, borders.[42] Consumer spaces (malls, movie theaters, and restaurants) compete with public spaces (parks, zócalos/city plazas, etc.) for the proliferation of middle-class intimacy, bridging consumer desire with romance.[43] In fact, professional women seek romantic affinities with men, locally or from afar, who share values embraced in professional settings: hard work, equitable relations, and a partnership based on communication, an open spirit to challenge oneself, and honesty.[44]

Laura is a hardworking single woman in her early thirties who often works six days a week for a company that imports and exports goods to and from Mexico and the United States. She lives with a relative and still has a hard time making the payments on a new small car she recently bought. Through her long e-mail courtship with Cody, a wealthy man from Texas, her e-mails are punctuated with affection, work success, family illnesses, hardships, and a deep determination to persevere. Her suitor, who visits periodically to whisk her away on romantic trips to the beach, wires her money when she needs it and ships her flowers and gifts for her birthday and holidays. Cody entered her life like a prince from afar who she could depend on, at least as long as the relationship endured.[45] In an early e-mail to him she describes her view on relationships:

> I'm not looking for a man to take care of me. I am looking for a man that is ready to share his life with me, that knows how to work, and who desires to grow alongside his partner. For me, it would not be pleasant to live with a man that sits around and hopes for good luck so that things go well. . . . I like to work, and I would like to work together with my partner so that between the two of us we could make something together for our future.

The kind of marriage Laura describes sounds more like a partnership than a patriarchal structure; in this partnership, intimacy develops in the shared vision of hard work and sacrifice toward securing a future together. This intimate vision makes no distinction between love and the economy, the public and private, the individual and the collective. In bed and in the workplace, a couple should be contributing equally and working hard to uplift oneself and the relationship. Mixing workplace culture with sexuality heated up, rather than cooled, the friction of bodies. For Laura, sex was no longer an obligation, geared toward male pleasure. Their romantic trips to the coast opened up a venue for sexual experimentation and mutual pleasure. This understanding of sex and love with the mutual ideals of capitalist exchange echoes the discourse promoted by U.S. magazines and psychological research on love. Eva Illouz's study on the parallels between love and capitalism looks to popular culture to trace these interconnections. Women's magazines suggest that instead of being "stricken" or "smitten" by love, a woman is responsible for her romantic successes and failures, that she must "work hard" to secure a comfortable emotional future for herself, and that she should guarantee that a relationship will provide an equitable exchange.[46] Magazines such as *Cosmopolitan* are quite popular with middle- to upper-class women in Mexico. This magazine mixes articles written in the United States with articles that are locally produced. Through this mixture of discourses, elite readers are asked to "vicariously" participate in emancipation, even though editors know that women are expected to abide by more traditional norms.[47] The middle-class women I interviewed are not satisfied with "vicariously" participating in new ideas of womanhood and marriage. Instead, they see themselves as actively working hard toward personal and work goals that alter their relation to the traditional and the modern and to Mexico and the United States.

In Tania Rodríguez Salazar's study of women and marriage in Guadalajara, she concludes that the older women she interviewed base marriage on luck and destiny.[48] These are ideas that coincide with appropriate gender roles for women under Catholicism. Women are encouraged to be spiritually strong, like La Virgen de Guadalupe, and passive recipients of God's will. A woman should not actively seek a partner but merely happen to be in the right place at the right time. Women I interviewed, however, described themselves within modern ideas of the self, as an individual actively seeking self-fulfillment and happiness through their use of the Internet and these matchmaking services.[49] As Anna explains her philosophy on love and life, she says, "I know from personal experience that if I need something, I can achieve it if I go and look for it, if I save in order to buy it, or if I work very carefully, I can earn it. . . . But I never wait for things to fall from the sky. . . . What's more, I think that happiness is found in the search and not in waiting."

Anna bases love and marriage less on destiny than on capitalist relations in which hardworking individuals achieve success. That Anna is Protestant rather than Catholic also shapes her understanding of women's role in the world. In fact, more than a third of the women who signed up with Mexican Wives identified themselves in their profiles as Christian or of no religion or wrote that they were Catholic but did not abide by all of the rules for women according to the Church. This shift from Catholicism to Protestantism reflects a broader trend of conversion to Protestantism in Mexico and Latin America.[50]

This version of Christianity, intertwined with Puritan ideals of hard work as well as capitalist relationships, asks followers not to be passive bystanders but hardworking individuals. Women base love and marriage less on a Catholic interpretation that teaches people to be passive recipients of God's will than on capitalist relations in which hardworking individuals achieve success. Conversion to Protestantism, the body's actual seizure by the Spirit, enacts the replacement of five hundred years of Spanish imperialism with a U.S. version that promises more power to individuals, spiritual renewal, voluntarism, and the search for new economic alliances and models of society.[51] American-style religion and corporatism offer values of personal improvement, the belief in meritocracy, and the promise of democracy. Joining a new religious community confirms these women's desire to question common-sense traditional values and to find moral affirmation in other ways of perceiving themselves and their goals. Similar to the accusations against women as *Malinchistas*, Protestant and especially Evangelical churches in Latin America are targeted for favoring foreign interests through the channeling of money and ideas from the United States and thus for compromising national sovereignty. Guadalajara is traditionally characterized as one of the more politically and religiously conservative cities in Mexico, as the majority of its citizens strongly identify as Catholic. In 1990, 96 percent of the population declared they were Catholic.[52] More recent data from the state of Jalisco reveals that from 1990 to 2000 slightly over 10 percent of the population converted to Protestantism each year.

Religious conservatism and women's status as part of the ownership class shape their political vision in contradistinction to feminist and other political struggles. For example, Jessica, a thirty-three-year-old dermatologist from Chiapas, Mexico, explains her reasons for seeking a U.S. husband in *Cowboy del Amor* (2005), a documentary that follows the tactics used by an Anglo-American cowboy to match U.S. men with Mexican women for over sixteen years. Jessica's middle-class background is evident as she shares how her father was killed defending his large ranch from the Zapatista guerrilla fighters during the 1994 uprising of the landless poor in Chiapas. Her pragmatic approach to finding a U.S. husband reflects her philosophy of survival more generally: "Rather than dream, I set goals. I am a person who works toward feasible goals, not dreams." Jessica depicts Latin men—as well as the economic, social, and political situation in their countries more broadly—as curbing their access to social and economic security and mobility. Women such as Jessica articulate their desire for U.S. men alongside the language of professionalism and the marketplace, as they recount the process of finding romance and/or marriage through ideals of hard work, self-sacrifice, and individual struggle. At the same time, they express their hope for self-improvement, what some women describe as *superarse*, or to better themselves and the lives of their families. Their moralizing of individual development with the sacrifice of patriotism sutures capitalist development with the collective good that justifies personal gain in the face of collective struggles for resources and land distribution, such as those fought by the Zapatistas. Guadalajara's placement in the northern region, symbolically weighted by gendered traditions of the rural hacienda as well as by its connections to agriculture and thus massive waves of immigration to the United States (in addition to its cosmopolitan growth as a high-tech hotbed), differentiates the city as one that sees, at least from many women's perspectives, its "modern" future as an intimate partnership and exchange with the United States.

Women look to the United States to be freed from a stagnant economy and cultural norms and hope to become architects of their own lives. This is a liberating prospect and has the potential for subverting the gender hierarchy in Mexico. But as seen earlier, for some women, this modern vision of remaking themselves relies on projecting the teleology of developmental backwardness and sexual excess onto lower-class, indigenous, and gay men. As women garner confidence and independence through professional careers and exposure to stories of love and marriages from abroad, they begin to imagine new possibilities for themselves. Yet Mexican women also do not accept everything about American culture or a capitalist framework. Aware that women in the United States are more liberal, that families are nuclear, rather than extended, and that many women are more materialistic in the United States, most of them state the importance of holding onto spiritual and family traditions. Furthermore, many of these women, especially those with children, know that they will have to "sacrifice" their professions and families in order to find happiness with a foreigner.

Internet Encounters

That women can turn to the Internet to commune with U.S. and other foreign men sharpens their sense of becoming someone new at the moment of intimate contact with another. These virtual intimacies rely not on proximity or even bodily contact, such as the exchange of breath and the friction of the body, but by the depth of one's commitment, communicated via translated e-mails. Women do not wait for the destined moment and person to come along; instead, they craft themselves as modern subjects conjuring life worlds from elsewhere into their everyday lives. In Ursula Biemann's film *Writing Desire* (2000), one of her participants in the cybermarriage industry states,

> After I decided to find myself a companion, I scrutinized my Mexican environment, which I call the "Cradle of Machismo." I realized that a woman like me—a fifty-year-old artist, nontraditional feminist, widow, and mom, university professor of a radical will of my own—would only scare any prospective man for fear of a fem-flasher. Since the listings within my reach were meager, I figured that the high-techs were here to help us find kindred spirits, wherever they may be. So I signed onto the Internet, and the famous online dating sites flashed up. I overcame the intellectual guilt that haunted me, and I posted my profile anonymously, again as "Fem-Flasher." I announced myself as an ideal partner for a very special person.

Fantasies, stereotypes, and utopic desires commingle on the screen through the act of Internet letter writing. The Mexican woman writes herself into a script in which she performs the ideal version of femininity, despite her feminist ethics, to find a loving, supportive, and gentle husband in a far-away land. Stories and images of the United States as a land of opportunity—where men respect feminism and love strong yet family-oriented women—make their way into this tale. The act of writing to a faceless man from the privacy of one's home or workplace adds an element of mystery, romantic enchantment, and the unknown. Away from strict families, the gossip of friends, Catholic teachings of respectable codes of behavior, the woman finds herself alone and hopeful that she can explore her new role with an audience that will interact with her with fresh eyes. Even in virtual space, however, she must negotiate traditional femininity, a gendered stereotype that clings to her virtual persona. Alongside the spread of the Internet in Mexico, women enact new gender identities not only as consumers of images but also as actors who forge new selves. Part of the lure of the Internet is that women can express themselves outside of local norms and customs, as their audience extends across national, cultural, and racial boundaries. The Internet is a springboard for acting out changing times, sexual desires, and new identities. Sherry Turkle describes the computer screen as the place where "we project ourselves into our own dramas, dramas in which we are producer, director and star. . . . Computer screens are the new location for our fantasies, both erotic and intellectual."[53] Women turn to the Internet to express their hopes, dreams, and intimate desires and, in the process, access other cultural frameworks and norms.

The use of the Internet and agencies rather than social networks to find relationships also marks a new way of thinking about love, courtship, and marriage. According to Mexican bourgeois traditions, a woman is expected to wait patiently and passively for a man to make the first move. Traditionally, once a man publicly claims his desire for a woman, she is marked as his territory, and she may not see anyone else. This courtship period may last a couple of years or longer. During this time, the woman, called a *novia*, must not allow herself to be in places in which she would be a sexual target for another man's desire. The man (*novio*), on the other hand, can have numerous sexual adventures with a variety of available women.[54] Though these courtship practices are outdated, the ideology of separate gendered spheres and the protection of women's honor and reputation through her sexual purity remain, as women express frustration over inconsistencies between married men's extramarital sexual conquests and the continued surveillance over women's sexual activity.

For these women, then, the Internet proves to be an ideal place for less restrictive forms of courtship. While women's bodies are guarded and

watched closely by social norms and codes of respectability, virtual connections open up opportunities to communicate or date multiple people
and to develop sexual intimacy in a society that heavily moralizes women's
sexual activities outside of marriage. Some women such as Laura also find
great pleasure in having men outside their social and family circles (and
the accompanying gossip) take them out or accompany them on romantic
getaways that lead to sexual encounters. Having sex is difficult not only
because of gender, class, and religious norms of respectability that dictate
women reserve sex for marriage. Many live at home and have little time
or private space for sexual or intimate relationships. In contrast, since
masculinity depends on expressions of independence and fraternity with
other males, men are afforded much more liberty to frequent bars, clubs,
and other social spaces. Blanca, the youthful-looking fifty-two-year-old
mentioned earlier, describes how she caught her husband—whom she
describes as having a large belly and as lazy, evident in his refusal to lift a
finger in the house—shamelessly having sex with her female neighbor in
the condominium pool one evening. She explains cracking open her social
world via the Internet, especially in light of her restricted mobility: "Right
now I am very confined. I almost never go out. I go out once in a while
into the street, and they follow me. People speak to me. But I don't like
to get to know people off the street because I think—I *think*—that they
think that I am easy. And I'm not easy. I'm not an easy kind of woman." I
asked her whether it was also difficult for women to meet people at bars.
She said, "Well, look, . . . another time I went out with some friends—only
one time, we went out at night. It's not difficult. They had come up to me,
but in reality they are people that are drinking, that think that if a woman
goes to a bar . . . the men think that if one goes to a bar alone, she is looking for a sexual encounter."

Blanca's reflection on the danger and lascivious nature of the street narrates a geography of class divisions across the deterritorialized spaces of the
Internet, spaces of foreign consumption, and local public zones. And perhaps
more to the point, women continue to fear sexualized violence when unaccompanied by men. I interviewed Blanca in her upscale home in a guarded
complex set off from the street by a metal fence and a security guard. As a
single woman, the zoning of public streets as male territory leaves her feeling
vulnerable to being sexually accosted.

The opportunities for women to meet a partner are limited to introduc-
tions by family and friends and thus are a challenge for older women who do
not have strong social or family networks. Anna, for instance, finds herself
isolated and unable to find a partner:

The truth is I've parted from my friendships and all social contacts that I could have had. But time has gone by, and apart from feeling alone— in spite of having my kids and family—I felt the need to have someone else whom I could express my feelings to and my thoughts about what is going on in my daily life. I realized that I couldn't have a life as a hermit. Men that I have known I had only known through work relations. And the truth is that due to my job, my work as a mother and as the head of the household, I don't have much time to have a social life.

Even though Anna lives at home and has the support and care of her family, she lacks the time or energy to build a social world that would allow her to meet and date people. In fact, almost all of the women I interviewed had weak social lives because of obligations to their families, children, and jobs. Not only is a woman's presence in public space questioned, but the squeeze on her time by work and family leaves little room for socializing with friends. Similarly, Blanca's busy schedule exacerbates her isolation within her home, as she hosted two female foreign students during a time when her son had returned from the university in the States. She cooks two to three meals a day for each student (oftentimes preparing distinct meals for each of the girls due to their dietary preferences), keeps the house clean, and does their wash, leaving her little time for much else. It was clear that without a man to help with the cost of her home, her son's education, and her middle-class lifestyle, she has had to hustle jobs with foreigners—whether in Mexico or previously as a nanny in California.

Women also enjoy having more control over the selection process through Internet dating. Teresa, a single and confident forty-two-year-old, was taking a break from a stressful life as a journalist to nurture and develop herself and her personal life. She said,

> At the bar, most people select each other by their looks rather than on intelligence. The atmosphere of the bar does not allow for more in-depth conversations where you really get to know a person. . . . Yet on the Internet, I can specify the man I want. I ask them personal and political questions, and if they are not interested in responding in this way, I know that they don't want a woman who is intelligent.

Rather than adhering to the concept of "love at first sight," many women want to get to know the "inner life" of a prospective partner before delving into an emotional relationship. Teresa tells me she can be playful and witty and see how men respond to her playful intelligence. She can read between the lines in Internet conversations and quickly judge whether someone is open-minded and whether he respects a woman's confidence and intelligence. Interestingly, through various e-mail relationships, Teresa finds Europeans more cultured, liberal, and open-minded than men from the United States and has opted to use various on-line dating agencies rather than to attend the Romance Vacation Tour parties. Similar to the lure of on-line dating in the United States, the use of on-line dating in Mexico draws from modern ideas of intimacy and selfhood based on the development of intimacy through communication, rather than "love at first sight," and on the desire for the advancement of the self through contact with others.[55]

Women's having a larger cultural context within which to compare themselves contributes to the rising number of them who feel that they do not have to settle for what is locally attainable. Through conversations with men on the tours and through Internet e-mails and chats rooms, women garner ammunition to construct new norms and gender roles. Anna shared her experiences with men from the GlobalLatinas tours and e-mail exchanges: "I think my country is renowned for having very deep-rooted people and customs. . . . And from here, that machismo is still very strongly rooted in the values of men. . . . I like to know other people who consider this [machismo] as a lack of maturity that provides guidelines so the woman has her place in society and in her life with men."

According to Anna, discussions with men who do not abide by the same cultural norms strengthen her convictions that men benefit from machismo while women do not. Anna also told me that she had received some very good advice from people with whom she had been communicating. Since women often condone and perpetuate *machista* behavior, there are not many confidants with whom she can share her inner thoughts and feelings.

In these cyber-exchanges, women must negotiate the tension between desiring to be liberated from local norms and gender roles and maneuvering the more insidious constraints of these more market-driven exchanges. Because men write to multiple women, this can be an expensive process, in which they pay not just for e-mail access and translating fees but for the cost of sending women flowers and gifts and even visiting the select few who have been screened out through writing. And because many men send women between $500 and $1,000 for English classes, women feel deeply appreciative and obligated to reciprocate in ways that would please the men they date. Monica wrote an e-mail to a man she was dating in the United States who sent her $500 for English lessons: "Regarding my English classes, I'm very proud because they named me as the honor student. . . . I still don't know much, but as I told you before, I'm doing my best to learn fast. . . . And also I don't want to disappoint you." Women can be constricted by the consumer's wants and needs and codes of reciprocity.

Conclusion

Guadalajara's economic future depends on promoting its rich traditions, which attract tourists, while also capitalizing on lucrative technological industries that are ever more critical to the transnational circuits of migration, commerce, and desire that wire nations together. Women's search for U.S. husbands demonstrates how the foreign circulates as an intimate force that translates women's desire to be more highly valued and respected. The foreign, and the Internet's capacity to translate written communication, consolidates women's hope to become someone new. The Internet entreats one to see the world differently and to find others who confirm this more expansive and pliable notion of one's self. Along with this is a hope for a more nuanced understanding of the ways emerging sectors of educated women from developing countries use global processes to step outside the limits of what is possible at home. Women are savvy excavators of opportunities that come their way, offering more stable, open, and exciting relationships, marriages, and futures. Sometimes these imaginaries produce ideal matches, and other times women may find men who want to reinstate the traditional family and gender arrangements that women are hoping to transcend. While Mexican women may turn to global circuits (such as tourism and Internet communication) and Western culture to participate in a mutual expression of modernity, women incorporate this sense of themselves alongside traditional notions of family unity and codes of femininity. Thus, these intimate exchanges demonstrate affinities and tensions between men's expectations for a traditional woman and women's expectations for a more feminist and equitable relationship with a U.S. man. In fact, women come to find that they are a good catch, even for U.S. men, while others find themselves too cultured and modern for the U.S. suitors they meet. Hope for a better future takes on a foreign profile, as streams of migrant money from the United States, new business opportunities, and romantic imaginaries propel their search. On the other hand, the circulation of success stories from women who have happily married narrates a migrant tale that compels them to continue their search, despite some women's experiences with men who fail to meet their expectations. Women themselves reproduce associations of the local and the national with the archaic, with the past, and with sexualized danger. In contrast, an ethic of hard work, coupled with the influx of U.S. capitalist development, promises to fast-track their lives into new futures.

Recent studies locate the "female underside of globalization" as the process whereby millions of women from "poor countries in the south migrate to do the 'women's work' of the north—work that affluent women [and men] are no longer able or willing to do."[56] Rather than extract raw resources from third-world countries, wealthy nations hope to import workers who provide better care, love, and sex. In a similar vein, U.S. men look to Mexican women as more able wives and mothers (more dedicated, feminine, and willing to serve their husbands), who will take on domestic roles they say feminist, career-driven women no longer want. Yet women, too, look to U.S. men as better husbands and fathers than Mexican men. Women's perceptions of men from the United States coincide with the image of the globe-trotter— the sensitive, loyal businessman who is economically savvy, successful, and hardworking. As we will see in the next chapter, outsourcing the American dream to Latin America and the project of empire building play out in the intimate desires of U.S. men who travel to Latin America to find more than a sexy wife.

3

Outsourcing the American Dream

Transforming Men's Virtual Fantasies into Social Realities

We are the disposable gender.
—U.S.-based agency owner

My whole life is abstract. . . . I don't find myself feeling really close
to people. I don't feel really close to my family. . . . I've realized I'm
just sort of going through the motions, so on some level, going outside the country is an attempt to, you know, get past that cynical,
detached experience that I have here.
—Jason

Stereotypical perceptions of "buying" women through mail-order bride cata-
logues no longer hold true for men I interviewed seeking a foreign bride. The
process, players, and reasons for seeking foreign women have changed; not
all fit the stereotype of the awkward and lonely guy with Coke-bottle glasses
searching the pages of a magazine from the privacy of his bedroom. Nor
are these solitary journeys in search for a wife. Chat-room discussants on
Planet-Love.com invest months, even years, sharing "travel reports," swap-
ping dating and marital experiences, and discussing cultural differences and
immigration procedures.[1]

Computers have dramatically altered the process and places of dating,
facilitating quick and accessible forums for men to communicate virtually
with women in other countries as well as with each other. As I followed
men in their search for a bride, it was not only their desire for a Latina that
interested me but the pleasure they found discussing their experiences and
perspectives with other like-minded men in chat rooms—a process that
had not existed in previous mail-order bride exchanges. Men logged on to

Planet-Love's chat room to seek and share advice, while others generated camaraderie and community in cyberspace and during their travels in search of a Latin American bride. Their fraternal bonding electronically generated virtual ties to a community of others who similarly sought to preserve family values at the bedrock of the nation. Through their journeys to Latin America, many described the need for better genes, for injecting the nation with more passionate and family-oriented women. Foreign marriage also breathes life back into the natural rights of man, an innocent past when men were unquestionably compensated for their role as the head of the home and, by extension, the nation. Their innocent ties to the nation resuscitate a ritual of cleansing and a sense of freedom forged through the erasure of the violent history of nation-building, as well as the legacies of conquest that haunt global capitalism.[2] In the process of discussing heterosexual love, relationships, and marriage in cyberspace, through guidebooks and with each other at tours, participants forge a transnationally oriented masculinity built at the crossroads of multiple technological, social, and global transformations. These transformations involve changes in gender roles and labor relations due to the outsourcing of production and migration; right-wing rhetoric on the crisis of the family in the United States; a burgeoning "sensitive male" ideal, as opposed to the stereotype of the hypersexualized, Latin macho man; a backlash against feminism; and the circulation of a particular feminine imaginary—the nurturing, docile, and family-oriented Latina.

In considering why, at this particular moment, transnational marriages are so alluring, this growing industry offers certain men, especially those who feel victimized and devalued by U.S. culture and feminism, a venue for conversion and a heightened sense of self, while images of Latinas flickering on the screen promise to turn fantasies into a reality. That erotic images of Latin American women accompany male transformation should hardly be a surprise, as the Orient and exotic landscapes and women's bodies have long allured the U.S. imagination, defining the Western self in relation to an "other."[3] While these international intimacies and marriages are not entirely new, the Internet provides a forum for participants to engage and act out these fantasies without having to leave the comfort of one's home or from one's computer at the office. Furthermore, these fantasies prove malleable enough to attract a radically diverse array of men—from the wealthy to men in the military; professional and working-class men; Anglo men, Latinos, and African American men; those in their late twenties to men in their sixties; and those from the religious and conservative to the politically left-leaning. Their search for meaning and purpose in a modern society driven by capitalist values of materialism opens up fertile terrain for discovering a spiritual "otherness," one that might transcend and transform the self, located in the "passionate heart" of Latin America.

Web companies reach men through ads in business and sports magazines and newspapers such as *Men's Journal*, *USA Today*, and *Penthouse*, pitched to men working at large corporations, and through the Internet, the most effective medium. International marriage brokers (IMBs) promise not simply marriage but a pleasurable vacation and the prospect of dramatically changing one's life. For example, one company owner explained to me, "Part of the challenge of this industry is that I have to find a way to get these guys off their chair—to do something about all their complaining. They have to know that this kind of thing will change their lives forever!"[4] Another said soberly, "It's a hard business because we're dealing with people's fantasies, their dreams, their neuroses."[5]

The critical role IMBs play in empowering male clients to maximize their return by importing what they consider to be a better breed of women situates this industry at the curious crossroads of self-transformation, social engineering, and global business values of risk. Even though men are not actually buying women, the process of virtual engagements with potential brides does tend to promote a consumer fantasy of change wrapped up in the exotic profile of a Latin American woman. Thus, I argue that outsourcing the fantasy of the nuclear family to developing nations follows the logic of transnational capitalism and corporate multiculturalism. Men can get a younger, more feminine woman who they are told "expects less" in developing nations, and women's difference is advertised as infinitely malleable, their bodies an investment that will revitalize oneself, the family, and the nation. The irony here is that while men turn to the marketplace of marriage to act more freely on their desires away from the scrutiny of social dictates and state laws, their search for authentic love and a more innocent woman reproduces state power and national ideology, as both men and the state rely on the arbitration of love to distinguish authentic from fraudulent foreign marriages.

Men lament that U.S. women are afflicted by their selfish pursuit of a career outside the home, while Latin American women represent the utopic prospect of rejuvenating and purifying the boundaries of the self, the nuclear family, and the nation. Latin American women embody the "last frontier," merging colonial and new cyber-frontier possibilities. Thus, finding a foreign bride converges with four discourses: colonialism, modern self-help movements, transnational capitalism, and futuristic ideals of flexibility, mobility, and a postracial society. These themes demonstrate how technology and ideas about globalization are incorporated into men's everyday lives as a yearning for a utopian, multicultural affinity to masculinity and citizenship that transcends skin color, profession, age, class, or attractiveness. As seen in chapter 2, these global shifts similarly inspire Mexican women in their pursuit of foreign men on the Internet to transcend local opportunities and confining parameters of femininity. As we will see in the next chapter, even Caleñas (women from Cali, Colombia) see potential in the global marketplace of marriage to invest in themselves via cosmetic alterations with the hopes of a brighter future. When these fantasies flickering on the computer screen and remade onto women's bodies fail to materialize, male participants redirect their search to farther frontiers less traveled or to Latin American countries less spoiled by tourism.

Producing Patriots: The Global Economies of Cybermarriage

I remember the sense of excitement and nervousness I felt entering the five-star hotel ballroom where about forty-five men eagerly sat in anticipation of the introductory meeting the day before the start of the Vacation Romance Tour in Guadalajara, Mexico. I sat up at the front of the room so that Harold, the Anglo Texan in his late forties representing GlobalLatinas, could introduce me as "the woman who was doing research on why you guys came all the way to Mexico to find that special woman!" Most laughed heartily, some skeptically, unsure themselves as to what was in store for them during this weeklong journey. That I looked like some of the women they sought out and that I was "vetted" through the agency contributed to the ease with which they opened up to me, asked me about my book, and prodded me for my opinion about women and the marriage agencies.

The Vacation Romance Tours fit perfectly into men's busy schedules and required a great deal of socializing during the three to four days they had to narrow their search to that one special woman. In order for the men to best maximize the tour and their trip, Harold strongly encouraged them to meet as many women as possible and then to narrow their search to one woman who would receive an invitation to attend the pool event on the last day. They should not worry if they did not find that "special someone" by day three, he reassured them. I could almost hear a collective sigh as he continued to explain that the agency invited a new batch of women to the final event. During this meeting, Harold gave them tips, such as how to meet as many women as possible (aided by young hired translators), and suggested meeting eligible dates for longer visits over breakfast, lunch, and dinner. I found out later that some men met with women they had corresponded with by e-mail during their break from the tour, sometimes being up-front about their attendance at the tour, while others found themselves in the awkward situation of not telling women for fear of hurting their feelings or for being misinterpreted as a playboy. Harold advised men not to ask questions about the political situation in Mexico and especially about women's economic situations. "Keep it light, gentlemen," he encouraged, "and have fun!"

I was completely tangled in a social web of relations at the tour and quickly realized how much work happened behind the scenes to satisfy most men's desire for the younger and most beautiful women. I finished one evening at the Guadalajara tour over dinner with the other agency representatives, a couple in their late twenties, the photographer, and several young Mexican translators who worked for the agency. Danny and Susie hustled to entice younger women to attend the tour (men were complaining that the majority of women were too old) by distributing ads at the mall across from the hotel, in the back of *Cosmopolitan* magazine, and at a local radio station. They explained how they set up a deal with the Mexican photographer, Javier (who easily energized alluring poses out of women from behind the camera), agreeing to pay him twelve dollars for every young model from his studio who showed up at the tour. He had been busy that day at the tour shooting photos of several of the young translators, paid fifty dollars each to act out a video for the website. The girls giggled at each other as they walked boldly into the camera and in sync exclaimed, "Come to Mexico, where the weather is warm and so are the women!" Javier also spent his days at the tour taking photos of women in a studio room next to the tour ballroom. Remembering a conversation with another agency owner in Hermosillo who told me women refused his request to post their photos on his website, I asked Danny how they wrangled women into doing this. He explained (off tape) that not all of them get on the Internet; only the prettiest ones were chosen. Plus, the agency did not tell women their photos might be posted on the Internet, since, Danny added, most women would not agree to this.[6] In shock, concurred by a quick glance at Susie, nodding her head in disapproval, I asked him how they got away with this. He flatly explained that women sign their name on papers not knowing that the small print on the back page authorized their company to use these photos for any promotional purposes. On the one hand, women do not have to pay for attending these events, for the photos, the food, and two free drinks, but on the other, the agency took away women's right to control how their images circulate. That agencies and even women carefully produce themselves to attract men's attention goes unacknowledged, a necessary fiction to the making of Latin America as an untapped frontier that is overflowing with young, smiling, and beautiful women.

In my notes at the Vacation Romance Tour in Guadalajara, I began to place men into four categories based on their descriptions of each other as well as my own observations and data collection: (1) socially awkward (15 percent), (2) divorced and disgruntled (40 percent), (3) good guys (30 percent), and (4) adventure seekers (15 percent).[7] Those with poor social skills could be found hugging the walls during the social event, approaching their female targets with the flick of an arm stiffly poised to hand out a photo or business card. Lucky for the women, there were very few of these kind of men, although more in this group tended to be shy, introverted, and inexperienced. The "divorced and disgruntled" group was the largest and most vehemently opposed to what they considered the feminist movement in the United States. This group overlapped with the "good guys," who were also in the majority. They saw themselves as ordinary guys, sincere in their search for a Latina who would appreciate them and their desire to find a lifelong marriage partner. The "adventure seekers" made up a small group of young and old men alike who frequented tours all over Latin America and were looking for a vacation and a good time and perhaps marriage. It is worth noting that men move between categories. This was especially the case for the "adventure seekers" in Colombia, who made sure that they had fun on their trip regardless of whether they met someone who caught their attention. Some men were horrified that some of the guys came all this way to hit up the strip joints, and they expressed their dislike for those who took advantage (sexually) of women in Cali. Yet, even as men come from a variety of class and racial backgrounds, they all see themselves as outside, in one way or another, the hegemonic construction of masculinity.[8] While *masculinity* is not the term they use, men see themselves as resisting a deflated, feminized, and "softer" masculinity brought about by feminism and modernization.

In this chapter, I combine chat-room discussions, interviews with three agency owners and over forty men at the Vacation Romance Tours, guidebooks, and websites to illustrate the continuities between cyberspace discussions, face-to-face interactions, and website images and narratives. With the ease of sharing hypertextual information in chat discussions, it is nearly impossible to create hard boundaries between interviews and textual data or even between on-line and off-line interactions; thus, chat-room discussions, tours, and guidebooks create a web of meanings that men internalize and recirculate.[9] The ethnographic interviews and web narratives explored here are not meant to define or categorize *all* men but to offer some clues as to how personal fantasies naturalize the global marketplace as the moral and patriotic force that propels men abroad.

The owners of two Texas-based Latin American IMB agencies, Michael (a former preacher) and Robert (previously an accountant), began their prospective agencies after they themselves married Latin American women. Michael is happily married, and his wife, Juana, helps him run the Colombia tours. Robert has since divorced his Latin American wife. Both expressed frustration with the lack of rights men have today and feel that the government should stay out of people's personal affairs. As a self-proclaimed Republican who opposes big government, Michael drew from his religious beliefs on the power of hard work and the family. He says, "Reagan had it right when he said the way of the family goes the country. . . . When people are happily married, the world is a safer place. Robbery and stealing would go down. We wouldn't have to build prisons—it's all about the family. Let's get to the root of the problem: people just don't feel good about themselves."[10]

Both Michael and Robert identify with men who feel deceived. Robert says, "Men were promised that if they loved their religion, family, and country, then they would be just fine." Michael concurred: "Men were told to work hard, but their wives left." Robert turned angry as he described how hard it is for men to get custody of their children, a struggle he fought in order to raise his daughter single-handedly for most of her life. And even men who manage to win equal custody with their ex-wives, he continued, pay half in alimony. He persisted, telling me how men die eight years earlier than women while all the attention goes to breast cancer, even though just as many men die of prostate cancer. Exasperated, he exclaimed, "We are the disposable gender!"

Agency owners (and many of the men I spoke with) blame this legal and cultural imbalance on the feminist movement and on women who persist in their hunt to track them down through the passage of legislation such as IMBRA. They ideologically defend the need for the Internet marriage industry and argue that shutting it would prove misguided and perhaps even unpatriotic. Robert, for example, argues that he spent sixteen years in this business "spreading international goodwill" between the United States and Latin America. Similarly, Michael pitched his business to me with as much passion as I imagined he inspires in his congregation, saying he was moved to open his business to help other disillusioned men and, in the process, to connect "North and South America to promote free trade, as one great nation." On both agency websites, women's bodies circulate as "free trade zones" and patriotic ambassadors of their country. Their photos are bracketed on both agency websites with the American flag on one side and the Colombian on the other. Women offer service with a smile, the seductive force luring in men and trade relations (including the marriage industry) to their country.

Free trade, or the right to exchange, is eroticized as distinctly American and patriotic. This pervasive ideology is hard to miss on Michael's website, where he proudly dons a collared shirt decorated in stars and stripes, while several busty women wear American-flag-colored swimsuits.

The friendliness and goodwill supposedly ushered by free-trade agreements, imagined on-line alongside women's bodies, instantiates U.S. values of unrestrained access to trade, intimacy, and development. The Internet fosters participation in global freedom, as advertising campaigns project the Internet as a space of unrestricted mobility and outside of state control, encouraging freedom of speech and equality. As a zone outside surveillance, men's turn to the Internet to cross into Latin America flaunts a culture of political correctness that automatically associates foreign marriage with exploitation, defined as a liberal and feminist ploy, now backed by the state, to confine their movement.[11] Ironically, the fantasy of moving women's bodies across borders signifies not exploitation and captivity but freedom and liberation—a perspective shared by those Latin American women who yearn to be "freed" from the cultural and economic restrictions in their country. Similarly, men hope to be "freed" from the local signification of their bodies and labor, enabled by their participation in the global marketplace. When I asked Michael about immigration restrictions in relation to "free trade," he described not liking walls: "Give 'em a job. I'm not afraid of competition." His wife, Juana, surprised him with her more conservative stance, supporting rigid immigration policies for those who flout the law.[12] Robert lamented that he has less rights than immigrants who can bring over their "large" Latin American families. Even gays have more rights, he continued, especially in their fight for equality and marriage (which he lamented they would eventually win), which would allow them to bring over immigrant family members—even though as a birthright citizen, he cannot bring family from Ireland to the United States.

Both agency owners personalize their role in making this world a better place, as Michael frames it, "one couple at a time."[13] They espouse a personal perspective on change, one as infectious as a good sermon, or a movement, where a single spark can ignite this "family" revolution that will make the world a better place for all. This passionate vision to get men to act refuses to take into account the historical and structural conditions that have limited various groups' access to the family, such as African American family formations decimated since slavery, laws banning interracial couples until 1967, the breakup and decimation of migrant families forced to separate due to restrictive immigration laws, or even gay binational couples.[14] The idea that the family structure is either rejected or embraced renders invisible the conditions that make the family a compulsory structure or even one broken apart by state laws and cultural norms.

These men's failure to feel valued by U.S. women and, by extension, the nation helps narrate countless stories of victimhood, of how they have been wrongly blamed as the "big bad men again."[15] On websites, potential male customers are entreated to "make your dreams come true!" with images of tantalizing women in skimpy swimsuits.[16] The actualizing of dreams on these websites appears as a man with his arm around a young Latina-mulatta in a swimsuit, but underlying these dreams are the desires of men "who want to feel beloved, valued, or cared for; to feel beautiful and desired; or to feel kind and generous, because they do not feel any of these things back home," according to Julia O'Connell Davidson and Jacqueline Sánchez Taylor. "These sentiments," they continue, "of course, highlight much that is very wrong with North American/European societies—the way in which bodies are constructed as beautiful/ugly, the refusal to recognize people with physical disabilities as sexual beings, the sexual value that is attached to youth, the class inequalities that deny people the opportunity to be generous, and so on."[17] IMB agencies market this longing to feel valuable as a natural right easily satisfied by the global marketplace, where men circulate as more valuable commodities. A website advertising women from Cali, Colombia, reflects this global identity: "Simply being an American gentleman puts you in high standing with these ladies. The truth is, you represent many things to them that the Latin man is not: a man who's devoted, enterprising, fiscally responsible, considerate, faithful and able to care for his wife and children."[18]

The beginning of the cybermarriage industry in Latin America coincided with the rise of multiculturalism in the United States, when racial difference was packaged in the media as a commodity that could add spice to the nation.[19] Just as discourse about globalization promises new markets and the comparative advantage that will solve all business problems, so too are men turning to Latin America to renovate their image back home.[20] Racialized "others" were targeted as the frontier of the future; their bodies and the products they represented promised spiritual vitality, a connectedness to nature, and access to a new rejuvenated self.

Whiteness-as-Alienation: Racialized Genes
and Fantasies of Connectivity

I interviewed Jason, who I introduced in chapter 1, who had married and divorced Mariana after a trip to Colombia. Jason's quote, in the epigraph to this chapter—"My whole life is abstract. . . . I don't find myself feeling really

close to people. I don't feel really close to my family. . . . I've realized I'm just
sort of going through the motions, so on some level, going outside the country is an attempt to, you know, get past that cynical, detached experience that
I have here"—demonstrates his exodus to Latin America as a way to, as he
says, "break out of the mold" and leave behind relationships overdetermined
by "competition and a focus on money." During our interview in a restaurant
in Northern California, he continues,

> The Silicon Valley is all about, you know, high energy, intelligence, . . .
> abstractions: abstractions like the Internet and computer chips and semi
> conductors. . . . In fact, that's why I got out of computer work, in part
> because I found it so impersonal, you know. I could just be staring at a
> computer screen all day and having nothing to do with anybody. I didn't
> like what I was becoming. I didn't like that kind of affect on me, and I felt
> like, I'm already an introvert. . . . Unfortunately by going into finance, it
> was an improvement, but kind of more of the same—an improvement
> because I needed to deal with customers. On the other hand, what am I
> providing to customers? It's abstract, it's numbers, it's a loan on a house.
> And what's a loan? It's not something you can touch. It's a service, but the
> results of the service I do is not tangible. I mean, it's not like . . . a farmer
> who makes vegetables or something, where there's a physical product
> as the result of his labor. There's no physical product as a result of my
> labor.[21]

What struck me in Jason's response was how the fragmented technological
labor he performed contributed to his sense of alienation and the longing
for heightened intimacy and traditional relations of labor. In his critique of
mechanized work (going through the motions), devoid of physical contact,
was a nostalgic return to a preindustrial time when a more holistic relation
between the production and trade of one's labor bonded one to an entire
web of familial and social ties. Latin American women epitomize the locus
of the "human," someone whose physicality and emotions—evident in her
lively connection to her family and community—render her superior to U.S.
women but also as outside conditions of labor or processes of commodification. Ironically, the outsourcing of U.S. production to developing countries
displaces families, as rural farmers are driven into mass-producing, export-
driven farms or are forced to migrate to the United States for work.

Jason's expression of alienated and fragmented labor also recalls conditions of routinized labor performed by mostly female *maquiladora* laborers
(although he is obviously paid much more for his labor). The potential for

critique and protest against the ways capitalist structures of profit squeeze laborers transnationally, however, cannot surface, as men's fantasies are framed by the logic of commodity fetishism in which an individual's mere consumption of objects promises change. In other words, women's bodies and "culture" promise personal transformation in ways that promote, rather than disrupt, the capitalist engine. Also noteworthy here is the centrality of trade and barter in fostering communal formation and intimacy, despite many cybermarriage male participants' beliefs that to be authentic, intimacy must be devoid of market relations.

The overlooked consequences of high-tech labor and alienation on men's lives, especially in feminist debates, and men's association of Latin American women with intimacy, family, and human connection make it difficult to build connections and alliances between high- and low-tech laborers. At the same time, the solution—turning to Latin America, naturalized as resembling a preindustrial past—erases the ways global capital, and the desire to maximize profit, has altered the conditions of labor and living for many people in Latin America. Women are fantasized as rejuvenating "life"—what Jason explains as the need to "import new raw materials." While at a Vacation Romance Tour in Mexico, I was told by Blake, a forty-two-year-old Anglo club owner from Los Angeles with a muscular physique and a tanning-salon glow, why he was looking for a woman from Mexico: "I think these women are culturally grown to want what we also want."[22] On-line guidebooks promoted on IMB company websites reiterate this logic by describing Latin American women as superior to U.S. women, as having "better genes" necessary to replenish the traditional family form, community, and domesticity lost in the United States. Here is a testimony from a male client who tells the story of why he is ready to find a mail-order wife, including a description of his mother's "feminazi" thought process:

My final decision to pursue a foreign bride resulted from an argument I heard between my mother and her new husband. Mother was bitching moaning and carrying on about how her life was a drudgery and how she felt unappreciated. Her new husband got tired of her whining and shouted, "Fran, you have a brand new $250,000 dream home in the suburbs with every furnishing and knick knack you wanted, a new Isuzu Trooper, a healthy bank account, a very comfortable living, a husband who has bent over backwards to make you happy. . . . what the hell more do you want!" . . . This is when I realized that the odds are stacked against me finding happiness with an American wife, which has led me to say, "it is time for new genes."[23]

In this Oedipal cybernarrative, the author envisions a better future by replacing his mother, rather than his father, and infusing whiteness with "new genes" in a transracial family. The author degrades "spoiled" suburban white women who do not appreciate what they have, women who do not reciprocate with docile bodies in exchange for a capitalist and patriarchal order in the workplace and home. Earlier in the story, he describes his mother's ideological participation in the feminist movement as the unhealthy "male-bashing environment" in which he unfortunately grew up. These women are labeled "feminazis," women who are hypermasculinized, driven to crush all opposition in their path toward power and success.[24] As a castrating force, feminazis create gender and sexual disorder within the family and nation. Male participants want a less liberated woman, someone less spoiled and materialistic than the women in their lives. In this excerpt, found on a link from Planet-Love's main web page, the testimonial serves—intentionally or not—to provide men with the language and ideology through which to understand and justify their desire for a foreign bride. This focus on genes continually reemerges during interviews, in chat discussions, and on websites. Men with the same resentful feelings are prompted to take action against ungrateful women, to pick themselves up by the bootstraps and take charge of their lives through a foreign and more appreciative wife. Many Latin American women I interviewed were aware that men wanted a woman who was more family oriented than U.S. women supposedly are. In fact, many rejected being labeled a feminist for fear of their association with white women popularly thought to be selfish, sexually loose, or too domineering. This did not mean, however, that women were not strong in their conviction that they want a man who respects them and who sees their contributions as carrying equal weight in the family.

Isolating a woman's body to her genetic material, scientifically "proven" as a stable and unchanging code of "natural" human life, serves up a ready-made ideology that frames men's journey abroad as moral and patriotic in their attempt to modify the U.S. national body with an injection of passionate genes. A genetic conception of women's bodies reinforces biological understandings of race, or culture, as fixed, albeit transportable. Unlike nineteenth-century constructions of racial mixing in the United States as *degenerative*, in this instance, foreign genes are constructed as *regenerative*. Men's concerns with replacing "natural" gender differences are part of a wider ideology endemic to popular men's movements, launched by the publication of Robert Bly's book *Iron Man* (1990), as well as within the religious right and even within academic debates. David Popenoe, a professor of sociology at Rutgers University, contributed to a lengthy study on the deplorable state of marriage and the family in contemporary times that was designed to help reinvigorate a dying social institution.[25] He says, "In order to restore marriage and reinstate fathers into the lives of their children, we are somehow going to have to undo the cultural shift toward radical individualism and get people thinking again in terms of social purposes."[26] By couching this moral quest as one in opposition to individualism, family values take on a social and even national imperative. In Wendy Kline's book *Building a Better Race* (2001), she argues that if we replace the word *social* with *race*, then Popenoe's statement resounds with the earlier project of his father, Paul Popenoe, who in the 1920s and 1930s warned of the threat of race suicide if eugenic projects geared toward the reproduction of white, middle-class families were not taken with utmost seriousness.[27] This shift in racial construction connects with individualistic ideals of multiculturalism in the global marketplace. Once again, diversity and race are products that promise to bring one closer to nature, one's "true self," and "natural" gender and racial hierarchies. The idea of genetic engineering emphasizes an understanding of women's bodies as flexible and mutable through the masculine hands and gaze of the Internet techie. Some bride-seeking men imagine themselves as the heroic engineers of the family and nation (contradicting the popular image of them as outcasts), and ethnic women embody the transformation.

Jason, who divorced his Colombian wife after realizing she was more interested in developing her career than in having children and a family, returned to Colombia with the idea that his ex-wife was the exception to the abundance of family-oriented women there. I met with Jason in California after he divorced Mariana and then again in Cali, Colombia, when he rented a flat from John (equipped with security guards and a glorious view of the city), along with a group of men who knew each other from the Planet-Love chat room. While both John and Jason were unsuccessful with their first wives from Cali, they returned for a longer stay, determined to find a woman more aligned with their needs and expectations. As Jason emphatically explained, "I think [Mariana] is probably the only woman in all of South America who didn't want to have children." Confident back then that she was the exception to the fantasy of Latin American maternalism and domesticity, in Cali, Jason expressed some frustration that most women he met in Cali already had children and, more vexing, ex-husbands who legally wielded the right to control whether the child could leave the country. Refusing to sign a parental waiver can make it difficult to bring women's children to the United States without a substantial bribe or an exhausting and expensive legal battle.[28] Notably, from men's perspectives, it is Latin American men who hold women hostage to a state of immobility and U.S. men who have the potential to set them free.

For men who do not envision themselves on the cutting edge of global business culture, bride hunting in developing countries symbolizes their entrance into the future. A former professor writes his reflections about his search for a traditional Filipina in his book *A Long Way to Go for a Date*. He says, "All my life I have been like a man facing the rear on a speeding train. I have always had my back to the future. Although the future is unknown, at least now I feel I am facing forward."[29] While international dating and romance are not new, men insert themselves into the modern future as members of a global class for which mobility is preconfigured by access to Internet technology, English, passports, and dollars, while women are conversely disadvantaged by their relative dependence on men in order to become mobile. Relevant here is R. W. Connell's discussion of business masculinity through colonial discourses of virgin markets engaged by men who enjoy a dominant position in the global marketplace. Connell does not, however, take into account the sense of disempowerment expressed by the men I interviewed. Many feel alienated in some way from U.S. culture, their family, and society. Michael's earlier quote, "Men are the disposable gender," reflects his frustration with the U.S. government and laws that he feels better protected his previous U.S. wife, the Latin American women men bring to the United States, and "illegals" who he lamented can petition to bring their whole families to the United States. Men's personal laments connect with the notion of empire, as chat-room discussants reveal men's anxiousness to push into new frontiers, to find countries with women less tainted by U.S. culture. The history of colonial contact, and the idea of the frontier, is cleansed of violence and instead imagined as a morphing of cultures in which women choose which cultural and genetic traits they will carry into the future.

Latin American Women as the "Final Frontier"

Latin American women's bodies are reconfigured within the global marketplace as young, untainted natural resources. For example, a former company out of San Diego called Sonoran Girls opened its website with a picture of smiling young girls from the northern Mexican town of Sonora; bold letters over the picture read "Discover Mexico's Greatest Treasures." These photos of young Latinas are positioned in front of the colors of the Mexican flag, as symbols of the nation. Young Mexicanas are the new resources or, as Arlie Hochschild describes them, the "new gold" whose laboring bodies are in need of men to import them to the United States, where they will become fully realized.[30] When I asked Steve, who owns an agency in Guadalajara, how he got into this business, he said, laughing, "I've been in the export business for a while, and the best export I found in Mexico were women!" Many websites advertising women from Mexico and Colombia describe Latinas in the United States as being tainted by U.S. values, unlike women found in their country of origin. For example, the FAQ page of the Latin Life Mates website addresses the question of why it does not advertise Latin women from the United States: "We tried many years ago and found that the caliber of women here [in the United States] was much lower than the 'pristine' members living in her home country, . . . Colombia."[31] These sentiments are echoed in the statement of a U.S. owner of a Colombian agency, Latin Encounters, in a newspaper interview: "Because of the drug wars . . . Colombia has been off the map for U.S. tourists for the past 15 years. During that period, the country experienced considerable economic growth. Now it is filled with well-educated women who have maintained 'pristine' values because they were isolated from U.S. tourists. . . . You used to think of drugs when you thought of Colombian exports. . . . But forget that. Now the big demand in the States is for Colombian women."[32]

Other websites depict women as cultural and biological *mestizas*, hybrid bodies that visually narrate the progression of history and the nation. In the web image in figure 3.1, titled "Lima Ladies," light-skinned young girls mark the transition between the indigenous past and the modern future, and they are figured simultaneously as individuals yet overabundant and technologically reproducible (and thus expendable).

Figuring women's bodies as light-skinned *mestizas* disassembles them from their racial past, cleansing their bodies as white, even as their genetic makeup ties them to this "colorful" past. Women are also visually captive to their indigenous past, as it frames how we "know" their genetic lineage. The artificial process of technologically pasting a woman's photo onto an archaeological site activates the fantasy of discovery (as if they might just pop right out of the screen), of finding gems among the "ruins," who when excavated come to "life" (and the present) thanks to modern development. Globalization repeats the colonial narrative of turning nature (raw materials) into culture (finished modern products). At the same time, global contact embraces difference, rather than obliterating culture, proof that one's membership within a modern nation reinforces one's status as tolerant and nonracist.

Virtually collapsing women's photos onto various backgrounds defies the stasis of the image, as women are poised for malleability and portability into a number of geographic locales and time frames. This fantasy is ushered by the Internet's capability to reassemble history, lineage, and one's sense of self.

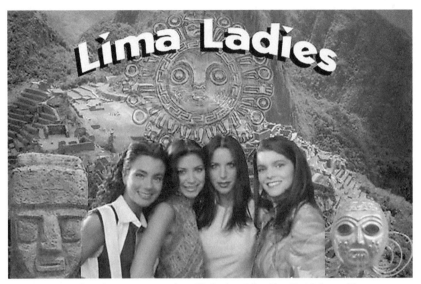

Fig. 3.1 Lima Ladies. (Image previously published in Schaeffer-Grabiel 2006b)

Marriage websites use the idea of *mestizaje* alongside globalization to high-light women's pliable affinity to foreign culture. Due to Latin America's long history of contact with other cultures and ideas, cyber-narrations of *mestizaje* define women as able to blend into a wide variety of cultural spaces, thus altering their history and genetic lineage toward a natural affinity with domestic life and multiculturalism in the United States, especially during the late 1950s and '60s. Michael tells me he loves going to Latin America because "it's like going back forty years. People say, 'Come over. Have some lemonade. Stay as long as you want.' Like we were forty years ago, before computers. Now everyone is in their own little world." Websites actually generate fantasies of erotic Latin women dislocated from a specific regional locale, set into an indistinct past, and alienated from the longer histories and politics of contact that inform the production of these intimacies.

The consequences of web images offering different shades and ages of women dislocated from time and space came to life when I talked to some men at the tours. For example, Donald, a white man in his early fifties from Alabama, told me that he is not attracted to white-skinned, red-haired women; he likes dark-skinned women.[33] Yet he does not like black women either. When I asked him about this, he said, turning serious, "Now, you know, I just can't take me a black woman home to Alabama. It wouldn't be good for her, and it wouldn't be good for me. It just wouldn't be a good situation for anyone." His family thinks he is crazy for going to these tours, but, he says, they just do not understand that he does not like those pasty, freckly-skinned, red- or blond-haired women. So I pushed on: "What do you think about taking a Latina home to Alabama? Do you really think she'd be happy there?" And he said, thinking, "Well, I hadn't really thought that far. Well, I never really thought about that. . . . But I just want a woman who stays at home. Well, . . . if she really wants to work, . . . I guess that's okay, but I just want a woman to stay at home." Like the images described earlier, men imagine home as the protective space away from the vagaries of racism, a space of containment severed from the outside world. Donald's attraction to brown skin evokes domesticity (a stable family), a space for containing his private appetite for exotic sexuality.

Contrary to media depictions and scholarship on the "invasion" of immigrant Latina bodies as hyperreproductive and contaminating threats to the nation-state,[34] Latin women here are revamped as the site of redemption from a breakdown of family values. Women are depicted in web images alongside nature, embodying anticapitalism (thus making these women's labor invisible), and as existing outside corrupting forces such as materialism and feminism. Many men and websites echo the idea that U.S. feminism is the polluting force of the family and nation. Thus, men see their masculinity as spoiled by industrialization, modern life, and feminism, which, Judith Stacey ironically argues, mirrors the beginning of the modern family.[35] Henry Makow reiterates this point: "Today feminism has morphed into a potent and virulent disease attacking the biological and cultural foundations of society."[36] The contemporary use of biological theories of gender reflect gender norms from the 1970s that followed on the heels of women's liberation movements.

Other versions of the frontier myth emerged in chat-room and interview discussions in which men described themselves as active participants in assimilating women into the "American dream" of upward mobility. The electronic frontier myth that promises to rejuvenate men through women's pure and youthful bodies extends to men's attempts to civilize, invest in, or offer opportunities to women they meet. At one of the agencies in Guadalajara, Mexico, I interviewed Stuart, an energetic, fit, and social seventy-year-old man (who told women he was anywhere from fifty-five to sixty), about his marriage to a twenty-seven-year-old Colombian woman. She had a child and came from an abusive family whose socioeconomic status had dropped dramatically due to social unrest plaguing the country. They divorced after living together in the United States for almost two years, even, Stuart tells me, after he gave his wife everything: plenty of spending money, English classes, and a membership to an exclusive gym.[37] He said, "All she needed to do was go to school, learn the culture, and be a mother and wife. I had yearly passes to the zoo, parks. . . . I just wanted her to experience American life, the American dream." There is a development narrative at play here in Stuart's expectations that, given his generous investment in his wife, she should make the most of herself. Even though women from Latin America are sought after because of their differences from women in the United States, ultimately, Stuart expected his wife to have the stereotypical gym physique, to cook meals he was accustomed to, to wear the thousands of dollars worth of clothes from Nordstrom's he bought for her, and to fill her time with goals of self-improvement, such as studying English and working out.

Like the female missionaries of the twentieth century who fulfilled their duty as moral citizens of the world by "uplifting" the natives, men such as Stuart similarly take on this role of the moral "good guys" who teach Latinas how to assimilate into the dream of liberal capitalism.[38] Chat-room discussions about women marveling over skyscrapers and washing machines in the United States and men's emphasis of women's "traditional" qualities easily slip into colonial ideas of the "natives" as backward, primitive, and uncivilized. Yet Latinas are also expected to be modern enough to appreciate technology when faced with its magnitude.

Stuart's philanthropic spirit, his desire to share the American dream with "less fortunate" women, mirrored his own personal genealogy, as he described himself to me as not simply a wealthy Anglo businessman but someone who came to the United States as a poor (and, at the time, racially marked) immigrant who worked his way up the social hierarchy.[39] For many men, the benefits of white masculinity can be tapped into through upward social and class mobility. Stuart, who grew up poor and worked as a steel worker and is now a wealthy and self-employed investment security business consultant, envisions himself as a self-made man. This perception is ironic as it promotes the very values of individualism and materialism that men consistently critique about U.S. women and U.S. culture in general. What Stuart had to do to gain his fortune as an insurance investor is less important here than his work ethic and desire to uplift others. Having a foreign wife reinvigorates the idea that the United States is an immigrant nation where those who work hard can make the American dream come true, while erasing the unequal system of power, slave labor, and colonial violence at the foundation of the nation's continuing global dominance. For those who do not achieve this dream, the blame falls on pathologizing the individual—which Stuart describes as his wife's "laziness"—rather than examining deeper structures of disempowerment. For other men whose marriage to foreign women failed, rather than question the formation of these fantasies and their own role in their construction, many returned to the tours in search of a more authentic woman.

Transformation of Self: Chat-Room Conversions

Men are told to expect an incredible status change once they leave the United States and enter Latin America. This status, based on what the Latin American man is not, assumes a middle- to upper-class subject. Even working-class men can attain a higher class standing in comparison to the earning capacity of the average Latin American man. Cody, an experienced client at a Guadalajara tour, remembers the first time he attended one of these parties, where over one hundred women compete for the attention of a small group of men.

> Actually, I don't know how you can prepare any of these guys for it, 'cause it's going to be a real ego charge for all of these guys. This is going to be the biggest boost they've ever had in their lives. . . . They're gonna understand what it's like to be a movie star, and they're gonna come out of here thinkin' there's nothing in the world that can beat this. I don't know any motivational speakers that can do what's gonna happen here. If it don't happen tonight for these guys, it's gonna be the first party that I've been to that it didn't happen.[40]

Cody reiterates just how powerful the tours can be as a space for transformation and for energizing men's self-esteem as hundreds of women vie for these men's attention. I too saw many men who would not necessarily attract attention in the United States change dramatically after days of being sought after by numerous attractive Latinas. This can be summed up with a striking statement by a white college professor in his forties: "I tell my friends that in the United States I'm the invisible man. I cross the border and I'm Tom Cruise."[41] In both accounts, men come to understand themselves not only as consumers but also as prized and visible commodities in the global marketplace.

While fantasy is usually relegated to the unattainable or the unknown, there is a realist aspect to these fantasies that is performed as "cultural anthropology." Men are taught to interpret the women they meet through their virtual interactions not as mere fantasy but as objects they can come to "know" and bring home through their own studies and research compiled through reading guidebooks, speaking to others, and traveling and meeting women in cyberspace and in person. Through an array of guidebooks offering an "anthropological" perspective on women and Latin American "culture," men are taught new ways of behaving, how to reshape their expectations when dating Latinas, and how to recalibrate their status, gender positionality, and relative power in relation to Mexico and Latin America. These fantasies can be engaged and scientifically "known" in ways that stabilize tidy boundaries between gender roles and the division of labor in the home and workplace, expectations that continually threaten to implode or disappoint, leading men to search for women in places less traveled or less exposed to tourists.

I discovered that even as a lurker (or invisible voyeur) and participant in Planet-Love, the stories men told me at the tours mimicked the stories repeated in the chat room. While I feared that just my being a woman from the United States would hinder the openness of my interviews with men at the tour in Guadalajara, I found that most men were eager to share their stories with me. My willingness to listen to men's stories and to talk openly with them in English and the fact that I was physically feminine, attentive, and racially visible as nonwhite (and thus nonfeminist in their eyes) contributed to my "insider" status as just "one of the guys."[42] While this was neither my intent nor a position I felt comfortable with at all times, I was able to engage men in honest and open discussions that, at times, I wished I was not privy to. Some felt the urgency to have their stories documented by a legitimate research project in the United States, others were curious as to my perspective and findings, and still others (who did not discuss their search for a Latina with family and friends) told me how good it felt to talk openly about their intimate relationships. One man, frustrated with the "poor" caliber of women in attendance (he even said his maid was better looking than most of the women there), thanked me for the three-hour group discussion that four of us had before the tour, saying it was the best part of his five-day trip in Guadalajara. This group interview was therapeutic, similar to a self-help meeting or confessional in which these men felt they could voice opinions they knew were not considered "politically correct" in the United States. My presence and interest in men's stories provided them a venue to tell the world how wronged they were by U.S. culture and feminism.

The Internet has been a powerful medium for reflecting on and performing ourselves in new ways.[43] That said, the Internet's technological capability for connectivity and interaction is not often discussed in tandem with other kinds of social formations. Chat-room boards share a history with the emergence of self-help and support groups popular in the United States. Influenced by Protestantism, self-help culture emulates the desire for personal growth, a strong work ethic, and the idea that confession and personal redemption, exemplified through sharing and honesty, bring one closer to one's true self. For the Mexican women discussed in chapter 2, their turn to Protestant values and the global networking capability of the Internet communicated their desire to shift from local mores to a more active role in changing the direction of their lives. Christian groups in the United States see their goal as reinstating men's authority in the family as ordained by God in the Bible.[44] Michael M. Messner studied one of the largest Christian male movements, the Promise Keepers, whose leader professes the crisis within the American nation to be the feminization of the American male—the kind of manhood that has produced "a nation of 'sissified' men who abdicate their role as spiritually pure leaders, thus forcing women to fill the vacuum."[45] Support groups help change behavior and reformulate the conception one has of oneself, combating social stigmas and redefining norms of behavior.[46] Men who do not have others to share their lives with find camaraderie and a place to express themselves without having to guard what they say. Several men I interviewed expressed frustration with having to self-edit due to popular pressure to be politically correct. Against the critical work of Michel Foucault regarding the turn to confession as a way of freeing sexual deviance, describing one's intimate desires is how men come to uncover an assumed "truth" about themselves, women, and the cyberbride industry in general.[47]

Groups such as Robert Bly's men's groups actively reclaim their own brand of masculinity or desirable masculine behavior. Bly believes in the biological gender dichotomy between masculine and feminine behavior and popularized all-male support groups focused on honing one's masculine essence through all-male mythology and ritual. While feminists, he argues, had their opportunity to reassert the "feminine voice" that had been suppressed, Bly argues that the masculine voice has been muted, and men have therefore become tame, passive, and domesticated. Masculinity must be recuperated through the resurrection of tribal rituals that exclude women.[48] Bly also believes that urban industrial society severed the ties between men, replacing them with alienated and competitive bonds.[49] While feminists have worked hard to make men's gender power visible, many men interpret this as limiting their ability to assert a dominant or overtly masculine performance of gender. Men's groups convey feeling disempowered by feminism and advocate empowerment, coming to self-actualization through the collective sharing of oneself. Based on women's consciousness-raising of the 1960s and 1970s, the self-help or support-group model inverts the radical structure of consciousness-raising by placing value on the collective self rather than on larger structures of power. Divorced from the original goals of the feminist movement, which aimed to make visible the ways social structures penetrate the individual, to highlight the privileges of race and class, and to connect the personal worlds of women with larger structures of power, men's groups focus on the individual and ignore rather than reveal these privileges.

In a similar vein, Planet-Love's chat room serves as a virtual and ritual space of male bonding and teaches lessons in manhood for men gearing up to adventure into unknown territories to find a wife. Masculinity is not natural but must be practiced and rehearsed through shared expression. Planet-Love offers men a fairly safe and secluded space to express their collective desire to find an alternative to U.S. women, to swap stories of dating in Latin America, and to practice new roles of manhood as they cross into Mexico and Latin America. For those curious or timid about the daunting process of finding a wife in Latin America, Planet-Love offers articles on the visa process, advice about translation services and immigration law, news articles relevant to mail-order brides, and reviews of dozens of agencies providing international "matchmaking" services. Participants vary from those seeking advice before they sign up with an agency and depart for Latin America to those who have extensive experience with travels abroad, to curious bystanders, to men and women already married. In the process of discussing how to find a bride, men confront questions about gender roles, cultural differences between Latin America and the United States, and the role of the family across national borders. Planet-Love's chat room is an increasingly popular space where social interactions happen simultaneously, across time and space, and new practices of transnational dating, marriage, love, and relationships are debated.

Part of the pleasure of the tours and men's participation in chat rooms is the male camaraderie. John, one of the more prolific participants on Planet-Love.com, sees it as a place to express himself and to make friends. He said, "I like planet love. I am a guy willing to talk about my life but wasn't before much. A lot of my friends were more aquantances [sic] or activity buddies. Plus I kind of impress myself sometimes, the way I can express. Something I was not doing elsewhere. Plus I met so many guys who are my friends."[50] In addition to the pleasures of male bonding, men enjoy the freedom to discuss and act out their desires in an unrestricted zone where they refuse to curb their speech or thoughts. I found Steve, who owns another agency a few blocks from the tour hotel in Guadalajara, lurking in the Romance Tour lobby with a couple of other men who did not pay the $1,000–$1,500 fee to enter the ballroom. He was on a mission to find a woman himself but also to recruit men (and women) to his agency.[51] Steve's agency, located in a residential neighborhood, offers a relaxing atmosphere, with its Spanish architecture and the central patio dotted with plants and fountains. Men pay a yearly membership fee to visit the agency as often as they wish. Once they arrive, they set up one-on-one meetings, aided by the energetic staff of local Mexican women, therefore bypassing the hectic pace and pressure of the Romance Tour. At the agency, Steve, in his early forties, expressed his pleasure in the male camaraderie generated through the collective gaze at women's bodies as erotic objects. He exclaimed, "I love this whole business. . . . I feel like I'm back in the fraternity hanging out with the guys back in the day, looking at all these photos of women: 'What do you think about her, man?'" This statement typifies the nostalgia for a time of unrestrained behavior and male bonding (while women provide the erotic glue).[52]

Men in chat rooms similarly bond as they circulate women's photos. One said, "There is a woman that some of you might find interesting . . . check out page twenty three. She is a professional dentist. It is worth a look. Let me know if your taste is the same as mine."[53] Others swapped pictures of contestants from Miss Colombia/Venezuela contestants as a means of collectively approving their decision to seek out Latin American women. While I was at the Guadalajara tour, it was challenging to arrest Willy's attention for very long as the constant flow of young women stole his gaze. In his early forties, he went to Guadalajara for six months to work in the international department of IBM. Looking at me sideways, he pulled me into his revelry as if I was one of the guys at the tour. "Yeah, see that one? She's *real* nice." He shared his preference for the young girls. "I find their moodiness and immaturity *so* alluring. . . . Yes, their mood swings, up and down, it's a lot of work, but I *like* it." The excitement building in his voice made me realize how close I was to an erotic underworld that I had not asked to enter, making me feel complicit as I followed his gaze, annoyed that my presence contributed to his peaking arousal. I knew, however, that my curiosity and willingness to open myself up to all sides of this industry meant that I could not walk away unscathed. Despite the fact that he hardly noticed when I slipped away, the consequences of his yearnings lingered within me like an unanswered question. After spending years following various chat rooms where men shared scantily clad photos of women they liked, and at times pornographic material, I was only partially surprised when Danny shared his disdain for a few of the men, especially those that call him at the tour agency, "getting off" as they share the photos of women they like best. Clearly, for some, the trajectory of desire is not confined to women's bodies, as a male audience augments the excitement and bonding between men.

Similar to support groups, these chat boards and tours re-create who counts as knowledge producers, as men with various levels of experience in the "bride business" gain authority as "experts" in heterosexual relationships, love, and marriage. These exchanges work within and against the increasing movement toward the professionalization of medicine, health care, and psychology, such that people with degrees prescribe appropriate behavior. Knowledge here is passed down from those seasoned members with the most experience to the "newbies" who may be "burned" by women if they do not arm themselves with a deep understanding of how the industry works. The passing down of knowledge enacts a ritual of male sociality that perhaps responds to men's desire to reverse how labor is valued, especially for those who feel the ever-present threat of their skills and knowledge being rendered obsolete and easily replaced.[54] For those men looking for brides in Mexico or Colombia, not only will coming to "know" Latin American women and culture improve men's chances of a successful relationship and marriage, but it also promises to stabilize a new self on-line.

While the majority of participants in Planet-Love are professional Anglo-Americans, there are increasingly more men of color as well as men from a variety of regions in the United States and from a variety of professional, class, and ethnic backgrounds. In a chat-room discussion, a Peruvian American participant named Doug Y. responded to another participant, "Hombre rosas," about the need for him to sacrifice time and money to fly out to Latin America to meet a woman with whom he had been corresponding. Doug Y. acknowledges, "It's easier for some than others. . . .You'll do it because good guys can always find a way. She's counting on you"[55] They bond on two levels, as U.S. Latinos who have had to struggle more than "others" and as professionals and citizens who now enjoy upward mobility.

On Planet-Love, there is often hostility directed at the few African American participants who bring up race as a marker of structural inequalities or oppression. Many participants refuse to believe that race influences why some African American men have less success than Anglo-Americans in dating women from various countries such as Mexico. Yet cultural differences, such as Latino participants' familiarity with Spanish and/or Latin culture, are interpreted as a positive asset. For Latino men, their travel back to Latin America supports pride in their national culture, much as Chicanos hark back to Mexican history and culture to authenticate and preserve a racial identity threatened by U.S. assimilation. "Hombre rosas" said,

So here I am, turning to LW [Latin Women], turning inward, towards the center of who I am, where I came from, it has made me once again count the ways I value my latin culture. But again, I never used to openly celebrate latin values or compare and contrast them with American, out of respect for the general American public, my neighbors, friends and family. But these days I see that I'm not alone in many of my sentiments and there is a general atmosphere of criticism of AW [American women] and their values, so I am less hesitant to celebrate being latino and saying where I'm from and all that.[56]

For "Hombre rosas," a critique of American women opens up a space to question assimilation and U.S. values. Turning to "authentic" Latin American women (i.e., women closer to traditional feminine values, unlike unruly Chicanas/Latinas in the United States) takes him on a journey to rediscover his true self, which he has had to hide in order to assimilate to Anglo culture. Situating Latin American women as the authentic other enables Latino men to construct an ethnic identity as white in relation to Latin American women, manual labor, and immigrants in general. Conversing on this board has connected "Hombre rosas" to other professional Latinos—as well as to white men who appreciate Latin American culture—and it becomes a safe place for him to openly celebrate his cultural heritage. The act of revealing oneself personally serves as an initiation or a rite of passage in which this new, "sensitive" masculinity is encouraged. In the world of self-help and male support groups, sharing one's experiences marks the journey of finding a bride, discovering one's self, and finding the "true man" one really is. In these groups, male camaraderie is founded on releasing the male energies the men believe are suppressed by domineering women from the United States and, for Latino men, by U.S. culture in general.

White men's self-conception as the good guy—sensitive yet in control—is fabricated alongside an idealized image of Latinas and in contest with hyper-masculinized Mexican/Latino masculinities. Pierrette Hondagneu-Sotelo and Michael Messner argue that white, educated, and middle-class constructions of the sensitive new male image must not be too quickly heralded.[57] This image builds itself on the backs of poor, working-class, and ethnically subordinate men who are the projected targets of aggression, domination, and misogynistic attitudes. Often overlooked, however, is how Latin men reassert their masculinity by feminizing white, Anglo men. A respondent called "The Watcher" said, "If any of these guys put down Latin men, they have some damn nerve! When they finally realize that 99% of the reason that any foreign woman would want to marry them and come to this country is for her own opportunity and benefit and that of her family, and not because American men are so special, then maybe they will check their egos and see the light."[58] Through his critique of U.S. men, "The Watcher" offers a disruptive moment of competing masculinities. He diminishes U.S. men's status by elevating women as creative survivors, thus negating women's supposed adoration of U.S. men. He also suggests women use men to improve their lives and that of their families. He continues, "Latinas need strong men. Men who are macho, that's right, I said macho, but in a good way. They don't want a man who will beat them around and treat her like trash, but they don't want some pansy who acts like a feminist sympathizer either. They want a Man who is not afraid to be a man!"[59] "The Watcher's" hostility reveals a Latin male perspective regarding white U.S. men. He turns the tables on Anglo-Americans who go to Latin America, feminizing them as the sort of men who not only support feminism but are also the ones who allowed women to take charge through feminism in the first place. By labeling feminist sympathizers as "pansies," he also implicates gay men and Anglo sexuality as feminized and overly domesticated, degrading the two alongside femininity. He also redefines his derogatory ethnic association with machismo from one that is undesirable to one that is highly desired by Latinas.

The discursive threat of U.S. white men's feminization in the United States has led to a refashioning of the cyberbride industry via popular culture. A yuppie sport magazine, *Men's Journal*, disassociates men from domesticity and thus femininity by depicting them as travelers, adventurers, risk takers, and capitalists on the hunt for women in virgin markets. An article titled "Project Wife" captures this spirit of adventure and cosmopolitanism. For readers unfamiliar with this magazine, this article can be found alongside other articles on topics such as how to increase one's testosterone and exotic sporting adventures all over the world. The article hopes to entice other athletic, heterosexual men to travel to places such as the former Soviet Union to dazzle and date beautiful white-European women. We see Spencer, the featured client in this article, as a middle-aged businessman, slightly balding and thirty-eight years old, crossing women's names off his list, dining in Italian restaurants, smiling in a club, and tantalized by photos of Russian women bracketing each page. Spencer "flies planes and rock climbs, but he's lonely. He hasn't had a serious girlfriend in quite some time."[60] Couched in this quote is a critique of the dark side of wealth and success: loneliness and alienation. A dose of a third-world encounter, however, can offset this sense of feeling ungrounded, overworked, and lonely. In the article, the problem is not that Spencer works too much, is dissatisfied with his job, and participates in perpetuating the capitalist system but that he is undervalued in the United States. While structures of corporate, white-male masculinity may be perceived to be in decline in the United States, the average Joe, or José, is enticed to enjoy the comparative advantage of women who value his work ethic, find him attractive, and are dying to marry a man from the West. Interestingly, men are encouraged to understand themselves not only as consumers but also as prized commodities in the global marketplace.

This comparative status can prove to be short-lived. Another Planet-Love.com participant, Doug Y., warns others about the possibility of falling from the ranks of a knight in shining armor: "All of us who've been to LA [Latin America] know what a rush it is to date and get the time of day with young, beautiful, mostly sincere, sweet LW [Latin women]. We also know that we are in a foreign country on a quasi-vacation. We are perceived differently because of where we are from, not who we are. Have any of you given much thought about the role reversal that can/will occur when that woman becomes a fiancée, and then a wife here in the US?"[61] Doug, who in another posting described himself as having "rural Myanmarese and Paraguayan heritage," raises the centrality of national origin in these interactions and cautions that men may be heavily influenced by the fact that they are on vacation in a foreign place. Doug reminds his readers that when they return home, the fantasy may dissipate once they return to being the modern, overworked "bad husband" who has no time to spend with his wife. Doug does not extend this critique of the American work ethic to the increasing loneliness men feel or to their inability to maintain relationships or marriages with women from the United States. Ironically, it is this need to work unfathomable hours that affords men the ability to travel, to own computers, and to accumulate the surplus capital that solidifies their affiliation with a dominant, heterosexual national identity.

Just as interesting is the way Doug shifts the gaze from the male perspective to that of his fiancée: "That same woman is no longer the lucky girl who found some 'rich' American (stereotype). She will be in a foreign country with only us. Any achievement or status she has earned as an individual will mean little if anything here. Right now I'm trying to gently convince my fiancée that she is not prepared to work as an accountant here in the U.S. even with fluency in English."[62] Doug disrupts previous conversations on bringing a bride to the United States by articulating the unspoken motives and inequalities that may burst the romantic bubble once couples live together in the United States. He subtly touches on the power inequalities, racism, and licensing laws of particular professions that bar Latinas from enjoying the same level of employment they enjoyed back home once they cross the border into the United States. He also tries to communicate Latinas' perspective, arguing that women may find American men attractive because they gain a degree of status from family and community members by dating and perhaps marrying successful men. John, who has participated in chat-room discussions on Planet-Love.com for five years, talks about his ex-wife, whom he married in Colombia after knowing her for only five days:

> One thing I notice is when we are in Colombia she always treats me better. It's like I get more respect from her because I get respect from her family. I'm sort of the main attraction, even with her friends that come over. . . . But back in San Jose [U.S.] back to the same old. . . . Two big things happened in 2002. She got a job. And she got her permanent residency card. Both made her feel a lot more independent.[63]

John's statement raises the question of whether men's dominant position is more fragile than suggested by popular understandings of men who seek Latin American wives. While men may enjoy a boost in status in Latin America, they may find this wears off once they return home. Similarly, women's subject positions and reasons for marrying U.S. men are also much more complex when examined from a transborder perspective.

The desire for a Latin American woman from outside the United States speaks to the power of the erotic imagination and the role of technology in transporting one's personal fantasies into a transnational social forum. The self-help model of individual transformation hijacks the feminist model of consciousness-raising, evacuating its radical potential through personalizing social transformation. It is this impulse toward the personal that makes evident self-help's genealogical roots within Christianity and Western individualism. Men's search for a Latin American bride necessitates a critique of U.S. capitalist culture, yet men and industry websites ghettoize this critique onto U.S. feminist bodies rather than onto larger structures of power. In other words, men blame consumption, materialism, and even greed on high divorce rates, on the fact that women leave them for wealthier and younger men, or on the fact that women seek their own empowerment through entering the workforce. Like the tension between, on the one hand, the role of the global economy and the state in protecting the unbounded needs of capitalism and, on the other hand, the bounded role of the state,[64] men justify their search for foreign genes outside the nation through a moral desire to improve the national family and, simultaneously, via fantasies of mobility, the tropes of empire, and the heroics of global manhood. Through their desire to build and improve the national family, they are caught in the dilemma of embracing ethnic, gender, religious, and national differences while maintaining global hierarchies.

As participants cybernetically debate cross-cultural dating and marriage, one participant self-consciously reflects on his own complicity in the creation of Latinas as a fantasy object. "J" posts a message titled "Warning: Prolonged Exposure to Fantasy Can Harm."

> I think there is something about *this process* that brings out the fantasy junkie in all of us, men & women. After all, falling in love involves a lot of fantasizing: preoccupation with the love-object's looks, manner of speaking & acting, finances, etc. The enchanting mystery of the Other. We tend to endow these people with idealized qualities, ignore their defects & project our own thoughts & feelings onto them.[65]

For men, the virtual "process" of finding a Latin American bride—searching websites, reading guidebooks, participating in chat-room discussions, and speaking with women who do not always speak the same language as they do—engages the erotic imagination more than other kinds of dating markets. Yet, while fantasy is usually relegated to the unattainable or unknown, these virtual fantasies can be known, contacted, and engaged—brought into the present through men's excavation of them from their "culture" and ultimately by importing them into the United States. Women's eroticized images can be domesticated into the marriage scene that finalizes most IMB websites. Through passion, faith, and determination (or as Michael exclaimed to me over the phone, "I believe in this!"), fantasies on the screen can become a reality, manifested by women in the flesh.

While some couples do successfully find that special someone, these fantasies can also elude men, as I argue in chapter 5. In the next chapter, I explore the influence of cyber imaginaries and global restructuring as they rearrange the very body shape of many women from Cali who refuse to see their bodies as natural and unchanging but instead see them as pliable and modern.

4

Bodies for Export!

The Pliable Economy of Beauty and Passion in Colombia

There are no ugly girls in Cali, only poor girls.
—female agency owner in Cali

In Cali, Colombia, I accompanied the same international marriage broker tour as in Guadalajara, Mexico, held at its sister five-star hotel. As one of the regions in Colombia with the highest black or *moreno* population, there were many more dark-skinned and working-class women at the Cali Romance Tour than there were at the Mexican tour. In contrast to the majority of women interviewed in Mexico, who drove nice cars, lived in middle-class neighborhoods, were highly educated, and had professional jobs, almost all of the twenty women I interviewed (except the translators and a handful of participants) had less education and/or lower-paying jobs.[1] And unlike Mexico, a large number of the female participants at the Cali tour were young and had undergone cosmetic surgery. Given Cali's more extreme political and economic climate, snatching a man at the tour and the possibility of migration was a more urgent desire.[2] Some women proudly flaunted extreme breast implants, while others exhibited a combination of breast and buttocks implants.

Cali's economy has experienced several booms and busts: from an initial urban explosion in the late twentieth century, generated by coffee production, to sugar during the 1950s–1970s, to the influx of capital from the Cali Cartel, which launched another industrial expansion in the 1980s–1990s that led to the rise of real estate projects (condos and shopping malls), the spread of new businesses, and the availability of luxury consumer items.[3] During the 1990s, the state further liberalized its economy, cutting social spending and opening the economy to foreign business. This last phase is one the state continues to expand, leading to former Colombian president Andres Pastrana's declaration in 1998 of an economic and social emergency; he instituted a neoliberal economic program including a cut to state budgets in health care, education, and development programs, while unemployment averaged 20 percent across the country.[4]

Colombia's reputation in the United States as a country plagued by drug wars and social strife ironically shares representational space with the region's globally renowned reputation for producing some of the most beautiful women in the world. Alongside other regions in the Caribbean characterized as sexscapes,[5] the broader transnational economy of beauty and sexualized passion makes Colombia the most popular destination for the international marriage industry. It is Colombia's racially diverse women and their reputation for winning beauty pageants that attracts thousands of men to Colombia in search of a bride and, for others, a good time. In fact, over 70 percent of on-line matchmaking companies with service to Latin America offer tours to Colombia. In line with the discussion in chapter 3 regarding male clients' and agencies' understanding of women's embodied value through their superior genes and as a natural resource to be extracted from Latin America, for some Colombian women, their bodies are a pliable resource to be remade, given the proper investment. As stated in the epigraph to this chapter—"There are no ugly girls, only poor girls"—making the body beautiful promises democratic access to class mobility. In fact, beauty is compulsory for those who want to get ahead.

My interviews with women reveal that they define beauty not as a natural state of being but as a set of bodily practices staged in relation to history and, more specifically, the present transnational economy between Colombia and the United States. Some Caleñas (women from Cali) described their turn to foreign marriage, and the process of beautification in particular, as the path to finding their *media naranja* (better half or soul mate) *and* as an investment in themselves. The intermingling of deep love and investment in foreign marriage signaled the need to situate my ethnographic encounters at the Cali tour alongside Colombian state-funded tourism campaigns and popular media to theorize women's amplifying of their beauty, or their "body capital," as not only a personal strategy but also one that binds them to the state.

Many women at the Cali tour understand the process of beautification (and for many, this includes plastic surgery) as a way to mold their subjectivity to be attractive to the demands of the global marketplace, including the influx of U.S. male tourists searching for beautiful Colombian wives. As I argue in the book, and in this chapter in particular, beauty and women's sexuality are not merely tools for the disciplining of state power or for the regeneration of the nation or even simply a discursive surface for meanings to circulate, but they serve as raw materials for women to express pleasure, to enact a sense of control over their lives, and to enter into transnational circulation. By positioning women's investment of their bodies in dialogue with the Colombian state's global investment campaign, "Colombia Is Passion," it became clear that women's sexual attractiveness and passion are not simply natural characteristics but are a required state of national belonging and of gaining transnational opportunities such as class mobility.

I employ the term *pliability* to describe a contemporary modality for Colombian mobility in relation to transnational capital. *Pliability* builds on the term *flexibility*, used to describe corporate models of efficient accumulation,[6] but *pliability* is more accurate in this case, as it describes a practice of remaking the body and self alongside prospects for future accumulation. As a practice, beautification reflects the discipline of self toward personal and political perfection—for a spiritual and entrepreneurial equilibrium that links the ideology of democracy and equitable exchange with the benefits of molding oneself to be attractive to the demands of the global economy. Similarly, pliable subjectivity extends a conception of the "natural" body to an understanding that the body must be cultivated through hard work. It is through great effort that women mold themselves into the fashion of their own imaginaries as well as outside expectations. Through the death of the old body (locally configured) and the birth of the new one (which takes on a new form within the transnational marketplace of love), this personal transformation is the first step toward collective self-improvement. For many Colombian women, by transforming the body through cosmetic surgery, fashion, makeup, and lifestyle, they transform themselves into both a spectacular glamorous body in their local milieu and a universal body in the transnational imaginary.[7]

Body pliability reflects not only a global tactic emanating from the West but also a local entrepreneurial strategy that shares conceptual space with other aspects of the in/formal gendered economy of Cali. As in other Caribbean and Latin American contexts, entrepreneurial activities outside the traditional marketplace or in proximity to streams of foreign capital provide an opportunity for upward mobility. For those who lack family connections to capital, middle-class status and consumption demand creative redress. Thus, foreign courtship is one component of this informal economy, mired in development capitalism, whereby both men and women must jump at the chance to help themselves or get left behind. The desire for romance and improving oneself are completely entangled in technologies of self-making that promise one's ascendancy to the global marketplace. In Cali, women's turn to cosmetic surgery and foreign men suggests a departure from the tyranny of locality that disables their ability to improve their social status and class position or even to move freely across national borders, to a body that has currency and can circulate in both local and world markets. Because beauty helps women express themselves as hardworking and ambitious, it promises a better life for them and their families. It is worth remembering that personal uses of the body's pliability also bind women's affections and aspirations of self-enhancement to flexible modes of production within the global economy, which can also adhere women's domestic labor to a highly heteropatriarchal and neoliberal order.

Sculpting the Body: Beauty as an Investment

In this chapter, I tell the story of Celia (a Caleña I met at the Cali tour) alongside the popular terrain of beauty, to explore the following ideas: (1) how contemporary understandings of the body as pliable articulate intimacy, mobility, and citizenship, (2) the binding relationship between women's bodies and the state's investment in the global economy and citizenship, and (3) the complex terrain of sexuality as both a modality of resistance and a practice that reproduces neoliberal values of individual uplift. Celia was one participant at the tour among many who interpreted cosmetic surgery and foreign marriage as a viable option to improve her life.

I followed several couples on dates during and after the tour and spent the evening with them as their translator. One evening, I accompanied an African American man, Seth (a taxicab driver from Virginia in his midforties, and his Afro-Colombian date, Celia (a twenty-three-year-old), to a restaurant.[8] The cab dropped the three of us off at the top of a lush hill overgrown with tropical foliage. As the restaurant was located next to the zoo, it was immediately apparent that it catered to tourists. The atmosphere was colored by a tranquil colonial nostalgia of dark-brown European architecture and traditional cuisine set against the brightly colored Caribbean attire of the Afro-Colombian female service workers. As we sat down at the table together, I waved hello to another couple two tables over whom I recognized from the tour. The Anglo-American man and his Colombian date giggled intimately as they gazed in each other's eyes with deep endearment, despite the presence of their translator. In my case, I could tell Celia and Seth were content, if not relieved, to have me along. Seth was a bit shy and awkward and appreciated my comfortable presence, not to mention the fact that Celia and I got along very well. They initiated the conversation with typical questions about what they liked to do in their spare time, music preferences, what kind of person they hoped to find, and their work lives. Celia asked about the town in the United States where Seth lived. He gingerly described enjoying his home-town, although he sensed an underlying tone of racism there, but he was not sure since his brother chided him as suffering from paranoia. I added that his intuition was correct, as this was a well-known region in which many African Americans experience racism. He looked at me with a mixture of disbelief and relief and then responded, "Yes, that's what I try to tell my brother, but he doesn't believe it." This did not seem to bother Celia, as she moved on to ask why people in the United States are so overweight. Before Seth could answer, Celia added that she had heard there is something in the water in the United States that causes obesity. A bit perplexed, neither Seth nor I knew how to interpret this outside our own cultural understandings. To compen-sate for Seth's awkward silence, I told her that our culture of fatty fast food is to blame, a much less exciting answer than she apparently sought. Soon after, Celia excitedly relayed the fact that she was going to have a liposuction pro-cedure done to transfer the fat from her belly to her behind. I was shocked, not so much at the fact of her surgery—especially since the cosmetic surgery rage has long proliferated across many Latin American and U.S. cities—but at the question of whether she wanted me to translate this statement to Seth, which I thought might disturb the aura of "natural" beauty that surrounded men's perceptions of women from Latin America. I began to ask her ques-tions about it, but Seth was eager to hear what he could tell were juicy details. I asked her if I should translate, and she nodded excitedly. Seth was similarly unsure how to respond. After digesting this for a few moments, Seth asked her why she would undertake this very dangerous surgical procedure when, he added, her body was already perfect. Seth may have been especially sensi-tive to this issue because he was shot in the face some years ago while driving a client in his taxi and now suffers severe scarring on his face.

I could tell that Celia's own appearance was extremely important to her, as it was for most women at the tour. The compulsion to dress sharply is predi-cated on a tight class hierarchy in Latin America that trickles down to the fact that most women, despite their humble living conditions, expend a great deal of energy on their appearance. Each of the four days I saw Celia, she was dressed in a new stylish outfit where everything meticulously matched, including her purse, cell-phone case, shoes, and earrings. She told us she is a student and an independent clothing retailer who sells her goods in people's homes. In order to afford the $1,300 for the liposuction, Celia explained that she had saved up money for several months, much of it sent to her by her previous U.S. boyfriend.[9] She shared with us her recent separation from her U.S. boyfriend, who had, for two years, visited her periodically, regularly sent her money, and had even met her family (a sign of serious commitment to most Caleñas). After waiting two years for him to propose to her, she ended the relationship. Apparently he was more interested in a Colombian girlfriend and having a good time than a serious marriage. Celia also relayed how her sister's positive experiences with liposuction and a U.S. marriage inspired her decision. Although Seth and I both told her that her body was perfect, she explained that while she liked her body, she wanted to improve it by thinning her stomach and fortifying her behind. Celia then said, "If I have the opportunity to change something about my body, to improve myself, then I will. Just like Seth made the choice to come to Cali [to the tour], I also decided to improve my life by choosing to do the surgery. It's an investment in myself."[10] After translating this to Seth, we both thought about it for a moment. Seth responded that he understood now, especially after seeing how competitive it was at the tour, full of hundreds of beautiful women vying for the attention of few men. He understood how valuable and important it was for a young woman to stand out.

Women's bodies are a sound investment for more satisfying romantic and economic opportunities in a region that suffers high unemployment, the displacement of over a million people from their land, and heightened violence. I do not want to misrepresent Cali, a place where the people I met were more joyful and generous than the majority of people one would casually encounter living in the United States. But for women who aspire to more than a meager-paying job, or for those who have to support their families and sometimes children, some kind of informal trade or hustle is often a necessity. Many women I met had multiple jobs, from selling food and clothes on the side to evening positions in restaurants and sometimes part-time sex work. I met women who were government workers, secretaries, hairdressers, restaurant workers, and students. Many juggled multiple responsibilities while supporting young children. For some women, even those in school or attending the university, sex work augmented meager salaries.[11] The small tourist zone surrounding the Romance Tour hotel was also populated by cosmetic surgery clinics, marriage agencies, clubs, and restaurants, as well as venues that catered to erotic dancing and sex work. As one of the safest and most well-manicured zones of the city, this tourist area contrasts greatly with the humble living conditions of the majority of Cali's working-class population. Celia's story, which I will analyze in more detail later in the chapter, speaks to the desire of some women in Cali to redesign the body, shifting the fat from the unproductive site of the stomach to the sexual protrusion of her behind. Although various women at the tour communicated their seriousness about marriage, other stories reflected the complicated nature of courtship in Cali. For example, an Italian American man I met at the tour showed up explicitly to investigate the disappearance of his fiancée. After having proposed to Mariana, Bill went back to his home in Jersey, New York, and, similar to many other men, spent about nine months and a good deal of money filing the paperwork for a K-1 fiancée visa to facilitate the migration of his soon-to-be wife. In addition to spending a great deal of time and money—traveling to Cali numerous times to visit and support his fiancée by sending her $500 each month—by the time his K-1 visa came through, his fiancée had disappeared. His mission in Cali to hire a private detective turned up evidence that she had been living a comfortable life with her Colombian boyfriend off the streams of U.S. dollars he sent her each month.[12] Bill described Mariana as a very attractive, light-skinned Afro-Colombiana in her midtwenties. Her youth and beauty gave her an edge in accessing streams of U.S. capital, while for Bill, the money he sent her each month solidified their agreement to a monogamous relationship and eventual marriage. Some women, such as Cecilia, are quite determined to marry and migrate, while others, such as Mariana, perhaps find the cash sent to them too tempting to pass up.

Beauty in Colombia

In Colombia, as in other Latin American countries, standards of beauty have imitated Western norms that link race with modernity. For this reason, blacks and indigenous peoples have long represented the antithesis of the modern nation.[13] Changes to the Colombian constitution and multicultural marketing circulate ideals about racial equality just as Spanish colonial legacies continue to permeate contemporary understandings of beauty and modernity, an ideal conflated with whiteness, the elite class, and Christian ideologies of sexual constraint tied to notions of the civilized.[14] As mentioned earlier, Cali, a Caribbean city whose mixed African population makes visible the historical legacy of the transatlantic slave trade, shares a representational space with the Caribbean, Cuba, and Puerto Rico, as a topography of primitive sexuality.[15] Cali's international reputation as tropical and hypersexual harks back to early beauty pageants, where women's bodies tied them to circuits of colonial trade and wealth in the context of emerging capital markets regionally and globally. In the twentieth century, local pageants provided a platform for plantation owners to display their wealth and power on the bodies of their jewel-adorned slaves. In national events, displaying women's bodies became the medium through which the Colombian state entered the domain of heteronormative trade relations, in which women's bodies were among the coveted natural resources and wealth of the nation. Women's beauty was central to attracting transnational business, to pitching the natural resources of the country, and to promoting foreign trade and tourism. In fact, the first beauty pageant held in Cartagena in 1934 choreographed a warm welcome for President Franklin Roosevelt and was meant to inaugurate foreign relations between the two countries. Early pageant contestants seduced foreign commerce, as women donned sashes draped over their bodies with titles advertising regional crops, such as Miss Coffee, Miss Petroleum, Miss Banana, or Miss Flower.[16] The shift from local to national beauty pageants accompanied new ideologies of beauty, as women now represented the icon for the nation's moral, pure, and modern resources. During these early twentieth-century pageants, when a woman's natural state was thought to be ordained by God, only the light-skinned elite women could represent the inner purity and spirituality of the nation.[17]

As a precursor to tourism, beauty pageants consolidated the marketing of regional differences and trade alongside women's bodies. For example, the coastal region became known for its tropical and exotic women, while inland regions with colder climates, such as Bogotá, were associated with women who were fair-skinned and more intellectually inclined. Since the 1960s, during the expansion of industrial capitalism and tourism restructuring, Cali has continued to define itself as sensual, playful, and carefree. Lise Waxer, who studies the production of Cali's world-renown music tradition, describes the city's reputation as "*la ciudad pachanguera*," "*la ciudad alegre*," and "*el sucursal del cielo*" (the partying city, the happy city, and heaven's outpost). Waxer also argues, however, that this fantasy image of pleasure and *alegría* "conceals darker ruptures: struggling new migrants and land invasions, escalating urban violence, the illicit trade of the Cali cartel, and renewed political violence in the national sphere."[18] These two opposing characteristics, violence and *alegría*, set the stage for the spirit of living in the eternal now, especially when tomorrow and the future in Colombia are uncertain for many people. There is a culture of immediacy in Cali that differs from Guadalajara. Unlike the Guadalajara tour, where courtships tended to last longer, in Cali, I witnessed at least five engagements after the four-day Romance Tour.[19] There is more incentive for women to leave Cali, where jobs are more difficult to find and violence and theft touch everyone's lives. For those who can leave, immigration represents a viable option for a better life: unemployment reached 18 percent in 1991 in urban centers (where two-thirds of the population lives), and by 2001, two-thirds of the total population lived below the poverty line.[20] In recent migration from Colombia, mostly middle- to upper-class residents have responded to violence, kidnapping, and land reforms by leaving the country, a total that as of 2003 is estimated to exceed 4.2 million, or about 10 percent of the total population.[21]

It is within the context of a mass exodus of the population that beauty and mobility coalesce. Many journalists comment on the ubiquity of beauty in Colombia, similar to other Latin American countries such as Venezuela and Brazil, to the point of labeling beauty a national obsession. Yet they fail to link this "psychological" obsession to material opportunities—including the state's reliance on beauty to pitch the nation's natural resources—within a highly gendered marketplace.[22] For women, labor opportunities and their access to state recognition and citizenship are mediated through their eroticized association with the world-renowned, vibrant beauty industry in Colombia, from beauty pageants, modeling, lingerie, and the fashion industries to the thriving matchmaking marriage industries, sex tourism, and prostitution.[23] Fashion and modeling visas enable women (mostly from the middle classes) to find more lucrative careers around the world. Academic scholarship and newspaper articles are numerous in regard to the national fervor over beauty contests; the most popular event lasts up to seventeen days and draws the attention of the majority of the country's viewers. Pageants have been theorized as an important event evoking a sense of hope, pride, and aesthetic decadence in a nation broken apart by violence, instability, and war.[24] Beauty not only functions as a powerful symbol in the recuperation of national identity but has also become a resource and symbol of hope, shaping women's expectations and access to the transnational circulations of goods, lifestyles, marriage, and migration.

The shift in the 1990s to multicultural marketing has had the effect of broadening the terms of beauty, romance, and marriage between the United States and Latin America to include Afro-Colombian women or *morenas*, those of mixed race. Recent changes in Colombia have also contributed to expanding expressions of beauty and desire. In fact, in 1991 a new constitution declared Colombia to be a pluriethnic and multicultural nation, with added articles mandating the protection of indigenous and black rights to land, education, and the ability to live free from racial discrimination.[25] In addition, various governmental positions opened up for blacks, while funding targeted NGOs working toward the empowerment of black development and communities.[26] A decade later, the success of these initiatives garnered national pride and global attention when, in 2001, the first Afro-Colombian beauty contestant in Colombia's sixty-seven-year pageant history, Vanessa Mendoza, won the title of Miss Colombia. It is uncertain whether the success of Mendoza's win marked a legitimate advance in Colombia toward the dream of "racial democracy"[27] or whether it represented the more sinister political intention to break the politicization of the Afro-Colombian population, to turn the resistant claims of racialized inequality into a celebratory discourse of multiculturalism.[28]

Today, Colombian women's entrance into the marketplace as consumers, as well as technological advances in the cosmetic industry, have shifted ideas about beauty from unaltered nature, or biology, to scientifically pliable understandings of the body that accompany democratic ideals of access to the marketplace. Colombian journalists spend considerable time debating the success or failure of cosmetic alterations as they focus the camera on a close-up of women's body parts. Cosmetic surgery has become a normalized aspect of everyday life, an enhancement that women discuss as openly as other forms of beauty modification such as makeup and clothes. But new technologies, science, and cosmetic corporations promise women (who can afford it) access to the rewards of beauty: success, mobility, and the ability to choose the life one desires.

The beauty industry's technological promise to uplift women from poverty to successful careers and a happy life, available for the exceptional few, makes this a contested practice that cannot be completely aligned with victimization or even patriarchal conformity.[29] Even women who lose pageants create professional possibilities for themselves as newscasters, actresses in soap operas, and nationally and globally renowned models.[30] These options are heightened for those who make it to Miami or other U.S. cities where modeling and fashion industries have exploded.[31] But marketing oneself via beauty and sexuality empowers only select women and does not completely evade complicity with heteronormative patriarchy. A popular example of women's success includes female performers of the diaspora, such as Shakira, who maintains her status and power as a sexualized object that is easily consumable through her performance of femininity and passion tied to the heterosexual order of Colombian nationalism.[32]

In a similar vein, there is a lucrative history that lurks behind the marketing of Colombian women on Internet marriage websites alongside the natural beauty of the country. Matchmaking websites, similar to the showcasing of Colombian women in tourism ads, market their commerce of romance, love, and marriage by displaying sexualized bodies of women. Images often depict women as sexy and playful ambassadors of their nation. In figure 4.1, the two women in swimsuits branded by the colors and stripes of the U.S. flag welcome U.S. marriage tourists to Colombia to enjoy some of the best natural resources in their country.[33] Like a Benetton ad, women are pitched as coming in all skin colors, shapes, and sizes, malleable to the desires of the client-buyer, while youth is depicted as the vital and abundant attribute. Romance tourism mirrors early national pageants in the way that women's bodies have become a medium through which the state, and now the marketplace, advertises its most coveted natural resources.

"Colombia Is Passion": Eroticizing Productive Citizenship

One of the most powerful and coordinated state attempts to rebrand Colombia's international image—from that of drug violence, social unrest, and outbound migration to a nation imagined as stable, happy, productive, and teeming with natural resources—found expression in the state-sponsored campaign "Colombia Is Passion."[34] Spread widely over television networks, the Internet, and newspapers, this ad appears on two agency websites that offer Romance Tours to Colombia.[35] Narrated by the voice of a young child who speaks English with a thick accent, the state's makeover of the national body projects itself as alluring, innocent, and nonthreatening to attract tourists, transnational corporations (which will hire their people as laborers), and investment.[36] This short video takes the viewer on a virtual tour of the nation's natural and man-made geography and showcases its most famous citizens and their accomplishments.

The video begins with tribal drums and music, accompanied by the familiar sounds of spilling coffee beans, adding to the indigenous musical riff that then inspires the camera's journey across exotic landscapes, with birds and oceans. When the voice-over begins, we see young children playing with their blond, light-skinned mother, laughing as she swings her child into the air. Then we see a business woman wearing a headphone. These images accompany a young child's voice who says,

> This is a why [sic] my country looks from the outside. Now, I want you to see it from the inside [shift to the dark eyes of a young girl], because this is how you will know who we are, how we act, and what we dream. Because if there is something we Colombians actually are, it's dreamers! And how we should not appear [sic], if this is a magical country, full of colors, flavors, places, good people, *many, many good people.* . . .We Colombians are ordinary people, people with problems, but who are, nevertheless considered to be amongst the happiest under the sun.

Fig. 4.1. "Chicas on the Beach." Advertisement for the Cali, Colombia, Vacation Romance Tour.

The camera scans to more images of a young, recently married couple about to kiss, then lingers on mothers playing with their small children. The clip introduces viewers to Colombia's diverse festivals and then its famous Colombian models. The video continues, "All this shows that there is more to this country than meets the eye. There are oceans, beaches, all possible climates all times of the year, . . . Spanish colonial architecture, modern architecture, handicrafts for export, there is progress [*reinforced by images of tractors plowing the country's rich soil to plant coffee*], countless beautiful women, and orchids."

Modern images of light-skinned, bikini-clad women casting seductive glances, including the crowning of a beauty queen, are tucked seamlessly between coffee and orchids, the women's bodies another valuable export and icon of the many natural resources Colombia has to offer. After a long list of all the famous artists, writers, and athletes of the country, the voice-over continues: "And all of them share one thing, passion! Passion for life, for family, for nature, and passion for peace. Perhaps now you will think differently about my country because what I have just showed you reflects who we truly are. Colombia is all about Colombians, that's why Colombia is Passion!"

The official website claims that passion is Colombian citizens' "best raw material."[37] It is the abundant resource that drives the nation's most creative and famous people, a natural resource that is unique, cannot be fabricated, yet is mined by the state into internationally renowned talent, exchange, and commerce. Passion here symbolizes not simply a personal attribute but a national drive common to all citizens: "The motor that drives us to give the best of ourselves towards the good of the country."[38] While the campaign is primarily international, the ad also works locally to "generate in all Colombians a sense of belonging and an emotional link to the country and its brand."[39] Passion—intimacy, sexuality, creativity, a strong work ethic, as well as the verdant land and hot climate—make it impossible to disentangle the erotics of the body from the productivity of the nation, thus intimately entangling personal success with the patriotic love of one's country. In other words, not only does the advertising campaign extend the productive sphere of the market to intimacy and patriotism, but it aligns citizenship with those who produce value for the nation.

In describing the importance of a national brand, the Tourism Board states, "It's to have an identity, a name and a reputation. In the actual articulation of globalization, it is important that countries differentiate themselves from each other, in order to compete in the international market."[40] In order for the country to project the malleability of its people and the plentitude of its natural resources, it projects itself as a pure and productive landscape for the influx of development yet also as modern and at the cutting edge of cultural trends and ideas. The country's projected innocence also works to wipe clean Colombia's image of drugs cartels, military violence, and social unrest. In contrast, the state website wants the world to know the country through the "Colombia Is Passion" brand, "in the direct path to development, with a stable economy, a privileged geography, great natural resources, but above all warm, friendly and passionate people."[41] Curiously, this passion achieves a moral place in the nation as long as it benefits the bottom line of the national gross domestic product.

The state also invests in *telenovelas*, managing the lines between moral and immoral sexualized passion, or governing which passion leads to happiness and which leads to death. For example, one of the most popular *telenovelas* in Colombia, *Sin tetas no hay paraíso*, funded by the Colombian state as well as the United Nations, tells the true story of a beautiful young heroine who uses her beauty to raise herself out of a life of poverty. A friend convinces her

Fig. 4.2 "Colombia Is Passion." Tourism campaign by ProExport Colombia. See the official website: http://www.colombia.travel/en/international-tourist/colombia/colombia-is-passion.

that the most lucrative route is to become a *prepago,* or a prepaid call-girl, for the leading drug cartels but tells her she will only command their attention if she transforms her flat chest into voluptuous silicone breasts.[42] The character, Catalina Saldana, spends countless episodes desperately searching for someone to pay for her breast implants, which she finally accomplishes (after being raped and having a miscarriage) by sleeping with a cosmetic surgeon in Bogotá. Her dream of living the good life violently deflate along with her silicone breasts, after she has them removed because of a painful infection.

Ultimately her world falls apart, as does that of her family, and she loses the hope to continue. In the final episode, Catalina plots her own murder, rejecting her alternatives: to work as a low-paid and badly treated prostitute like some of her acquaintances in local bars, to return to her neighborhood boyfriend, Albeiro (who slept with and impregnated her mother), or to work hard hustling odd jobs here and there like her mother, who barely makes ends meet but appears fairly happy. The message here is painfully clear. Young girls who use their eroticized sexuality and get mixed up with the underworld of drug lords ultimately end in misery and even death. This popular Colombian *telenovela*, remade to air in the United States and over fifteen other countries, contrasts greatly with the images of models, beauty queens, female high-tech workers, and mothers in the "Colombia Is Passion" advertisement. Their sexuality, beauty, and maternal labor reproduce the moral image of the nation and a future-projected notion of gendered citizenship split between the reproduction of bodies and productive labor. Prostitutes, and especially those who get mixed up with the drug cartels, are blamed for their own demise and the violence tearing apart the nation.

Erotic Citizenship: Agency during a Neoliberal Age

In Colombia, women's exhibition of their beauty and sexuality reflects the ways the Colombian state meets with the demands of global capitalism. To aid in this goal, the state ensures economic compensation, trade, citizenship, and benefits to those who transform their body into consumable icons and labor to fulfill foreigners' desire for alterity, pleasure, leisure, and sexuality. M. Jacqui Alexander argues in her theorization of the state, sexuality, and tourism in the Bahamas that state power continues to be consolidated through heterosexuality. She contends that the state perpetuates the colonial project of policing sexualized bodies by locating subjectivity in the body—if only to deny it—as if to convey legitimate claims to being civilized.[43] She argues that states premise citizenship on physiognomy, or judging individuals' inner characteristics by their outer appearance, refusing citizenship to those deemed to be sexual Others. Similarly, in Colombia and many other Caribbean and Latin American countries, the state uses sexuality to sell these countries as a tourist destination. For Alexander, the neocolonial nation-state draws together powerful processes of sexual commodification and sexual citizenship in order to create a population of "loyal sexualized citizens to service heterosexuality, tourism, and the nation simultaneously."[44] Julia O'Connell Davidson and Jacqueline Sánchez Taylor contribute to this debate to argue that Caribbean states rob their own citizens of rights through an economy of consumption in which tourists have more rights to resources and safety (including water usage, phone lines, Internet, etc.), while the natives are left in the position to capitalize on their role as service providers.[45] North American and European countries similarly endorse heterosexuality and the rights of nationals by extending citizenship rights (partially and reluctantly) to the spouses of their nationals.[46]

In Cali, some women's use of beauty foregrounds a contemporary way women demonstrate themselves as "fit," not only as citizens of their own nation reorganized around erotic sexuality but for citizenship and rights in the global marketplace and arena. Citizenship is increasingly configured not only through skin color but, for Colombian women, through their ability to commodify their bodies into a hyperfeminine aesthetic that continues to define normality and citizenship in relation to heterosexual desire, consumption, moral sexuality, and middle-class relationships. With few other outlets for expressing themselves as enterprising, valuable, and savvy, the pursuit of beauty for women at the tours is an appropriate outlet to translate a sense of themselves that cannot be expressed otherwise.

Some women also use foreign dating and/or marriage to upgrade their body capital, refusing to remain confined by their class standing. Because women cannot afford to buy the signs or products of modernity, what Coco Fusco calls in her article on *jineteras* in Cuba "el highlife"—the lifestyle of dining out or wearing the latest fashion—foreign romance is inseparable from consumption, modernity, leisure, and affluence.[47] Even while local working-class women in Cali popularly associate marriage with domestic slavery or drudgery, foreign marriage translates as providing a higher return on women's intimate and erotic labor. Maria Cristina Tenório analyses popular texts alongside interviews with working-class women in Cali to argue that young women are turning away from marriage because of the extra burden it places on them.[48]

My turn to popular narratives of beauty in Colombia demonstrates that women's beautification of their bodies operates at a social and state level, as a collective form of citizenship but also as gender complicity and resistance. It is important to remember that women's experiences and desires are incredibly diverse and that the thousands of women who participate in the international marriage industry are a small percentage of the overall population in Colombia. Colombian popular culture is a significant avenue, therefore, for uncovering the broader cultural and feminist refusal of hegemonic standards of beauty and social mobility. Another one of Colombia's most popular soap operas, *Betty la fea* (Ugly Betty),[49] became a platform for Colombians to voice their discontent at beauty's use as a model for women's advancement. Against the grain of most *telenovelas*, where a woman's glamorous appearance miraculously offers an escape from whatever downtrodden situation she finds herself in, Betty and her friends are from the working class and do not embody global hegemonic constructions of beauty (constructed through whiteness, straight hair, current fashion, large breasts, etc.). Able to attract over eighty million viewers worldwide,[50] this popular *telenovela* depicted Betty as a woman who uses her intelligence, hard work, humor, sensuality, and most importantly, her integrity to navigate and improve her socioeconomic position (wealth and status), regardless of her looks. Since men are often paired with hyperfeminine women in most *telenovelas*, women from lower socioeconomic classes may have a more difficult time securing a romantic relationship. Thus, one of the themes of *Betty la fea* is that through hard work and intelligence, anybody can "make it," a similar narrative driven by the consumer marketplace.[51] Yet success comes at a cost, as Betty must finally alter her physical appearance; she cannot be an "ugly" professional who desires to marry her boss. Millions of female viewers hoped "ugliness" would be resignified from its hegemonic understanding as that which has little currency or cosmopolitan cachet—indigeneity, dark skin, poverty, and locality. Despite Betty's strong credentials, her frumpy looks resign her options for employment to the ranks of a secretary position in a fashion company, until she falls in love with the owner. It is the *telenovela's* gesturing to reality that evokes such loyal viewers. For example, many jobs available for women in Cali request that women have "good appearance," a requirement confirmed by applicants' inclusion of a photograph in their application. Betty, in order to successfully court her boss's attention, ironically turns to a beauty pageant consultant to undergo her painful transformation from *la fea* (the ugly one) to *la bella* (the beautiful one). Her physical renovation is equated with a rearticulation of the character's subjectivity and future prospects.[52]

It is the *telenovela's* promise to transform the "common" female body into a spectacular subject who enjoys upward mobility that speaks to the widespread popularity of *Betty la fea*. Yet the depiction of the transformation of the outer body as proof of one's inner beauty led to a public outcry by feminists, professors, and fans alike. The revolutionary appeal—that an average woman can get ahead through her inner strength, her moral values, and her intelligence—was replaced by a hegemonic definition of modern, female beauty as it is made visible on the surface of the body. A well-known feminist journalist and professor in Colombia wrote, "Betty . . . Nos enfadaste" (Betty . . . you pissed us off).[53] This statement reflected the widespread disappointment and feminist anger from middle- and lower-class Colombian women whose hope for a different model and narrative possibility ended up being a recipe for more of the same. Betty ultimately transforms herself, her subjectivity, and her power by becoming an object of desire. In other words, female subjectivity accrues value and visibility through heterosexual attraction, in which the male perspective determines a woman's actions and desires.

In a country where corruption is rampant, the most popular episode with the most viewers came after Betty refused an $87,000 bribe to curry favor with her boss. In this episode, Betty contemplates taking the bribe by imagining herself in stylish clothing and driving a Mercedes-Benz.[54] Journalists and millions of viewers called in to the show, pleading that Betty not take the bribe. Newspaper headlines regarding this episode demonstrated the blurring of reality and artifice in *telenovelas*: "We need your example, Betty"; "You still have time to save the country." And still others suggested Betty run for office, after politicians in Congress had been discovered taking kickbacks for public contracts.[55] After a discussion with her father, a hardworking man who implores her not to take the money and tarnish the family name, Betty refuses the bribe, resulting in a sigh of relief for many of her fans.[56] The desire for hard work to pay off comes at a time when wages and jobs are low paying and hard to find. The "high life" is reserved for the wealthy and/or the corrupt—the elite, politicians, drug dealers, and those who can afford to migrate out of the country.

Kamala Kempadoo argues in her study on sex work in the Caribbean that since the colonial period, the Caribbean has entered the popular imaginary through sexuality. Because of this, women and men have utilized this stereotype for their own benefit. The logic of sexuality, she argues, is not only proof of women's continued status among the colonized but has in fact become a decolonial tool against racism and sexism:

> I speak of sexuality as embodied practice and as a "rebelling pillar" in Caribbean society. . . . It is with these ideas that the physical body becomes more than an entity that is inscribed or marked by discourse, or is seen to exist as a fixed or presocial national condition, but is conceptualized as an organism that actively responds to change and contingency, that is self-organizing and a self-actualizing agent, constantly in process of transformation and development.[57]

I build on the work of Kempadoo and others to argue that in Colombia, beauty and women's sexuality are not merely tools for the disciplining of state power but have become resources for women to find meaning, pleasure, and a sense of control over their lives and to enter into transnational circulation. I agree that sexuality has become a tool for women's own benefit.[58] Yet in

saying this, I also want to make visible the neoliberal discourses and consequences that accompany this notion of agency. In positing women as pliable
or, as Kempadoo describes, as "self-actualizing agents who actively respond
to change and contingency," this notion of flexibility may work to reinforce,
rather than to break down, the production of subjects by neoliberal capital.

The popularity of pageants and beauty industries, as intimately associated
with modern development, democracy, and new patterns of entrepreneurial activity for women, dangerously blocks from view, rather than exposes,
the very unequal system of capitalism. Rosemary Hennessy, in arguing that
postmodern theories can collaborate with capitalism rather than provide
a critique, finds that the success of neoliberalism is directly related to the
"triumph of ways of knowing and forms of consciousness that obscure its
enabling conditions."[59] In making connections between neoliberalism, commodification, and sexual identity, she argues, "The knowledges that promote
or demystify neoliberalism are varied. . . . They are most often identified with
the advocacy of entrepreneurial initiative and individualism—in the form of
self-help, volunteerism, or morality rooted in free will and personal responsibility."[60] Hennessy's quote reminds us of the dangers of perpetuating individualism in scholarship by advocating democratic ideals embedded within
private, personal, or individual solutions, especially when the majority of
women do not benefit from marketplace values promoting one's "innovative"
entrepreneurial motivations. I am also reminded of Donna Haraway's claim
that not all subaltern knowledges (or even practices) are innocent, progres-
sive, or unproblematic.[61]

Beauty industries across a broader comparative context enable many
women to enter discourses and practices of entrepreneurialism and capitalism. In various countries across Latin America and Asia, women turn to
cosmetic industries such as Amway and Avon as an opportunity to remake
themselves alongside the promise that the glamorous life can be gained
through working hard and making oneself over as a marketable product of
current capitalist restructuring.[62] For some of Ara Wilson's female subjects
in Thailand, they were drawn into the selling of cosmetics through various
transnational companies' cultural correlation with "self-advancement" and
an "entrepreneurial self-help" model rooted in an appealing egalitarian narrative.[63] Through hard work and motivation, some women envisioned themselves as burgeoning entrepreneurs, using beauty's association with modernity and progress to break from the social hierarchies and class limits of Thai
society. In Cali, it was apparent that a similar narrative of opportunity and
even democracy emerged out of women's explanations as to why they turned
to cosmetic surgery and foreign marriage.

Cosmetic Surgery and the Reproduction of Democratic Citizenship

Even if illusionary, the promise of a democratic future, where opportunities and rights dangle within women's reach, resonates in beauty industries and exchanges in Colombia. As argued by Alexander Edmonds, beauty in Brazil may rearrange class divisions and catapult the poor into the national imaginary of modernity.[64] The proliferation of state-funded cosmetic surgery clinics extending low-cost services to the poor in Brazil holds out the promise of democratic access, the "right to beauty," at a time when rights are increasingly medicalized and diminishing for those at the bottom. For some of the Caleñas I met, cosmetic and erotic alterations of the body are part of women's participation in democratic access to modern (self-) development on a global stage.

Celia's desire, like that of many other women I interviewed, to invest in her body with the hope of improving her chances of finding a husband indicates how women imagine beauty, and in this case, hypersexuality, as a tool to further their own aspirations and to willingly transform themselves into marketable products of exchange. Women at the tour who were more than thirty years old complained to me that they had a much harder time securing employment and attracting foreign men at the tours; in both cases, young pretty girls are specifically sought out. These women participate in a well-worn development narrative, similar to the one that many men congratulate themselves about regarding their journey to Latin America. If you can change your life, you should; if you do not, you deserve the consequences that await you. Modern states encourage a citizenry organized around self-help, or what Foucault labels self-cultivation, as it shifts the gaze from larger social critique (revolution) and the state to the self.[65] Celia's careful sculpting of her body mimics the state's entrepreneurial spirit; women's eroticized bodies become the object of self-improvement, self-help, and the promise of a democratic future. Hard work on oneself is equated with modern subjectivity and citizenship imagined as a glamorous lifestyle. The state's support of market forces remakes its image from corruption and violence and channels change and mobility through science, new technologies, the marketplace, and consumption (rather than production).

Cosmetic alterations ironically accompany a discourse of hard work and uplift, without the laborious and time-consuming task of exercise and watching one's diet. Celia said she tried exercise but did not care for it. Like the drug culture of fast money in the telenovela Sin tetas no hay paraíso, women get hooked onto foreign boyfriends and their accompanying streams of U.S. currency, enabling women to afford visible markers of the glamorous life.

They work toward improving their beauty capital quickly, rather than wait months or years for the hard work of exercise to pay off. Furthermore, working in a dead-end job with paltry wages pales next to the influx of dollars that quickly inflate women's abilities to invest in their body and future, something otherwise impossible with a low-paying job.

For example, after Monica married John (who lives in Silicon Valley in California), he wired her family in Colombia about $300 each month, quickly transforming her family's living conditions. These remittances financed their move from a modest home and neighborhood in Cali into an upper-middle-class spacious home with new appliances. Her mother had lost her job making dolls after the production site was transplanted to China; thus, the additional money John sent her mother provided enough for her to invest in her own flower business. Although now divorced, John asked Monica to marry him just five days after they met at a Cali tour, and though she hardly knew him, she soberly accepted.

In contrast to the many women in Guadalajara who dressed professionally, many Caleñas wore outfits that accentuated their body capital. It is important to note, however, that Celia, a dark-skinned Afro-Colombian, chose to alter her body by augmenting her buttocks, rather than her breasts, thus complicating the equation of beauty in Colombia with hegemonic standards characterized by whiteness, straight hair, and large breasts. While many women at the tour had breast implants, or some combination of breast and buttocks implants, it was significant to see women use surgery to augment their ethnic attributes rather than to erase the embodied signs of racial difference. In the majority of U.S. studies on the historical and contemporary uses of cosmetic surgery, most nonwhite subjects are theorized as turning to surgery to "pass," to erase the stigmas associated with ethnic body parts, whether the nose for Jews, African Americans, and Peruvians or the eyelids for Asians.[66] Kathy Davis argues that for white women in the United States, augmenting breasts or doing face-lifts is merely a tool to correct women's sense of dislocation from social norms of femininity, or women's desire to just be "normal."[67] In this instance, surgery for white women becomes an acceptable form of psychotherapy, an individualized technique disconnected from the wider context of modernity, visual culture, body mutilation, and privilege. In Davis's more recent book, she understands ethnic surgery, such as the many procedures of Michael Jackson, as connected to the desire for more neutral racial features, androgynous sexuality, and the desire to get beyond race.[68]

For Celia, her soft voice, graceful gestures (reminiscent of women groomed for beauty pageants), and desire for an enlarged behind articulate a complex longing for a more pliable construction of identity, ethnicity, and

sexuality that has both local and global currency, that situates her subjectivity as both embodied and translatable in a broader context. Depending
on the spaces and social situations Celia moves through, she can rework the
meanings of her race and class. In line with the tour's location at an expensive hotel and many men's search for "high quality" women (and the class
implications that accompany their desire for quality),[69] women must upgrade
and beautify their bodies to blend into these tourist zones so they are not
mistaken for prostitutes or "green-card sharks." Yet at the same time, these
women garner currency in their local context and with foreign men through
the embodied signs of authentic difference and hypersexuality.

Large behinds have had a long history of fascination in the European
and American imagination, such as the exhibition of Saartjie Baartman, or
the "Hottentot Venus." Spectator fascination and horror at the sight of black
women's behinds and genitalia instantiated African women's primitiveness
and hypersexuality.[70] Frances Negrón-Muntaner acknowledges the contemporary legacies of colonial reactions to racial and sexualized excess. She says,

> A big culo (butt) does not only upset hegemonic (white) notions of beauty
> and good taste, it is a sign for the dark incomprehensible excess of 'Latino'
> and other African diaspora cultures. Excess food (unrestrained), excess of
> shitting (dirty), and excess of sex (heathen) are its three vital signs. Like
> hegemonic white perceptions of Latinos, big butts are impractical and
> dangerous. A big Latin rear end is an invitation to pleasures construed
> as illicit by puritan ideologies, heteronormativity, sodomy, and a high-fat
> diet. . . . In Simone de Beauvoir's classic words, "the buttocks are that part
> of the body with the fewest nerves, where the flesh seems an aimless fact."[71]

Celia's desire to move the flesh from the stomach to the behind rearranges
this narrative of excess, as her body is not simply discursive but a resource
for her to sculpt her body into one that is (sexually) productive, a body with
more value. Pumping fat into the behind, I argue, is connected to the productivity of the behind, rather than its excess. To move the fat from its unproductive location in the belly to the behind shifts the meaning of the body
from a site of ugliness to beauty and from its disuse in one area of the body
to an excess of meaning and value in another. In addition, accentuating her
behind, coupled with the meticulous attention to her manners and a feminine appearance, confound the lines between hypersexuality and respectability, the modern and the primitive, leisure and labor, and so on. Similar
to beauty pageants, where women are groomed for respectable femininity,
Celia alters her body in ways that confound the boundaries between sex

work and marriage, beautifying her body to increase her class status, even as she accentuates an area of the body long associated with racialized sexual appeal, attributes highly sought out by some men at the Romance Tours. This rearranging of body fat augments her own sexual pleasure as much as it may abet her ability to procure love, romance, and marriage.

Women's sense of their bodies as a pliable commodity is also a response to foreign males', and especially African American men's, erotic desire for large buttocks and a curvy body. Unlike the tours in Mexico, where the majority of men were white and Latino, 20 percent of the men at the Cali tour were African American (including two black men from Europe). For Afro-Colombian women, emphasizing their physique may be an act that does not merely conform to the demands of the tourist market and patriarchal desire but that also provides a chance to pleasurably accentuate characteristics (such as large buttocks) that have been degraded by mainstream notions of ideal beauty in Colombia.[72] Accustomed to being scrutinized on the grounds of physical beauty, these women capitalize on new cosmetic technologies and foreign configurations of desire to display their motivation and self-enterprising spirit in the face of limited opportunities for jobs, travel, and mobility at home.

Women's ideology of pliability resembles popular narratives of cosmetic surgery in the United States that promise to uplift women from poverty, as seen in the onslaught of television reality programming. The horror and violence of cosmetic alterations are not solely located on third-world women's bodies, as these surgeries are widespread in U.S. culture and gendered practices. Cosmetic surgery proves to be an apt practice and popular metaphor for individuals to turn poverty into a personal flaw that can be remedied through willpower and technology, rather than a social problem based in unequal structures of power, opportunity, and the continued repercussions of racial inequalities. In the popular reality show in the United States called *The Swan*, the power of science is embedded in the array of heroic male surgeons (and one female psychologist) who turn visible physical characteristics, such as crooked and yellow teeth, an overweight body, small breasts, and droopy facial features, away from a potential discussion of an economic system that fails to provide health care and education to those most impoverished and into a feat of science in which those who choose to improve themselves witness stunning possibilities.[73] This narrative is repeated in Colombian pageants in which television respondents focus on the success or failure of women's cosmetically altered additions, emphasizing an understanding of the body not as whole or natural but as an alienated surface composed of pliable parts, as well as a democratic surface available to all through scientific and artistic uplift. Beauty pageants and *telenovelas* also individualize beauty and romance as qualities attained through the entrepreneurial motivation of the woman, rather than as larger questions about how beauty is related to a patriarchal society, questions of access to expensive (and dangerous) surgery procedures, or examinations of the lucrative industry of beauty and fashion that accompany these popular events. In these contexts, it is evident that women's success, whether romantic or otherwise, is the responsibility of their own enterprising spirit. The focus on the self distracts one from questioning the role of the state in providing for its citizens. For many subjects of the Global South, the use of technologies is relegated to the increased marketability of the body, which then reinscribes race, class, and sexual differences, rather than enabling its pliable transcendence from markers of difference.[74]

The prevalence of "choice" as a central tenet of neoliberal market values and individualism corresponds with recent constructions of the body as pliable via popular discourses of technology, science, and genetics. These new discourses and uses of technology to remake the body continue the propaganda of neoliberalism but also offer the possibility of providing Latin American women a strategy for becoming ideal global citizens with superior reproductive and moral characteristics. The dangers of cosmetic surgery are downplayed in order to highlight the ways this technology offers people the flexibility not only to *be* themselves but to *produce* themselves, to alter the inner and outer reproduction of the self. It is worth recalling that early surgeons used cosmetic surgery to erase marks left on the body from diseases such as leprosy, enabling subjects to pass as able-bodied and free of illness. In this contemporary case, cosmetic surgery projects individuals as upwardly mobile, rendering invisible from women's bodies the violence and harsh economic conditions of everyday life in Cali. This turn to self-management corresponds with what Emily Martin describes as an increase in the role of the individual as taking over the arm of the state in promoting the "right conduct" of orderly citizenry.[75] The state apparatus is surely not in decline as it extends its disciplinary power to individuals.[76] Rather than look to the government or community to advocate for improving the social body and access to resources, the state fosters democratic inclusion or citizenship through individual uplift. Similarly, the body as a malleable resource can serve as the raw material for making oneself into a more appropriate citizen whose skin stretches its meaning across global space.

Men's investment in women's beautification reproduces the logic of freedom and democracy for the exceptional few worthy of foreign investment. The statement by a Colombian agency owner, "There are no ugly girls in Cali, only poor girls," was repeated by one of her U.S. male clients.[77] This statement reinforces the idea that women can be malleable given the proper resources and aesthetic care, an idea that extends to Latin America more broadly, as a region infinitely capable of development given the proper investment. While beauty here is uncoupled from nature, assigning women's femininity through beauty may also reinforce their association with docility, with the desire to please. Furthermore, similar to *Betty la fea*, class and beauty go hand in hand.[78] Colombian women make themselves into subjects of glamour and in the process make it difficult for men to imagine the harsh living conditions that life in Cali doles out to many of its inhabitants. Like many women, Celia lives in a humble home with other family members. Most men described being quite surprised by the simple living conditions women came from in comparison to the amount of money spent on their clothes and appearance. And the appeal of foreign marriage is upheld by the select few women whose success stories materialize when they return home with luxury items and when there is a dramatic change to their family's class standing thanks to the remittance money they send home to their families every month. A young woman at the Cali tour (accompanied by her mother) accepted the marriage proposal (after the tour) from a wealthy man from the Midwest, who promised to buy her working-class family a fancy new condo in Cali. In case his Anglo-American identity was not enough to convince women of his class standing, the thick diamond rings glittering on several of his fingers instantiated fantasies of a wealthy American lifestyle.

Conclusion

Women's classed comportment is also compulsory at the Romance Tours held at five-star hotels. The tourism industry demands narrowly scripted interactions, as spatial hierarchies—overdetermined by relationships between the consumer and service class—are heavily surveilled, protected, and cleansed of danger. The safest places in Cali are located within privatized spaces of consumption and ownership, such as middle-class homes, tourist zones, hotels, malls, and restaurants, guarded by military men strapped in heavy armor. In a similar sense, through beauty modification including cosmetic surgery, women's bodies are cleansed of the memory and reality of struggle and violence. Their beautification contributes to the idea that true pleasure, leisure, and the body are void of economic considerations. In fact, this ideology perpetuates women's appeal to U.S. participants of cybermarriage, to the U.S. immigration apparatus, and in the image of the Colombian nation in the international marketplace, as more pure, moral, and naturally family-oriented than U.S. women (and workers), who are viewed in comparison as greedy, selfish, and too demanding of their worth. As we saw in chapters 1 and 2, women's proclamations of love have consequences for violently confining how women express their actions and needs, especially in light of their precarious legal status. And because romance and love in the United States are associated with leisure and consumption, any percolation of economic motives threatens to soil women's reputation and diminish their ability to attract a foreign husband.

The fact that rates of breast and buttocks implants have soared in countries across Latin America such as Brazil, Venezuela, Mexico, and Colombia since 2000 speaks to the racialized economy of desire wrought by globalization, tourism, and the media. During Carnival in Brazil, women with breast implants are now famous for painting the Brazilian flag over their swelling new additions, making women once again complicit with sexualized state regimes that rely on women's erotic symbolism to attract tourism, trade, and attention into the country, while these women also use the new signs of status for their own pleasure and advancement.

It is also apparent that a new grid of privilege and modernity is articulated through cosmetic alterations. It is through one's adherence to the norms of heterosexual femininity and male desire inscribed onto the body, rather than merely skin color, that one acquires a new language of global ascendancy. Cosmetic advances rearticulate long-enduring colonial legacies of racial difference as biologically entrenched in nature to reflect identities that are pliable, "democratically" available, and reliant on innovative technologies. Being civilized is equated with technologies of self-cultivation, with working hard, taking a risk, and jumping at opportunities that come your way. This is directly related to the role of U.S. state immigration in discouraging citizenship to those who may become a public charge, in other words, accepting only those whose enterprising spirit will contribute to the surplus labor of the nation.

There is a truth to be found in women's bodies, as the sight of the "real" in both ethnographic methods and men's own theorization of their "experience" with women, that perpetuates incommensurate notions of who these women are, what they want in life, and why they hope to marry U.S. men and migrate to the United States. By the end of the tour, Seth and Cecilia decided to continue to date and remain in e-mail contact. I could not help but wonder whether they could understand the realities of each other's lives. Celia's surgery communicated her strong desire for a U.S. husband, as Seth's desire for a foreign wife was communicated through his travel all the way to Colombia. But this is only part of the story. It is through a transnational lens that we can better understand the complexities of intelligibility across cultural divides and as a framework to piece together the array of actors who contribute to everyday forms of desire, violence, and meaning making. Women's ability to participate in globally mediated constructions of hyperfeminine beauty offers them the chance to play a part in the glamorous life of visibility and leisure. This is significant given the invisibility of women's domestic labor in the privacy of the home. Yet, for many women, the glimmer of hope to "be somebody," or even just to have an ordinary and stable life with someone, compels women to surgically cut apart their bodies and to jump into romantic and marital relationships with men they may know little about.

In this chapter, I have analyzed the centrality of the body in forging new aspirations for class, citizenship, and transnationality that are malleable rather than stable. Access to the freedom of movement across local spaces and national borders demands conformity to hyperfemininity and sexuality, as well as to neoliberal practices of self-care and entrepreneurialism that are evacuated from the language of need, welfare, excess, and disease. Women's desire to prove their inner respectability and worth through aesthetic alterations speaks to the tension between their reputation as women who know how to have a good time and the rendering of bodies in motion that today signifies sexual danger. For example, Colombian sex workers are turning up in high numbers in Spain, the Dominican Republic, and western Europe. In fact, a veteran of the Romance Tour circuit in Latin America shared his strategy with me about how he finds a "quality" woman at the tour. He makes sure to ask women where they have traveled in order to ascertain whether they have engaged in sex work. If women have traveled key routes, he explained, then he has a pretty good idea that she traveled to these places to work in the sex industry rather than to enjoy an expensive holiday. Many men attempt to find women and places less tainted by U.S. culture and/or industries when they discover that too many women in Cali are learning how to use foreign marriage for their own needs and desires. Convinced that the pure, precapitalist woman does in fact exist, they fail to see the larger context that contributes to the importance of beauty for many women, as they continue their search for less-traveled Latin American countries to find that unspoiled image of the perfect woman.

As in Mexico, heightened media attention to the trafficking of women in Colombia, while important in depicting the lives of some women, is happening at a time when women in Latin America are migrating in larger numbers regionally and internationally via sex work, marriage, and other feminized patterns of migration such as domestic labor. Thus, women's bodies simultaneously characterize the aesthetic of beauty and the purity of the nation as well as the dangers, dislocation, suffering, and violence that globalization can wreak on the bodies of women, family life, and the nation at large.

The scrutiny of women's mobility through marriage unfortunately continues even after women marry and migrate to the United States with their new husbands. There are challenges to migration and to leaving one's home that are eclipsed by the glamorous images of life in the United States.

5

Migrant Critique

Love and the Patriot

In discussing my research topic with others through the years, most people want to know how these marriages work out. On numerous occasions, people would come up to me after I had given a talk on this project and ask, "Do men *really* find a 1950s wife?" Or "Do Latin American women *truly* enjoy a more traditional domestic role?" In part, these inquiries question whether these virtual fantasies work out in ways that match expectations. I am wary, however, of drawing from statistics that would prove whether foreign couplings are more or less successful than U.S. marriages. I have not personally heard any cases of physical abuse, although it is clear that given the unequal citizenship status and sometimes gendered expectations between men and women, these marriages carry uneven obligations that can generate, I argue, heightened intimacy but also the potential for painful misunderstandings and hardships.

The desire to know the outcome of these marriages, including in my initial own interviews with couples, swerves uncomfortably close to practices of governmentality in wanting to settle on a "truth" about foreign marriages.

This is especially the case given the official dialogue of "mail-order brides" in state reports and research that base legislation reform on the two exceptional cases of homicide, one of a "mail-order bride" from the Philippines and one from the former Soviet Union, to argue for more surveillance and monitoring of foreign marriages in the name of protecting women. Despite these admittedly harrowing examples of the extreme abuse that can occur, shutting down cybermarriage industries seems an extreme response. There have been positive policy outcomes from these debates, especially in arming women with more information about their rights, yet the use of these two extreme and anecdotal cases has served as the evidence, alongside films, to render cybermarriages as abusive, unequal, and exploitative. Even debunking the stereotypes that men are power-mongers and women are green-card sharks does not address how everyday structures of gendered citizenship compel women to emotionally situate themselves as patriotically in love.[1] Furthermore, what it means to have a "successful" marriage varies greatly. Since authentic, or enduring, U.S. relationships are popularly based on commonalities (age, ethnicity, culture, religion, etc.) and their duration over time, which versions of difference and sameness define a successful marriage? After how much time is a marriage successful? After a woman obtains permanent residency or citizenship status? Does a marriage have to demonstrate equality to be successful, and how do we measure equality? The only attempt to gather statistical data on the success rate of international marriage has been a study compiled by Planet-Love.com. It found that international marriages have a 40.76 percent divorce rate, significantly lower than the slightly over 50 percent divorce rate of U.S. marriages.[2] At best, this statistic serves as an estimate, especially given the difficulties of tracing couples whose marriage records are scattered across the United States.[3]

While chapter 1 questioned the state's role, and more specifically immigration procedures, in determining "authentic" marriages through the presence or absence of romantic love, this final chapter argues that the capillaries of state surveillance continue to pervade women's everyday lives even after they move to the United States. Various couples sense an acute scrutiny of their relationship by friends and family who disapprove of a coupling they presume is plagued with unequal power dynamics. Furthermore, women's precarious position as dependent on their husbands until they secure citizenship haunts chat-room debates and interviews, as men fear they are merely the transit point to legalization. This preoccupation puts extra pressure on women to prove their love—or their disinterest from economic considerations—to authenticate their marriage as well as their fitness for citizenship. Unfortunately, Latin American women themselves guard each other's authentic status through love, care, and sincerity, thus extending the arm of the state to men and women themselves in determining appropriate gendered behavior. Just as participants of cybermarriage rearrange how bodies and affinities are aligned, disturbing the boundaries between the natural and the unnatural, the lines between the "foreign" and the "native" and between the traditional and the modern continually shift in cross-national marriages.

Bonnie Honig, in her book *Democracy and the Foreigner*, turns the attention away from immigration as a negative inflection—as a national problem to be solved—and seeks out the unexamined and positive uses of foreignness that prompts her to ask instead, "what work does foreignness do" for stimulating founding ideals of nationalism, democracy, and citizenship?[4] She asserts, "Again and again, the cure for corruption, withdrawal, and alienation is . . . aliens."[5] In other words, Honig argues that the immigrant has long remobilized the idea that national membership is consent based and voluntarist rather than inherited and organic.[6] Throughout this book, I explore how the "foreign" promises to rejuvenate U.S. men and the nation (while also threatening to implode its most foundational institutions and beliefs), as well as rejuvenating some Latin American women, who find foreign intimacies more closely aligned to their own status and goals. Here, I demonstrate that Latin American women's assertions of love and care determine their proximity to gendered ideas of domesticity, national belonging, and citizenship. Influenced by Chicana/o / Latina/o feminist and queer scholarship, I contend that marriage migrants toe a fine line in maintaining their status as exceptional patriots through proper marital femininity and thus bodies deserving of rights and life. Those women who do not conform can easily slide into the category of the "antipatriotic immigrant" who threatens normative structures of the nation and thus must be deported or left with few rights.[7]

In this chapter, I question how popular investments in normative love prevent us from recognizing the possibility for outlaw intimacies. By "outlaw," I mean the misaligned affinities that disturb cultural norms and expectations, as well as national laws and borders that define how and why people belong together. Given global economic changes and the deterritorialization of people, what ties people and places together can disturb our expectations and warp moral legal maps. In fact, our gaze as arbitrators of a genuine relationship shares a complicit role with the state in the exclusionary demarcation of national and racial boundaries. It is within this broader context that this chapter frames our participation in ossifying the lines between the foreign and the native (difference and sameness) through the scrutiny of love and the desire to demonstrate the "true" motives of "foreign" female marriage migrants. In this final chapter, women's erotic sensibility and comportment continues to legitimize moral claims to inclusion and exclusion and to govern gendered behavior.

Categories of sameness and difference are not static but rather orbit around the gravitational pull of "otherness."[8] Latin American marriage migrants negotiate a spectrum of categories of otherness that range from the foreign to the exceptional citizen through their patriotic alignment with love and, thus, citizenship. Outlaw citizenship invokes a disordering of kinship, the nation, or relatedness. Women's dependency on marriage for citizenship places even more pressure on them to prove their patriotic fervor through love of husband and country and reorients women's foreign status as rejuvenating, rather than in opposition to, the nation-state. While love transmits secular patriotism, governing women's civic allegiance, affect also transcends the political and territorial to communicate proximity to a spiritual or translegal domain. Akin to previous chapters that map out the embodied forms through which women align themselves in relation to foreign intimacy and opportunities, this chapter reworks the transcendent force of love to communicate women's universal value as human. In other words, through claims to love, women can make demands under the radar of the political (or as seemingly unmotivated by selfish demands in the relationship). At the same time, I demonstrate the limits of love as a myth that affords women pliable citizenship, as they are confined to a narrow repertoire of behavior to be taken as sincere in their marriage and as potential citizens.

After I conducted interviews with six couples in person and on-line, participated in and followed marriage chat-room debates, and analyzed legislation and films concerning transnational marriages, a contradiction emerged between popular understandings of foreign marriage as plagued with difference and thus exploitative and couples' own emotional descriptions.[9] Given that couples move to various locales across the United States, I followed men's and women's discussion of marriage and life in the United States in chat rooms to get a broader sense of the challenges and pleasures of foreign marriage. On Planet-Love, web monitors organize the relevancy of a post by the number of respondents who engage with the topic. Similar to my own sense of the relevancy of a particular post, certain experiences or speech acts reverberate in virtual communities in ways that resonate with others experiences, even shaping expectations as they become part of the everyday lives of others despite the heterogeneity of experiences. For this reason, I have chosen debates on-line that sparked the liveliest debate, in addition to selecting utterances that clarified something universal in the experiences of others. Particularly useful were women's discussions of marriage and life in the United States in cyber-communities that created intimate affinities (and hardships) for recent migrants from across the Americas. In these electronic spaces, women debate appropriate behaviors and norms while foregrounding their role as ideal feminine subjects in ways that deepen the cleavage between exceptional migrants eligible for citizenship and those undeserving migrants who should be sent back home. As in other chapters, women maneuver within the parameters of eroticized emotions such as love to reinforce exclusionary parameters of citizenship but also to critically expand Western notions of love and governance.

Various couples responded to my interview questions about the challenges regarding cultural difference by emphasizing feelings of affinity, especially in comparison to cultural codes forced on them by friends and family in the United States and Latin America. After I questioned a young couple living in an upscale suburban community in Houston, Texas, about the kinds of cultural differences that came up between the two of them, they corrected my assumption by instead describing themselves as culturally, racially, and socioeconomically on par. This was the case for Lorena and Paul, who had been married for over a year when I interviewed them in their large, suburban home in Texas. Lorena, a cheerful and light-skinned twenty-four-year-old from Guadalajara, Mexico, met her husband, a thirty-seven-year-old computer programmer who gained his skills while serving in the U.S. Army, at a Romance Tour. Lorena feels there are fewer differences between her and her husband than between her and the Mexicans in the suburb where they live, whom she finds unhelpful, as they do not reach out to other Mexicans. They both agreed that they share more commonalities than she does with the majority of Mexicans there, characterized by her husband as mostly "illegal" working-class migrants (the gardeners, maids, and day laborers). Lorena playfully hit her husband and said, "Hey, you're talking about my relatives," who, unbeknownst to her husband, live in Los Angeles. For Lorena and Paul, perceived cultural and class similarities trump national origin.[10] As with other couples, Lorena expressed their relationship as equal and based on their complementary contributions to the greater good of the collective, rather than a definition of equality based on similarity. In their case, Lorena cares for the home and later their child, while Paul works and manages home repairs. Ironically, many of these "traditional" roles Lorena learned in the United States. She was raised in a middle-class home in Guadalajara with a live-in maid, so it was unnecessary for her to cook or clean until she moved to the United States with her husband. Most couples are conscious that the harmony they build in their relationship—relationships that resurrect more traditional gender roles—conflicts with modern U.S. couplings, such as those in which both people work, necessitating a more equitable distribution of domestic and financial contributions (or at least the ideal of equality). Even though there is much more fluidity between what a traditional and modern marriage looks like, my point here is that various couples are conscious that their relationship flouts the norms of socially acceptable behavior in both the United States and Latin America.

A chat-room debate between two men, one married to a Russian woman and the other to a Latin American woman, explains the couples' sense of dislocation from more modern or feminist gender roles:

> Some friends had a bridal shower for Ingrid my wife. . . . While I was in the other room talking with some friends of the family, Ingrid had started to make me a plate of food. My cousin, who is very much an American woman (has a great job as a consultant for Oracle and very much loves to show how she can take control and loves to put people in their place) ran into the room where I was and insisted I get up and help my wife. I think she assumed I had the nerve to ask her to get me a plate of food and bring it to me. While Ingrid was making the plate, many people told her to make me do it myself. When I got into the other room, I saw the shock of horror on many of the younger women in the room, watching my wife do something nice for me out of love. I told these women that I had not asked her to do that for me, and that she had done it to be nice. Then everyone got on my case about me not treating her good. They have no idea what goes on between us, and do not know about all the nice things I do for her (helping with the cleaning, laundry and cooking, as well as getting up everyday at 5am to take her to work without one single complaint). Ingrid defended me, but none of these women wanted to hear it.[11]

This respondent's post (and others similar in tone and genre) offers a glimpse into the everyday forms of scrutiny that international couples endure. Unacknowledged are the extra burdens of these relationships but also how their reliance on each other may build trust and deepen a sense of intimacy. Other chat discussants similarly complained that feminist gender norms cast men as traditional and exploitative. Another chat-room thread extended this discussion to men's estrangement from masculine roles in Latin America:

> I remember one of the first times my wife and I visited the home of my wife's uncle and aunt together. . . . Her uncle, the perfect host, who was sitting right next to his refrigerator, asked me if I was thirsty (notice, he

didn't ask the both of us). I replied that yes, I was. He turned to my wife, who was sitting further away from the refrigerator than either he or I, and said in Spanish, "serve him." . . . What we've done, when it was necessary, is that we've separately told both sets of relatives, as well as the friends we hope to keep, that we are behaving toward one another exactly the way that suits both Z and I, and so they all now know that the two of us may be "odd" or "wrong" (from their own particular cultural perspective, although they always mistakenly believe that they're seeing things from a universal perspective). . . . By the way, after my wife's uncle told her to serve me, I stood up and served all three of us. I imagine that I may have somewhat screwed with his "hospitality" by that act, but after a few years he's come to a personal realization that gringo men (meaning me) just won't behave like men "ought to," and so there's nothing he can do about it and there's no need to get worked up about it either.[12]

These chat-room exchanges reinforce participants' sense of themselves as "outlaws."[13] Stories shared here, however mundane, provide a glimpse into the ways couples interact within and against gender and social norms in the United States and Latin America. As self-perceived outlaws, acts committed from the heart register as more authentic than the gendered cultural norms policed by supposed feminist women in the United States or *machista* men in Latin America. It is this shared outsider perspective that accentuates social alienation but also fierce feelings of closeness. Taking seriously these intimate feelings challenges normative lines between traditional and modern relationships and opens up the shared border space that couples occupy between national contexts. At the same time, their enactment of what appear to be more traditional roles marginalizes them from the social, especially due to popular perceptions that men and women strategically turn to foreign marriage out of self-interested goals. Thus, these marriages prove even more challenging as unsupportive friendships and family ties may have to be severed. On one hand, there appears to be pleasure in going against perceived gender norms that place them, and especially the men, on a higher moral ground than the Latin American male uncle or the feminist women at the party. On the other hand, they refuse to abide by cultural norms in either country, as acts that come from the heart defy premeditated mapping. Exclusion can be painful, but it also holds couples together.

As migrants, women may affiliate as outsiders with men who similarly feel estranged from norms in the United States. However, women also sense their difference from U.S. culture, especially during their initial relocation to the United States. Though the initial migration may prove exciting and even romantic, once the daily regimen sets in and men resume busy work schedules, many women describe intermittent to protracted feelings of loneliness as they navigate a foreign and oftentimes alienating linguistic, cultural, and geographic terrain. In fact, chat-room discussions attest how critical it is for men to acclimate their wives within the first six months to a year during this initial period of total dependency on their husbands due to language, culture, and legal barriers that prevent women from working or obtaining a driver's license.[14] Unlike other migrants who confront the stress of arriving to the United States with little money and sporadic access to labor but who usually live within migrant enclaves that provide access to networks, women in foreign marriages typically move to suburban zones of the city or remote rural areas.[15] Further complicating the success of marriage, after arriving to the United States for the first time on a fiancée visa, women have three months to marry or return home.

As a society heavily geared toward financial gain, U.S. culture, especially values of privacy and individualism within suburban and rural communities (and even larger cities), is described by many women as a cold, lonely, and sometimes hostile environment in comparison to the dynamic lives they left back home. Milagro said, "I miss the human warmth in Colombia; people are happy, attentive, and caring, etc. North Americans are friendly but reserved."[16] Against the popular idea that migration and financial security are the primary reason for women to seek foreign marriage, Milagro understands the benefits and costs. She says, "For me and my children, coming to the United States meant having to leave our entire family, . . . in addition to giving up a very happy culture of family reunions, parties, etc. for a calm city, where we didn't know the language and didn't know anyone."[17] Despite her initial feelings of loss, she has been happily married to her U.S. husband for over five years. Women often miss the bustling streets of Latin America and the daily interaction with others, in contrast to the quiet culture of the United States, where most people relish their privacy. Many miss the smells, sounds, and colorful sights of home.

Differences between the United States and Latin America were often expressed through emotional language that resonated with humoral descriptions of the human, social, and national body's health through characterizations of hot and cold. Women's expressions of affect resonate with medicinal and scientific understandings of the body as it communicates health and disease through food intake and climate, while extending to a discussion of social bonds. Latin America has long been associated with a warm, if not hot, climate and culture where social relations and kinship ties play a stronger role in everyday life than in the United States, where social ties are constrained (or proliferate) through one's relation to work, time, and money.[18]

For Milagro and many others, regardless of the imagined affinity they shared with the West before their arrival, everyday life in the United States moves to a foreign tempo. The pace of both countries differs across rural and urban zones, but the source of movement motivating people in hot zones versus cold cultures has consequences for understanding broader sentiments of belonging between Latin America and the United States. Milagro gestures to the liveliness of social interaction in Latin America, in contrast to the culture of efficiency that severs social exchange to privilege an economy of individualism in the United States.

Migration to the United States cannot be understood within the individualistic paradigm of choice when for so many women their dream of a better life necessitates the support of others, given great instability back home. Milagro was a chemical engineer in Colombia in charge of one of the most important textile plants in the country. Even her prominent managerial position earned her only enough to pay for her three children's school expenses, food, and clothing, with little left over for anything else. While she laments having to leave her family and her culture behind, she realizes too that the United States offers the ability to live a higher quality of life now that she has much more time to spend with her children, who currently enjoy a range of extracurricular activities such as sports and arts programs. She also appreciates that her husband cares deeply for her and her three children, despite the fact that he also has four children of his own from a previous marriage.

Against popular and feminist concerns that foreign brides are forced into domestic slavery, the ability to stay home, to care for one's children, and to enjoy a higher standard of living than one could as a middle-class professional back home can be a welcome relief. In Nicole Constable's study of "mail-order brides" from the Philippines and China, she argues against universal feminist paradigms that associate traditional gender roles with exploitation. Through her interviews with Filipina "mail-order brides," women described marriage as a relief from the backbreaking work of factory or field labor.[19] While this sentiment is similar for Milagro and other women who prefer to remain at home with their children, the variety of sentiments expressed as to the material costs and benefits of U.S. culture temper popular sentiments disseminated in many men's chat discussions that the life and the opportunities women will enjoy in the United States are uniformly superior.

Citizenship and Cyber-Communities for Latin American Wives

For those recently married Latin American women who join e-mail exchanges, these cyber-communities provide an important space for negotiating the norms and expectations of them as wives in the United States. Not all women feel alienated from, or a sense of belonging to, U.S. culture in the same way. To combat women's dislocation from Latin America, in 1999 an Argentinean woman named Marisol began an e-mail exchange, Latinaesposa, for the wives of U.S. husbands.[20] She advertised the exchange to men during conversations on the chat room where she also participated regularly, stating, "The first year together I was locked in the house without the possibility of a car and no transportation in this county of Atlanta. I suffered a lot without friends or family but the Internet helped me to cope."[21] With the advent of cheaper communication devices such as phones and computers, as well as the explosion of Latino culture in most U.S. cities, home can be experienced within the context of the everyday, although these middle-class migrants may find that technologies, rather than face-to-face communities, more often broker this relationship to an elsewhere. Furthermore, the Internet serves as a critical tool to territorialize women's familiarity with their new home across ethnic, gender, linguistic, and national differences. As women from Mexico, Colombia, Brazil, Guatemala, Bolivia, and Ecuador swap strategies on how to be a wife, mother, and feminist and/or how to survive and interpret U.S. cultural norms, they do so not only in relation to U.S. culture but within a larger hemispheric community.[22] Women exchange critical information as diverse as how to fill out immigration paperwork, how to acclimate to U.S. life, and where to find Latin American grocery stores, restaurants, and communities. They also share advice on legal rights and lawyers, intimacy, and money management—including how much remittance money should be sent home, how much spending money men should give women each month, and how much to spend on credit cards.[23] Sharing stories on-line shifts individual experiences into social norms that help women garner the confidence to make demands and raise issues with their husbands, an important exercise in interpreting oneself as part of a collective voice and as a citizen.

In order to defend women's right to have chat rooms exclusively for themselves, Manuela explained the difference between Latinaesposa and men's chat rooms: "We talk to each other with caring, almost . . . everyone finish[es] our messages with phrases like: las quiero mucho, les mando un besote, son mis hermanas, las he extrañado, etc. I have never reed [sic] something like that in this (LWL) [Latin-Women-List] list, and I hope I won't, because that makes the difference between men and women."[24] Gender differences become the basis for protecting an all-female space based on sentiments of care, against the more aggressive format of the male-oriented chat room. Manuela prioritizes the chat-room list's goal of care, comfort, and emotion as the condition through which exchanges are respected and valued. While differences exist, Manuela explained to the men on LWL, "we don't try to impose our points of view."

Problems arose, however, in this on-line community as intimate information from Latinaesposa leaked to women's husbands and sometimes to the (mostly) male listservs, Planet-Love.com and LWL.[25] Ensuing chat discussions raised questions about women's genuine sentiments for their husbands and created contentious divisions among women, reinforcing the damaging effects of love as a barometer of authentic femininity and citizenship that continued to discipline what women could ask and express to others. On Latinaesposa, most interactions were positive, although some women brought to the list urgent complaints about their husbands or the marriage. Age played a formative role in shaping women's expectations, including middle-aged to older women who were happy to leave careers or a working life behind. One younger woman, however, bemoaned that her husband refused to support her desire to attend the university while she juggled raising their son. She also accused him of using gifts to win over their son's affection. The heartfelt advice varied from those who thought her husband's damaging behavior against her and her son constituted reason for therapy and possibly divorce to those who suggested she may want to endure the marriage for the sake of her young son's future. Across the lively exchanges, it was evident that most women expected U.S. men to be supportive of those women who wanted to better themselves through education, a career, or other extradomestic activities (as long, some women added, as these activities did not compromise the marriage).

In response to the divisions and fissures created on Latinaesposa, a woman from Mexico named Gabriella began another e-mail support group, called Hispana-N-US, so people could discuss "immigration, culture shock, language, family, relationships, food, parenting styles, traditions, etc."[26] Gabriella explained why this support group is for both Latinas and their husbands:

> That would give them the opportunity to share their experience and learn from one another since it's not only the women who are in this boat, right? My experience when I was in one of those [women-only] lists I told you about was that my husband often felt left out and the other women sometimes didn't advice [sic] you thinking of the best for you and your family. Some may even be a little too radical and tell you to do things that could hurt your marriage or damage your relationship with your husband.[27]

Some participants on these lists considered discussions that were too negative, or that put into question a woman's allegiance to her husband and the family, as "too radical." To be radical within these Internet communities is associated with critique, with negative expressions regarding U.S. men and the family. By excluding men, the tenor of the conversation poses the danger of creating an opposition to, or fostering too much difference between Latin American women and U.S. men. Gabriella's fears that women may be too radical mimics the stance many Latinas take against a feminist perspective associated with the U.S. context from which it springs: individualistic, antagonistic toward marriage and the family, and selfish.

Even within the more private space of an invitation-only Internet community, women do not escape technologies of surveillance—the Department of Homeland Security, husbands, dominant U.S. culture, family and friends back home, and even other married women. The imagined "gold diggers," "visa hunters," and "goodtime girls" are a threat not only to men and to the boundaries of the nation but also to the legitimacy, status, and honor of women who choose marriage for the right reason, those who are "truly" in love with their husbands and the United States. There are codes of behavior that monitor participants' communication: women expect other women to be sincere in their desire to be a good wife and, by extension, a citizen of the United States. For those who desperately want to leave their marriage, they must prove abuse in order to be eligible for legal protection and benefits. Claims to intimacy, then, figure centrally in not only intimate interactions but also broader claims to citizenship, or access to both local legal structures and deterritorialized forms of belonging.

Affectionate versus Legal Contracts: Love and Citizenship

> If you come here, you have to *love* the culture, you have to *love* the country. Otherwise go back.
> —Karina

Josh and Karina have been married for nineteen years, the longest international marriage I have encountered. They met by writing personal letters to each other, brokered, in the pre-Internet era (1988), through classified ads in a Brazilian newspaper. Once the AIDS epidemic hit the United States in 1987, around the same time that Josh turned forty years old, he decided it was time to settle down and marry. This was when he decided to leave a carefree life of traveling as a chef on ships and engaging in free love during his Harley-Davidson days. As an avid traveler, he preferred to marry someone from another country, such as Brazil, where a year's stay in the country deepened his appreciation of Brazilian culture, especially the strong family ties, since he lost both parents when he was young. In Brazil, he met Karina, who practiced English with the Americans she met while working as a model at the international trade shows. After weeks of letter correspondence, they describe the first time they met as "fire and passion."[28] Despite enduring many ups and downs in their long relationship, our three-hour conversation in a small Latin American diner in Southern California made it quite evident that they adore each other. Probably one of the most unique aspects of the story relayed by Josh (in contrast to the majority of men I spoke with) is that he lived in Brazil for more than a year as a tourist and resident and thus developed a good sense of and deep affinity for his wife's culture, family, and aspirations. During the pre-Internet era of the early 1990s, they comanaged an international marriage agency for "distinguished" and influential political figures from the United States. Even though they no longer run their agency, they often consider opening another. They also recently wrote a screenplay about their experiences of romance and marriage across national boundaries.

When we broached the topic of immigration, I asked them for their thoughts on U.S. policy and immigrants more generally. Josh joked that I was asking an "Irishman" what he thought about immigration laws, a nod to early 1900 exclusionary laws against Irish, German, and Jewish immigrants that complicate his attachment to the category of whiteness.[29] Besides his acknowledgment that the laws privilege the wealthy, white people, and exceptional individuals, he understands his status as a U.S. citizen as giving him the right to bring a spouse to the United States. When I asked Karina, she said she is not against people coming here but that immigrants must learn how to adapt to the United States, to love it and learn the language and rules: "If you come here, you have to *love* the culture, you have to *love* the country. Otherwise go back."[30] When I asked her to explain what she meant, she relayed a story about a friend of hers from Italy who, despite her aversion to the United States, petitioned for citizenship so she could be close to her daughter, whose father was a U.S. citizen. She also had a Brazilian friend who divorced her U.S. husband, hated the United States, and never learned English, emphasizing the connection between divorce and the absence of affective ties to the country.[31]

In contrast, Karina sees herself as someone who has long admired U.S. culture, even when she was living in Brazil. As a model in Brazil who could speak good English, she worked at international trade shows pitching the benefits of various companies to a variety of businesspeople, including Americans, whose accents she adored. Karina's adoration for Americans predates her migration to the United States. In fact, Josh and Karina only petitioned for her citizenship status once Brazil changed its law to enable her binational citizenship.[32] Thus, love cannot be contained to the migrant story of assimilation. For example, as Pamela Haag argues, claims to love have historically symbolized immigrants' proof of assimilation or the idea that citizenship articulated a "growing allegiance of the heart."[33] At the turn of the twentieth century, immigrants' initiation into America often involved images of a "love match" between newcomer and state.[34] Nationalism, Haag continues, needed to be revamped from a duty compelled by laws to "patriotism" or the sentimental love of country.[35] In contrast to placing the burden of proof of attaining citizenship solely on the migrant, Karina's statement about love demands mutual responsibility in marriage and can be extended to the relation between individuals and the state. In addition, claims to love are meant to foreground citizenship as a mutual exchange between the migrant and nation, between the two cultures and individuals. Against the teleology of assimilation, I argue that claims to love resonate within a transnational terrain and must be explored more carefully.

Karina's expression of love signifies a mutual relationship of obligation between individuals, kin, and the state. It is expected that cross-national marriage will guarantee women's humane treatment through citizenship rights and obligations. Her expectation that the man she chose to marry should love her culture can be extended to the mutual obligation of the state in respecting the transnational orientation of migrant subjectivity. Placing people within an emotional social field that extends to Latin America shifts an understanding of love from a passive sentiment reflecting the desire for assimilation into U.S. culture to an active demand for empathy and humanity that counters an alienated view of people. Claims to love can be seen as reinforcing women's contributions to U.S. culture through a knowledge structure that privileges the affective and human dimensions of actions, remoralizing their attachment to patriotic inclusion.

Foregrounding love as proof of one's eligibility for citizenship suggests that women in Latin America are influenced by the intertwined obligations of kin relations and the state. As stated by L. A. Rebhun in relation to Brazilian definitions of love, "In addition to its nature as a personal sentiment, love in the sense of caring about and taking care of others constitutes a social duty. In some societies, all social relations refer in some way to kinship; in others, states take on obligations toward citizens."[36] Various women's statements characterizing the United States as a cold culture can be read as a critique of the universal foundation of the law as the basis for a system of governance. A popular saying in Mexico reinforces an alternative way of understanding the relationship between intimacy and the state: "For my friends, anything;

for my enemies, the law." We consider law in this country to be the founda-tion for a system of meritocracy, against the elitist model that privileges peo-ple with family or friend connections. In Mexico and many regions of Latin America, this universal approach to social relations, distance, and objectivity is at the root of self-gain, individualism, and violence, in contrast to kinship ties legitimated by intimacy and mutual obligations. As argued in chapter 2, many women lament that their government and system of law in Latin America is corrupt, inept, and violent and thus alienated from the needs of the majority of people. Affectionate ties in the United States, however, articu-late a moral contract that buttresses legal dictates. Women's desire for U.S. men cannot be severed from the hope for a system of governance they imag-ine as more caring and equitable than those they left behind. For this reason, various women such as Katrina support strong protection of the border as part of their moral support for the rule of law, despite the exclusionary status of immigration law dictating who can enter versus who must be kept out.

Karina's expression of love also shifts citizenship claims to the endur-ing but also contingent life of interior feelings, rather than static biologi-cal notions of blood ties, race, class, sexuality, or gender. In authenticating citizenship claims through love, Karina raises interesting questions about how individuals understand ties to cultural and political belonging as well as rights that transcend national boundaries, biological lines of affiliation, and rational law. In other words, Karina's focus on feelings inverts the direc-tion of exclusionary national and cultural notions of "foreignness" based on physiognomy, such as skin color, and privileges interior emotions. Just as love has the potential to embrace a wider range of subjects into the nation, focusing on one's interiority is also dangerous for its privileging of morality and choice in distinguishing those who truly desire to become an "Ameri-can" from those who do not.

Migrant Critique and the Absence of Love

Intimate expressions of belonging turn the focus to an emotional interiority that reallocates the moral and human from the collective to the individual, a shift that justifies the retraction of rights from migrant laborers who lack individual subjectivity due to their surplus association as "economic" ver-sus "affective" actors. Marita, one of the few participants from Guatemala on LWL, has been married to her U.S. husband for several years and now lives in Alaska. Although she was highly respected by others in this on-line commu-nity, one response from her on the list ignited a heated debate. Marita stated that U.S. men oftentimes do not value Latinas as equals or appreciate the fact that men have a "better deal" in foreign marriages, as they are able to remain in their country, while women must leave everything behind. In solidarity with another Latin American woman married to a U.S. man, she translated a section of this woman's e-mail from an all-women's e-mail exchange for men to read: "If you need us, then learn to value us as equals, not to think that we are mean because once you had a bad experience. Learn to value the sacrifice that we made in leaving our family, our country because we are looking for a good man and a great love."[37]

The following response to her e-mail provides a poignant example of how Marita's critique (and especially her use of economic language, that men have a better "bargain" than women) was met with an accusation that perhaps she is one of "those" migrants who complains about the United States and thus is undeserving of citizenship:

> While a Colombian woman married to a guy in the Midwest was here on her second visit to the U.S. she decided to try working at a Mexican restaurant as a hostess to save a little money for her family. . . . One of her biggest concerns was her Mexican coworkers who spoke terribly and in very derogatory and demeaning terms about the U.S. and its citizens. She told me of the things that these people used to do to the food being served to unsuspecting Americans as a way of getting even for their "plight." . . . Maybe it's time for the people of our country to ask for the fair deal that you want. It is evident that Mexico will never change and the ruling caste will continue to beat your own people down. If the citizens of Mexico want a fair deal, why don't they demand it in their own country instead of coming here and complaining, complaining, and complaining?[38]

The respondent adheres to the idea that some migrants are more appropriate marriage migrants and patriots. Alongside neoliberal values of proper citizenship, the Colombian woman in the story stands in for the exceptional "good" migrant against the disgruntled masses who, the author argues, mistake the "opportunities" available in this country for exploitation and should target their critique toward their own government rather than the U.S. people and the nation-state. He continues,

> I am sure that Felipe Calderon would listen so intently to these poor hungry masses. Mexico needs to get a spine and have the courage to create what they whine about wanting. Maybe it is just easier to march in our streets where they know they will not get killed or beaten for voicing an opinion contrary to Mexico's ruling class. If a Latin woman really wants

to have a good husband and a new life for their future children, she needs to re-evaluate her own priorities and her allegiances. She needs to realize that this is a new life, new country, and new future where she can excel and see herself, her children, and her family grow and prosper beyond their wildest dreams through education, hard work, honesty and perseverance. It makes no difference where she is from as long as she loves and supports her husband as he should love and support her.

Oddly it has already been successful with the Germans, Dutch, Africans, Danish, Koreans, Chinese, and many, many others who have come and fulfilled their dreams. However, if the Latin woman only wants the perks and benefits while remaining a staunch and loyal supporter of the old Latin regimes and caste systems which she ran away from . . . maybe she just needs to go back where she came from as that is too great to give up![39]

The response works to silence and ostracize Marita and any other female marriage migrant who shares her perspective. Consistent with hostile responses by male chat-room respondents that I highlight in chapter 3, this type of diatribe accuses women and immigrants who complain or are critical of the United States of antipatriotic sentiments. These chat rooms are not only "intimate publics" that rehearse the boundaries of citizenship but also forums for extending the surveillance of the state by disciplining responses into narrow scripts of what can be said versus what must remain unspeakable.[40] The most vocal members guard neoliberal values that define the individual and the nation as infinitely pliable and innocent, untainted by the past or structural inequalities. The idea of the nation, both in the past and in the present, as a benevolent force protects men's global attractiveness as U.S. citizens. The respondent equates criticism of the United States with the masses of poor migrants who should be sent home (deported) for threatening to "corrupt" the United States with what he calls the "old Latin regimes and caste systems." In this familiar narrative, the immigrant threatens to pollute the modern West with anachronistic forms of governance, proving that most migrants cannot be sovereign or self-determining citizens. In line with other chat responses that equate Latin American women with child-like dependents, such criticism targeting migrants invokes a latent critique of racial melancholia, or the inability of most immigrants to separate from their motherland, a refusal to let go of the past that enslaves them mentally and physically and disables the proper mature transition from the past to the future, from a Latin American caste system to American-style democracy, and from tradition to modernity.[41] In the face of great opportunities, so this thinking goes, immigrants trek disempowering ideologies with them to the United States, such as the belief that structural forces prevent them from the freedom to pliably remake themselves and their lives, an onslaught against the ideology of the American dream. Foreign cybermarriages, premised on one's ability to virtually travel unmarked, to partake in the "free" marketplace, necessitating hard work, a healthy dose of risk, and the ability to think outside the boundaries of the nation, fortify individuals' adherence to the doctrine of democracy and equality for all regardless of race, class, nationality, and citizenship status. Feelings of patriotic love, an entrepreneurial spirit, and virtual disembodiments are the networks for enforcing pliable citizenship in national and global economic terrains.

Americans may not be able to visibly differentiate immigrants working in restaurants from other exceptional figures (the same can be said for those who respond in chat discussions to others they cannot see). Positive affect such as determination and perseverance, then, distinguish between *individuals* who choose to make it here versus the *masses* of migrants who "complain" that unequal structures limit their success in obtaining the American dream. In fact, individuals, rather than broader transnational processes or even structures of racism, are blamed for migrants' failure to "make it" in the United States. The story of the exceptional romantic and middle-class immigrant contrasts with the "mass" underclass of undocumented migrants who embody negative affect such as criticism, anger, rudeness, and a lack of appreciation—further proof that they themselves "choose" not to obtain citizenship. Marita's potential critique of some U.S. men and her structural movement from gratitude to a position in which she makes claims and demands is silenced by the threat of her deportation, or her association with the masses of migrants who should stop complaining and return home.[42]

Transnational processes, such as U.S. empire or policies such as NAFTA, that place the United States in a complicit position with the displacement of migrants from their land and communities are rendered unthinkable through the binary position of the old regime in Mexico and the modern democracy in the United States, where all can become successful, "self-actualizing" citizens with the proper affective disposition (gratitude) and hard-work ethic. Love, as positive affect, is differentiated from the migrants working in restaurant kitchens who slip seamlessly into the masses of angry immigrants who, in 2006, protested the increase of penalties and inhumane raids and deportations of "undocumented" migrants.[43] The e-mail exchange quoted earlier emphasizes what is at stake when cultural rifts emerge in chat rooms and, by extension, in some marital relationships.

Positive expressions of love as the precondition for citizenship reinforce exceptional paradigms of inclusion (via heterosexual marriage) yet also communicate a demand for inclusion by those who feel marginalized from dominant national imaginaries. This complex positioning can only be interpreted if we expand the rich scholarly ideas on migration and trauma that document the psychoanalytic sentiments of loss in relation to national forms of belonging.[44] In other words, inclusion is possible for those groups that forget their past, institutionalizing loss as the precondition for belonging. David Eng and Shinhee Han's article "A Dialogue on Racial Melancholia" (2000) opens up space to interpret Asian migrants (an ethnic group assumed to successfully assimilate into U.S. culture as the "model minority") as collectively suffering similar sentiments of dislocation and loss as other migrants excluded from national memory. Yet the question is what do we do with Latina immigrants who claim love as the precondition for citizenship? Women's romantic attachment not only to their husbands but, by extension, to the nation can be interpreted only if we broaden the continuum of responses to forms of marginalization and exclusion. Is there space to envision love as a technology that transcends pain, exclusion, and inequality but also serves as a passport to transmit positive affect in the destination country that otherwise would render these migrants' mobility a threat and constitute them as foreign? While Karina's husband, a white man with Irish roots, does not have to defend his placement within the national order, her description of love as proof of patriotism may be another form of survival in which love, as positive affect, is compulsory when negative affect carries the weight of being unpatriotic. While heterosexual marriage and love are depicted as foundational to nationalism and citizenship, Karina and her husband continue to see themselves, like many others I interviewed, on the margins of normative social relations in the country they live in. In addition, affirmations of national belonging do not necessarily correspond with assimilation into hegemonic U.S. culture, as both of their lives reflect a worldview forged across national contexts. In migration studies, assimilation assumes a linear model of belonging that demands migrants sever themselves from their feminized and racialized "motherland."[45] In the case of cross-national marriages, most women are supported, however unevenly, in maintaining ties to Latin America. For instance, men and women travel back and forth between the United States and Latin America; family and friends from elsewhere permeate the nuclear U.S. family structure; women and men continually negotiate cultural norms between countries; and women (and their husbands) oftentimes continue to financially support family members in Latin America long after they have married and moved to the United States.[46]

In fact, many men help their wives send money home to pay for household expenses and unexpected job or health costs and to cover the cost of a university education for siblings. John, who we met earlier and know divorced his Colombian wife, recalls the look of appreciation on his wife's face, during an earlier moment in their marriage, when he asked her (several months after she had arrived in the United States) whether they would need to send her family money to compensate for her absence. After a spirited dialogue on remittances on-line, John realized how hard it must be for Monica's family now that he had taken away their primary contributor to the family income. Monica described a sense of relief when he brought this up, as she felt she could not ask him outright to send money home to her family, for fear that he would think she was taking advantage of him. In an e-mail exchange in which men debated whether remittances were their responsibility and, if so, how much to send, John couched this monetary gesture not simply as an "obligation" but as charity. He said,

> So maybe, just maybe, fate, or perhaps something more significant has given me an opportunity to help someone else. And me being an economics type guy I really like what I call "Bang for the buck," no sexual innuendos intended. . . . Where $50 a month can mean the difference between a family living in a very bad neighborhood and house or a pretty good one, as an example. The need plus the bargain prices can come together for a very satisfying way to help someone else. Of course a guy needs to be cautious about just being used.[47]

Seeing remittance contributions as charity, instead of an obligation that may place women in a position of making demands if the funding dries up, shifts the focus from the woman to the man. Charity implies giving without reciprocity from the actual receiver, causing an imbalance in the relationship. After John and Monica's divorce, John lamented that he had actually sent his Colombian wife's mother about $30,000 in total to help her launch her flower business, including the purchase of a truck, and money to cover the cost of upgrading Monica's family into a middle-class neighborhood, a gift that Monica could not reciprocate. That John frames remittance payments to Monica's family as charity connects his actions to the rise of philanthropy and the making of the moral self in relation to transnational development. Seeing remittance exchanges as a gift also solidifies kinship ties to Monica's family in Colombia, a gift that indebts the family to this marriage. Divorce entails a sour option for the entire family.

These gendered and sexualized imaginaries are heavily mediated by both colonial regimes of otherness and contemporary equations of value hidden within the intimate structures of labor in the global economy. Women's intimate labor is highly valued and potentially a lucrative site for rebuilding one's life. Yet it is also cause for emotional and physical pain and suffering, as their behavior must fall within normative structures of affect to be rendered legitimate. In chat-room debates, John (like other men who described a variety of lacking qualities in women as "deal breakers") threatened to send Monica back to Colombia if she did not comply with his demands for more sex. Ultimately he did not force her to return, since he felt responsible, and partially to blame, for bringing her and her son to the United States. Regardless of his personal sense of obligation, John is legally responsible for the economic welfare of his wife for ten years, even in the case of divorce. He explained how he lost his house and was forced to retire in Latin America on a pension plan that would be difficult to live on in the Silicon Valley. For Monica, she carries the burden of silently juggling multiple obligations in the United States, going to school, working, and caring for her son (from her previous Colombian marriage) in the United States, as well as supporting her family back home.

Virtual Intimacies

Monica complained that John spent his entire day on the computer participating in chat rooms and surfing pornography websites. Conversely, John lamented on the chat board, and to me, that Monica spent her whole day watching one *telenovela* after another, making it evident that both found more joy in the possibilities of virtual love and intimacy than in its actuality. John later realized that his feelings of "love" for Monica were based more on fantasy than reality. This mediated imaginary was one that John realized caused him to make a hasty marital decision. Back in Colombia, John thought Monica acquired what he called a "boob job" to please him (he realized later she was merely wearing a push-up bra). This thrilled him, as it provided "proof" that she intended to do what it took to make him happy. After only a handful of dates in Colombia with Monica, John proposed. On the eve of their honeymoon, after taking Monica and her son to Disneyland, John was angered by the fact that Monica lacked sexual interest in him. The second night after their wedding, John relayed (in an e-mail interview with me) that he must have found the most conservative woman in bed. His new wife did not want any foreplay, and when he tried to direct her hand down *there*, she recoiled as if a snake bit her. "So much for assumptions and hot Columbiana stories. I was way off reality in my mind," he wrote.[48]

As Monica described to me, her own fantasies of marriage with John were also thwarted. She said, "My dream, and that of my son, turned into a nightmare." Her husband was easily angered and much different from the gentle and sweet man she met in Colombia. Monica described her husband as having no understanding of the process of intimacy that develops through time and with trust. How could she have sex and feel intimate with someone she hardly knew? Years later, while speaking with a marriage counselor, Monica defended herself against John's claims that she never truly loved him by stating that her proof of love was evident in the great sacrifice she made to leave her home, family, and life behind for the possibility of a life with this man. Her emphasis on sacrifice shifts her actions from the level of the individual to a collective feminized script of pious suffering without end. Again, the difficulty of articulating loss in relation to U.S. immigration and marriage renders unthinkable the cost of leaving one's home behind. Some women feel they sacrifice more than men in moving to the United States, while men feel they shoulder both social estrangement and a tremendous economic burden despite remaining in place. After over two years of marriage, John reflected that the times he felt something akin to love from Monica were the times when he felt a deep and true appreciation from her for his help in adopting her son in order to facilitate his migration to the United States and for sending money home to her family. These were times when their relationship was the most intimate. This form of intimacy (and her agreement to sex) situates love within structures of reciprocity, or as gratitude and repayment of debt, which defies the idea of "pure love" as divorced from economic relations.[49] Instead, Monica proclaims love through sacrifice, of leaving everything she knows in Colombia for the hope of a better life. While not explicit, the narrative of sacrifice also serves as a "hidden script"[50] for articulating the limited choices many single mothers have in supporting themselves, their children, and family members who depend on their income.[51] The stereotypical image of Latinas as more traditional and family oriented, yet also more passionate and sexual, turns patriotic through gendered claims to sacrifice. Monica's description of love through her desire to give up something for the greater good of others reorients her actions as moral across a transnational sphere. Ultimately John and Monica both saw the structures of reciprocity as not able to sustain the differing understanding of a mutually satisfying relationship.

The consequences of men's imaginaries are best reflected in an e-mail interview I had with Manuela, a Mexicana who participated in the Latinaesposa e-mail exchange for married women who moved to the United States to live with their husbands. She has been married to her Anglo husband for more than three years. She described to me one of the many contradictions discussed by women:

> While men want a Latina because she is supposedly more passionate, when we have this passion, they don't know how to respond. Men prefer Internet pornography than to make love with us. They'd rather watch perfect women than normal and real women. All of us agree that we can't compete with these unreal bodies, that don't fight, that don't get angry, who don't veer from the norm. . . . It's easier for los gringos to masturbate in front of the computer, where they don't have to put forth any effort to satisfy anyone. Like many things here [in the United States], [they are] the most convenient, . . . the most individualistic, and self-absorbed.[52]

Manuela's theorizing of Western individualism, masculinity, and whiteness in relation to technological power ends up deflating Western fantasies as some men become lost in the maze of their own simulations. The role of the Internet in facilitating visual and interactive fantasies and even marriage speaks to yet another way U.S. individualism and the capitalistic gaze become a potentially powerful means for men to experience themselves as a decentered subject rather than the center.

Certainly it is not true that all men are junkies for Internet porn (nor are all women against it, as long as, one said on-line, she is included in the fun), but the reemergence of various renditions of this statement by women to me and in chat discussions serves as a trope for a broader critique of U.S. culture. This act of betrayal opens up a space for women to express the disjuncture between Latin American and U.S. culture through the lens of hot and cold, passion and rationality, sexuality versus prostitution. As stated by one woman, "You go to Latin America, running away from American women because they are cold, but after a Latin Woman gives you all her love and passion then you treat her as a prostitute."[53] This woman places men in an equivalent position with U.S. "feminist" women for objectifying women's sensuality as an object of trade or use rather than privileging an orientation to others through a complex prism of needs and desires. Women are often accused of scamming U.S. men or using them to come to the United States for a better life. The irony, however, as women point out, is that men place them on a high pedestal in Latin America for their warmth and sensuality, despite the reality that men are more attracted to an ideal that eludes them in the flesh. Some men's erotic fantasies are locked in a virtual maze of perfection, where access is mediated by visual representations and frames that solidify women into a feminized ideal. Bodies that deviate from femininity prove a woman's lack of authenticity, her lack of genuineness, or a failed contract. Men's intimacy with Latin America and women's expectations of men in relation to the United States are visually mediated through signs of difference that tell us more about intimacies of empire and globalization than the messy realities of everyday life tell us.

In contrast to the seduction of virtual fantasies, another genre of e-mail responses from men detailed their sense of wonder and disorientation that accompanies seeing the world from women's perspectives. One of the previous moderators of Planet-Love, Justin, described the pleasure of foreign marriage through his wife's newly arrived perspective, which suspended his command of interpretation and provided a sense of wonder at how differently he could interpret the world when he did so through another worldview. His sense of pleasure resembles the feeling of eros that entails the suspension of knowledge, of opening oneself to deterritorialized pleasures of the body, otherness, and the self that extend prefigured expectations. The erotic warps a sense of time and space and has been described as opening up a momentary sense of union with the universe or the divine. The self melts away, and time protracts, expands, and fills the space with wonder. This experience of vertigo, a sense of temporal and spatial displacement, reflects how Justin describes for other men on-line the possibilities of being decentered, in contrast to Internet porn, where men's pleasure is confined to a sense of mastery over the situation, while the repetition of the sexual act and narrative guarantees the same pleasurable outcome.

Conclusion

A film, *Love for Rent* (2005), reinforces the need to extend citizenship status to exceptional female migrants whose reproductive capabilities, love, and determination provide surplus intimate labor for the nation. The film details the plight of two Colombian women who migrate to the United States through their marriage with two Anglo-American citizens. A Colombian woman marries a man she calls a "harmless gringo" in order to pursue her fledgling entertainment career and talks her cousin into doing the same. The cousin, Sophia, the main protagonist, claims from the very beginning that she is not interested in marriage but rather in obtaining her law degree. After being robbed of everything she owns by her U.S. husband, who ultimately divorces her for another foreign bride, she encounters a proposition too good to pass up. A British-American couple offer her $50,000 to be the surrogate mother for the American wife, who is unable to bear children. Both cousins wonder why the couple chose Sophia, besides her "super Latina reproductive capacities," and find at the end of the film that she was also chosen for her moral character and her desperate situation. In the film, Sophia defies and reassembles stereotypes as she embodies the hyperpassionate Latina who has sex with a doctor on the first date (while pregnant with the British-American couple's child); the passionate law student who wants to empower those who are disenfranchised; and then, in typical Hollywood style, the wife of a doctor living in a middle- to upper-class home. In other words, she realizes the "American dream," but with a slight twist: they adopt a child who has been neglected by foster families and the state social services.

Thus, in the film, it is the U.S. nation, the state, and broken-down families that become healed and rejuvenated through this Colombian's reproductive, domestic, sexualized, and passionate desire for social justice. It is the erotic passion of Latinas that provides the moral fabric at the foundation of a nation incapable of the moral reproduction and values at the heart of claims to citizenship. Yet the British-American couple recuperate a moral position in the film when the wife shows Sophia her appreciation for bearing her child by offering her a paralegal position in her brother's law firm so she can avoid deportation, get her citizenship papers, and remain close to the baby she bore for the couple. Neither of the protagonists become fully human until they commit acts of care or love that shatter normative boundaries around the legal, natural, moral, and foreign. In fact, Sophia becomes human when her worth transfers from that of labor and exchange value, as an alienated productive body for the good of the nation, to an exceptional individual deserving of citizenship. Her moral status exceeds legal dictates of inclusion/exclusion and sameness/difference. Women's bodies signify the traditional role of morality framed within the heterosexual family but also gesture to a broader spiritual presence that generates a critique of capitalism, productivity, mass wealth, corporate greed, and imperial anxiety.[54] The affective pull of unlikely affinities in the film destabilizes national boundaries but also reproduces the violence of exception and individualism at the center of Western categories of the human. These plots only work through the exceptional cross-cultural romance in which love motivates characters toward a host of spiritual acts and transformations that position them morally above the state or as exceptional civil and state actors.

This seemingly benign arena of everyday cross-national intimacies provides an opportunity to query how difficult it is to escape our complicity in reinforcing national boundaries and exclusionary notions of the legal and the citizen. My goal in tracing the malleable lines of sameness and difference arises out of the need to chart more carefully intimate alliances but also the breaks. *Love for Rent* and other media accounts of abusive "mail-order bride" marriages clearly demonstrate that some men take advantage of the control they wield over women through various levels of abuse. What I found to be more widespread than physical abuse, however, were the more intangible forms of violence that migrant wives might confront. Especially significant are the compulsions of belonging and citizenship that bind women to enactments of emotional care and unselfishness. Throughout the book, I have traced the compulsions of love and passion for women's access to national visibility, global capitalist labor, and moral routes to migration and citizenship. In this chapter, I have followed the consequences of women's disruption of the caring, passionate, sexual patriot as it relegates her as ungrateful, too traditional, or locked in the past.

I center intimate claims to love alongside access to citizenship to make irrelevant hard boundaries delineating the political. Our sense of the political is stymied and opened up through the confluence of U.S. and Latin American understandings of love that traverse the individual and the collective, the secular and the spiritual. While I have outlined the dangers of love as another exclusionary and exceptional paradigm for making citizenship claims, I have also tried to open the possibility for other meanings to permeate. Claims to love enable one to transcend social norms, to access the universal, but also to transcend secular spaces of calculation, scrutiny, and technologies of governance. Women's diverse forms of loving are embedded within and expand individual paradigms of sociality. Bringing back love as a social obligation refuses Western paradigms of "enslavement" and takes us back to more humane expressions of closeness that bind us to each other, rendering unthinkable an individual outside the terrain of the social. I am not advocating a return to marriage or heterosexual kin ties, especially at a moment when inclusion and citizenship demands conformity to heterosexual norms evident in debates over gay marriage, thus limiting sexual-intimate forms of living. I am hopeful that unlikely affinities may arise out of a range of "outlaw" social formations requiring an ever-expanding engagement with otherness beyond sentiments captured by national boundaries and structures of citizenship. At the same time, I hope to have provided a glimpse into how gendered and sexual inequalities pervade these relations due to women's precarious standing as migrant wives dependent on patriotic expressions of love, and ultimately their husbands and the state, for citizenship. I end the book highlighting the everyday challenges and pleasures of navigating eroticized forms of belonging on-line. It has been my goal to hold open the possibility for deep intimate and sexual lives, while rendering visible the structural challenges that may contribute to deep misunderstandings of these marriages, especially the deeper investments in sentiments and marriage structures made compulsory by law.

NOTES TO THE INTRODUCTION

1. Countries such as China and the Philippines have had a longer history of intimate exchanges, made popular with U.S. men in the military who kept in touch with women they met through writing letters. This form of communication was later brokered through pen-pal agencies that advertised friendship, romance, and marriage with Asian women through letter correspondence.

2. The United States–Colombia Trade Promotion Agreement was signed in 2006, although the governments of Colombia and the United States have long negotiated substantial trade relations. In fact, the recent trilateral trade agreement signed by President Obama on October 21, 2011, with Colombia, South Korea, and Panama will continue to devastate lower-level economies in these countries, especially for farmers (which make up about 20% of Colombia's workforce), while increasing social unrest, migration, and even the need to produce lucrative drugs such as cocaine.

3. I am thinking here of the passage of Operation Gatekeeper in 1994 at the San Diego–Otay border region.

4. For some of this groundbreaking work, see Fernandez-Kelly 1983; Hondagneu-Sotelo 1994, 2001; Chang 2000; Parreñas 2001; Choy 2003; Ehrenreich and Hochschild 2002a; Hirsch 2003; and Wright 2006.

5. The prices for men to attend vary, but most U.S agencies charge from $1,000 to $1,500 for this three-day event (not including hotel, airfare, and other travel costs), whereas the women are invited free of charge. When I began this project, there were no other ethnographic accounts of the cybermarriage industry. Recent ethnographic studies have provided a more nuanced critique of studies that equate "mail-order" brides and foreign marriage with the exploitation of poor women in Asia and Russia. See Constable 2003; Johnson 2007; and Thai 2008.

6. Of the fifty-four men, twelve were Latino, two were African American, and the rest were Anglo-American.

7. I use pseudonyms for all participants in the book.

8. There has been a great deal of scholarship in the United States and Latin America on romance. For some of the more influential work on the

subject, see Radway 1984; Modleski 1982; Franco 1989; Sommer 1991; Allen 1995; Illouz 1997; and Berlant 2008.

9. For a more in-depth discussion of the intersection of neoliberal market rational and exceptional modes of citizenship see Ong 2006.

10. See Povinelli 2006.

11. Ibid., 9.

12. See Ong 1999 and Grewal 2005.

13. Schmidt Camacho 2005; Fregoso 2006; Wright 2006; Inda 2002; Falcón 2007; Fregoso and Bejarano 2010.

14. Not only do the majority of web companies offering services to Latin America advertise Colombian brides, but chat-room discussions confirm that the majority of men travel to Colombia to meet Colombian wives. Mexico, because of its proximity to the United States, sends some men looking for women less tainted by Western culture to farther Latin American destinations such as Brazil, Costa Rica, and Peru.

15. I changed the names of each of the cybermarriage agencies I address in the book.

16. Parreñas 2011.

17. Kolodny 1984; Glenn 1986; Yuh 2002; Bouvier 2004; Enss 2005.

18. Said 1994; McClintock 1995; Young 1995.

19. Chávez-García 2004.

20. Paz 1961; Limón 1998; Pérez 1999.

21. Limón 1998; González 1999.

22. On websites and in chat-rooms discussions, Russian women are often described as American women with an exotic flair, Asian women as petite and service oriented, and Latin American women as passionate and family oriented.

23. For a critique of the turn to flexible identities heralded in cyber studies, see Schaeffer-Grabiel 2006a, 891–914.

24. The strategic turn to the Internet by the Zapatista indigenous movement (the EZLN) in Chiapas, Mexico, is an effective and powerful example of the subversive uses of the Internet. This technology enabled them to turn their local struggle into an international movement that helped to put some pressure on the Mexican government against further displacement of and violence against indigenous peoples and to spread support against trade policies such as NAFTA. I would like to thank Russell Rodriguez for reminding me of this example in relation to the many revolutionary uses of the Internet in Mexico.

25. This fantasy of global connection and transcendence is only available for the middle and upper classes, who have access to computers, although the spread of Internet cafes reaches more of the population.

26. Massumi 2002.

27. Moore 1994, 66. Sherry Turkle also describes the Internet as a space where we can project ourselves into our own dramas as the producer, director, and star. See Turkle 1995, 26.

28. Nakamura 2002, 3–5.

29. Colonialism and U.S. imperialism around the world make this a common sentiment for those who remain at home in occupied territories. See Rafael 2000, 2005; and Tadiar 2004.

30. See Coontz 1992, for her critique of the nostalgic turn to the ideal family during the 1950s.

31. See Zelizer 2005 for a sociological analysis of the economic aspects of intimacy. Also see Villipando 1989 and Glodava and Onizuka 1994 for a discussion of mail-order brides that associates marketplace values of exchange with women's exploitation. Wendy Chapkis (1997) counters early Marxist feminist critiques by engaging in an ethnography of women who work in various sex industries. Against the theorization of women's exploitative relation to the marketplace of sex and intimacy, she opens up space to consider the performance of erotic labor and pleasure. Also see Kamala Kempadoo and Joe Doezema's anthology *Global Sex Workers* (1998), which argues for the need to interpret women's association with the erotic as a form of labor. Constituting sex as labor politically shifts the tendency of feminists to morally condemn sex industries. Rather than attempt to pull women away from sex work, they hope to ameliorate exploitative conditions for women in the sex industries.

32. Donna Hughes has been one of the most vocal feminist scholars advocating for policies to shut down sex tourism, sex trafficking, and mail-order bride agencies. Hughes is the education and research coordinator of the nongovernmental organization the Coalition Against Trafficking in Women and holds an endowed chair position in women's studies at the University of Rhode Island. She worked closely with the Coalition Against Trafficking in Women to push for the International Marriage Broker Regulation Act (IMBRA), which passed in 2005 as part of the Violence Against Women Act (VAWA).

33. Given the increase in attention to sex trafficking in Latin America, foreign marriage industries now symbolize growing fears that foreign commerce and trade may generate new economic activity at the cost of the continued theft of natural resources, including women.

34. Constable 2005; Johnson 2007; Simons 2001.

35. In fact, since the early 1960s, mostly middle-class feminists associated the family with patriarchy, gender oppression, and the exploitation or devaluation of women's labor. The widespread feminist critique of marriage gained force with Betty Friedan's book *The Feminine Mystique* (1963). Friedan brought to visibility the unacknowledged depression

that many middle-class white women were feeling, despite "having it all" (marriage, economic stability, etc.), which was expressed as the utter boredom and drudgery of their domestic roles in patriarchal marriage. Maria C. Lugones and Elizabeth V. Spelman and other women-of-color feminists countered the association of the family with women's exploitation and deprivation. They argued that while to a Western, middle-class, and white feminist, divorce and/or economic independence may be preferable, for an unwed Hispanic mother in the United States, marriage with a man who serves as the economic provider may offer relief from wage labor and may even constitute "liberation." See Lugones and Spelman 1983. Furthermore, Chicano sociologists in the 1970s argued that for Chicanos, the family constituted a bulwark against assimilation and colonial exploitation. This was later tempered by Chicana activists and scholars who argued that women's role in the home defined their domestic contributions to the Chicano political movement of the late 1960s and '70s. For a discussion of marriage's conncection to prostitution, see Barry 1979, 1995; and MacKinnon 1987.

36. Some of this vast scholarship includes Enloe 1989; Alexander and Mohanty 1997; Hennessy 2000; Tadiar 2004; Brennan 2004; Alexander 2005; and Cabezas 2009.

37. Beck and Beck-Gernsheim 1995; Illouz 1997, 2007; Giddens 1992; Hochschild 1994, 1997.

38. Kelsky 2001.

39. Giddens 1992.

40. Bourdieu 1984; García Canclini 2001; and O'Dougherty 2002.

41. A burgeoning field of study takes on new ways of understanding the global through everyday intimate engagements. See Altman 2001; Manalansan 2003; Parker 1991; Wilson 2004; Hirsch and Wardlow 2006; and Padilla et al. 2007.

42. Coontz 2005. Recent ethnographies analyze the links between cultural expressions of love, sentiment, and marriage alongside the political economy and local changes. See Collier 1997; Rebhun 1999; Constable 2003; Hirsch 2003; and Padilla et al. 2007.

43. Padilla et al. 2007, xvii.

44. Illouz 1997; Ahearn 2001; Freeman 2007.

45. Doris Sommer and Benedict Anderson both interpret nationalism through cultures of feelings that accompanied the rise of the printing press and literacy, especially patriotic sentiments of love. Anderson 1983; Sommer 1991.

46. Rather than see intimacy as "an interactional description," Giddens understands it as the training ground for rights, obligations, and responsibilities "that define agendas of practical activity." Giddens 1992, 190.

47. Sandoval 2000.
48. Lauren Berlant follows the privatization of citizenship through a host of intimate injuries of exclusion from the nation in *The Queen of America Goes to Washington City* (1997).
49. Berlant and Warner 1998, 5.
50. Appadurai 1996.
51. Tadiar 2004.
52. Some of this vast scholarship includes Hondagneu-Sotelo 1994, 2001; Chang 2000; Parreñas 2001; Choy 2003; Ehrenreich and Hochschild 2002a; Hirsch 2003; Brennan 2004; and Agustín 2007.
53. There has been a recent surge in scholarship on the consequences of migration on the families left behind, including the children. While not an exhaustive list, some of this scholarship includes Parreñas 2001, 2005; Hondagneu-Sotelo and Avila 2007; and Dreby 2010. There is also a documentary called *Which Way Home* (2009) that follows the consequences of migration on young children who travel, unaccompanied, by foot and train from Central America to the United States. Of course, it is not simply families who suffer, or women who do care work. The stories of transgendered migrants from the Philippines who care for the sick and elderly in Israel is poignantly addressed in another documentary, *Paper Dolls / Bubot Nayer* (2006).
54. Parreñas coins this term in the documentary *Chain of Love* (2001).
55. Hochschild 2002, 26.
56. Ibid.
57. See Constable 2005; Suzuki 2000; Faier 2009; and Yang and Lu 2010.
58. Alexander 1994.
59. Kempadoo 2004; Frank 2002.
60. Parker 1991; E. Bernstein 2007b; Shimizu 2007; Agustín 2007; Cabezas 2009.
61. Foucault (1978) 1990.
62. Kempadoo 2004; Alexander 1997; Brennan 2004; and Cantú, Naples, and Ortiz 2009. State surveillance and immigration policies also demand conformity to heterosexuality when people cross borders and bypass state inspection. Luibhéid 2002, 2005b; Luibhéid and Cantú 2005; Coutin 2003. And still other scholars demonstrate the continuing salience of national borders for migrants whose journeys afford them new intimate expressions and sexual identities: Espín 1999; Zavella 2003; González-López 2005; and Cantú, Naples, and Ortiz 2009.
63. The feminist contributions to ethnographic understandings of experience are immense. The political project of documenting women's voices was critical to the resurgence of Western feminist activism in the 1960s and 1970s. The insights of the women's movement during that time came from women's organizing and discussions within

consciousness-raising groups. To document those voices that were most oppressed was a radical move because it destabilized Eurocentric and elite paradigms by locating authority and "truth" in the perspectives of those who were marginalized from history, politics, and scholarship. In the 1980s and 1990s, anthropology took a narrative turn that began to question the fictive contours of ethnographic work. Some of the formative work in the area included the writings of women of color who spoke from their marginalized positions, as well as scholarship more centrally located within anthropology, such as Clifford and Marcus 1986; Spivak 1988; Behar and Gordon 1995; Visweswaran 1994; and Heilbrun 1998, in which the author explores the intersection of gender and genre, or the ways that typical or expected narratives may constrain what women can say (and what listeners or readers can grasp) about their experiences. I have also been influenced by Patricia Zavella's ethnographic critiques in "*Talkin' Sex*" (2003), in which she gestures to poetics as a useful paradigm to understand the broader gendered constraints that limit how Chicanas talk about sex. Also Zavella's article "Feminist Insider Dilemmas" (1993) was helpful in addressing how her Chicana identity was complicated by factors such as age and national origin that challenge and shape our interactions with others in the field.

64. Mohanty 1991, 2003.
65. Zavella 1997, 2003.
66. Kamala Visweswaran, drawing from Adrienne Rich, also views women's silence (or misinformation) as a critical aspect of feminist ethnographic inquiry into the power relations and cultural norms that shape speech acts. Visweswaran 1994, 30–31.
67. In Mexico, respectable femininity is contrasted with *la puta* (the prostitute), who, because of her excessive sexuality is blamed for an array of brutal violence enacted against her body. See Fregoso 2003, 2006; Schmidt Camacho 2005; Wright 2006. In addition, Jasbir Puar (2007) draws from the work of Giorgio Agamben to discuss the boundaries between queers destined for death and those whose exceptional sexual status guarantees them life.

NOTES TO CHAPTER 1

1. Although I did not attend this party, two women separately shared this same moment with me during interviews about their recent marriage with U.S. men.
2. In *All about Love* (2000), bell hooks seeks to understand the absence of love in the United States through an excavation of people's family backgrounds. She also draws from self-help books that, unfortunately, leave out a discussion of the transnational political economy, such as slavery and capitalism, that contribute to cultural expressions of love.

3. Men's expectations for more authentic love and family traditions are reproduced in feminized labor patterns set up since the colonial period, such that mostly women from the Global South migrate to the West as domestics, nannies, caretakers, and nurses. See Choy 2003.

4. There have been many scholarly debates as to whether romantic love belongs to the lower or the upper classes. In a Marxist model, love represents an opposition to capitalism and thus belongs to the proletariat, which is opposed to capitalist relations of exchange. Edward Shorter, in *The Making of the Modern Family* (1975), for example, locates love-based marriage among the working class, especially as women's extradomestic wage labor freed them from arranged marriages. Others, such as Lawrence Stone, in *The Family, Sex and Marriage in England, 1500–1800* (1977), see love as more naturally flourishing among the upper classes of northern European descent, revealing the bias of positing the lower classes as possessing a less-refined character. Any sentiment of the lower classes must be for lust or, conversely, for material gain. Also see Rebhun 1999, 95.

5. Men's distance from home at the Vacation Romance Tours and their anonymity in chat-room discussions (where belonging and intimacy depend on prolific self-disclosure) facilitated their openness in interviews, while women's stories were told with much more caution. For more on the problematics of subaltern speech, see Spivak 1988, 296.

6. Zavella 1997, 2003.

7. Zavella 2003, 229. Zavella's use of "poetics" is a practice of deconstructing the boundaries of meaning between the said and the unsaid, or of highlighting the discursive limits of speech acts. The poetic nature of analysis has been attributed to the New Historians, such as Stephen Greenblatt, who purposefully refuted the boundaries between the literary and the nonliterary. For more on the "poetics" of cultural and historical analysis, see Greenblatt 1989.

8. Illouz 1997.

9. The Center for Immigration Studies is a think tank created in 1985 that advocates for less migration since, as they say, "many of our researchers conclude that current, high levels of immigration are making it harder to achieve such important national objectives as better public schools, a cleaner environment, homeland security, and a living wage for every native-born and immigrant worker." They continue, "In fact, many of us at the Center are animated by a 'low-immigration, pro-immigrant' vision of an America that admits fewer immigrants but affords a warmer welcome for those who are admitted." See CIS, "About the Center for Immigration Studies," http://www.cis.org/About (accessed December 18, 2010).

10. Seminara 2008.

11. The year 1953 was also the year the Congress, after the Supreme Court decision in *Lutwak v. United States* case (in which three veterans were caught using the War Brides Act to bring over "fraudulent spouses"), passed the law that marriages entered solely for immigration would be criminalized.

12. There have also been controversies raging in the Indian diaspora community over "sham marriages." A woman from India was placed in jail for confessing that she did not love her husband. See "Wife Jailed for Sham Marriage" 2004. There is also a website dedicated to marriage fraud: www.Fraudmarriage.comRelatedNews.htm.

13. While ICE does not keep track of the numbers of marriages deemed fraudulent, Nina Bernstein published an article in the *New York Times*, "Do You Take This Immigrant?" (2010a), and determined that, nationwide, U.S. Citizenship and Immigration Services (USCIS) rejected only about 8 percent of the 241,154 marriage petitions filed by citizens for their immigrant spouses in 2009.

14. Pew Research Center 2010.

15. Alexander 1994; Luibhéid 2002; Luibhéid and Cantú 2005.

16. In the introduction to *Entry Denied*, Eithne Luibhéid mentions, but does not discuss in much detail, "the gold-digging hussy intent on snaring an American husband" as one of the peripheral sexual figures under scrutiny by the immigration apparatus (2002, xv).

17. Kerber 1998, 11–12.

18. Cott 2000.

19. Kerber 1998, xxiii.

20. Pascoe 2009, 2.

21. In the book *Why Marriage?* (2004), George Chauncey provides a detailed historical account of when and why homosexuality is constructed as a threat but also why, at this particular historical moment, gays are fighting for their right to marry. He structures the book on five key structural reasons behind the push for gay marriage: (1) There is currently more equality between the sexes. (2) More rights are conferred to married couples. (3) AIDS hit during the 1980s causing even more social disarray for gays and lesbians who lost their job when they became sick and had little family support to turn to. Without the structure of family and marriage, or the workplace to provide insurance, many lacked the funds to go to the hospital. For those who did, their partners were constituted strangers by law and thus were stripped of their visitation rights. (4) More lesbians had children without a man in the 1980s. (5) The church had less say over the morality of heterosexual marriage. Chauncey's book is a necessary companion to queer debates that understandably interrogate the desire for inclusion into marriage,

for fear this normalizing move will further stigmatize queer intimacy and sex outside the confines of marriage and the private sphere.

22. Guy 1991; Nathan 1999; Fregoso 2003.

23. Luibhéid 2002.

24. The INS is now the Bureau of Citizenship and Immigration Services (BCIS), one agency under the Department of Homeland Security (DHS) that is greatly devoted to security and surveillance.

25. Stern 2005.

26. Luibhéid 2002, 6.

27. Cott 2000, 135–136; Haag 1999.

28. Cott 2000, 151. Japanese "proxy marriages" were performed in the home country by someone who substituted (as a proxy) for the groom so that when the woman arrived in the United States, she arrived as a married woman. Most "picture brides" landed in Hawaii, where immigration inspectors—infused with the idea of marriage as a bargain based on consent—investigated the character of the alleged husband before permitting the bride to land. If the proxy bride was allowed to disembark, she had to remarry her "alleged husband" right away in an American ceremony at the port. Ibid., 152. The 1924 Immigration Law excluded all Asians who practiced proxy marriages, due to rising anger against Japanese migrants who arrived not only as wives but as horticultural laborers for their husbands who displaced white farmers.

29. Cott 2000, 148. Cott finds that because of a 1917 provision, seventeen thousand European "war brides" of World War I American soldiers were scrutinized for "immorality" before acquiring citizenship by marriage.

30. Haag 1999, 94–118.

31. Kerber 1998, 41–42; Johnson and Burrows 2003, 550.

32. Moran 2001.

33. The Treaty of Guadalupe Hidalgo during the U.S.-Mexico War of 1846–48 ushered in the time when the United States agreed to allow Mexicans living in the newly occupied territory to have naturalization rights. See Almaguer 1994.

34. While this interracial mixture was not barred, California Civil Code Section 60 stated, "all marriages of white persons with Negros, Mongolians, members of the Malay race, or mulattoes are illegal and void." Yet, in the 1948 case *Perez v. Sharp*, a Mexican American woman attempted to marry an African American man in California and was denied a marriage license. See Johnson and Burrows 2003, 532. They fought California's antimiscegenation laws as unconstitutional in 1959, when the California Civil Code eliminated racial restrictions on marriage. This pathbreaking case led the way to the well-known legal precedent against

interracial marriage, *Loving v. Virginia*, in 1967. See also Pascoe, "Lionizing Loving," in *What Comes Naturally* (2009), 287–306.

35. The IMFA was a section of the IRCA (Immigration Reform and Control Act), a reform aimed at cracking down on illegal immigration. The impetus for this legislation was not only to curb fraudulent immigration through marriage but also to protect the men who were conceived of as victims of the crime. Karen L. Rae says, "The Subcommittee's concern focused not only on the sheer number of perpetrators of marriage fraud, but also on the victims of the crime. In particular, the hearings highlighted the plight of innocent American citizen spouses who are duped into what is termed 'one-sided marriage fraud.'" Rae 1988, 183. This legislation set in motion a series of studies and accounts that documented the abuse of foreign women, such as M. Anderson 1993.

36. The Cable Act of 1907 mandated that no longer would a U.S. man's foreign-born wife be allowed citizenship simply through marriage. Rather than wait five years to obtain citizenship, women could obtain citizenship after a one-year conditional status. See Cott 1998, 1465. In 1952, the Immigration and Naturalization Act allowed "aliens" who married a U.S. citizen the ability to adjust their status and become a legal permanent resident using a K-1 visa without having to leave their country.

37. This shift in the law (alongside new Internet technologies) transformed the international matchmaking industry from a magazine format to one that incorporated tourism through Romance Tours as well as e-mail and letter contact.

38. Constable 2003, 185.

39. INS 2001. In the 2009 *Yearbook of Immigration Statistics*, these numbers were only slightly lower: 93 percent of Mexico's total migration and 74 percent of Colombia's. See the Homeland Security web page at http://www.dhs.gov/files/statistics/publications/yearbook.shtm (accessed December 6, 2010).

40. Reddy 2005.

41. Sponsors must show bank statements, proof of home ownership, and any other assets. See Fragomen 1997.

42. Reddy 2005, 110.

43. Luibhéid 2005a, 81.

44. Smith 2001, 315.

45. Bell and Binnie 2000, 60.

46. U.S. Senate 1986, report J-99-43, 17.

47. Without statistics, an INS deputy assistant commissioner for investigations was quoted as saying he thought overall marriage fraud to be at approximately 30 percent of all foreign marriage petitions. See Zaldivar 1985.

48. U.S. Senate 1986, report J-99-43, 16.

49. According to Chandan Reddy, the Immigration Act of 1990 capped the number of immigrant visas for so-called unskilled workers to 10,000, while it increased family-based immigrant visas to 480,000 annually, beginning in 1995 (one year, I might add, before DOMA was passed). This shift to family migration enables the federal government, Reddy argues, to appear as if it is a benevolent force in reuniting broken families, while meeting capital's need for immigrant workers. Reddy 2005, 109.

50. Similarly, there was speculation that these could also be persons who would ordinarily not be allowed entrance into the United States on the basis of their status as illiterate, as mentally retarded, and as potential prostitutes. See U.S. Senate 1986, report J-99-43, 7.

51. Povinelli 2006, 176–177.

52. Ibid., 184–185. Of course slavery, the genocide of Native Americans, and the colonization of people by the United States also provided the backdrop for colonial imaginaries of self-governance, freedom, and democracy.

53. Ibid., 185.

54. For a more in-depth discussion of the complex terrain of power relations in cross-border marriages in Asia, see Constable 2005.

55. Interview, February 8, 2005.

56. For a discussion of the legal ramifications of race in citizenship claims, see Haney López 1996.

57. Anagnost 2000, 392. Renato Rosaldo, in "Cultural Citizenship and Educational Democracy" (1994), similarly describes "cultural citizenship" for those who have full citizenship as being expressed through "notion[s] of dignity, thriving, and well-being" (402).

58. As described in later chapters, some women from Mexico prefer U.S. Latinos, while some women from Cali, Colombia, prefer black men.

59. Chavez 2001; Santa Ana 2002.

60. Falcón 2007; N. Bernstein 2008.

61. Interview, February 8, 2005.

62. Journalism is especially dangerous in Colombia, as many journalists have been kidnapped and murdered for disclosing sensitive information in relation to narcotrafficking, kidnapping, and injustice.

63. Interview, March 28, 2005.

64. Ratna Kapur notes that arranged marriages in India were a consequence of colonialism, to prove that nonconsensual marriage was a higher form of love than that in the West. Kapur 2005, 157. Also see Niklas Luhmann (1986), who argues that love gains significance in the transition from feudal societies to market ones. While a market society privileges choice and social mobility, premodern societies dictated strict restrictions on what group one could love. In an article titled "Rishtas: Adding

Emotion to Strategy in Understanding British Pakistani Transnational Marriages" (2006), Alison Shaw and Katharine Charsley question the opposition between "love" and "arranged" marriages and the unemotional portrayal of the latter. Through interviews, they illustrate that oftentimes young people's choices and descriptions of love accompany family-based arranged marriages in transnational Pakistani marriages.

65. See Honig 2001, 91.

66. Illouz 1997.

67. Newspapers and scholarship speak to the rapid shifts in places such as China, where democratic forms of capitalism and ensuing sexual revolutions are quickly displacing socialism and Confucianism: Farrer 2002; Farquhar 2002; Rofel 2007. In other parts of the world, the importance of intimacy, and especially new patterns of love and sexuality, reveals the affective dimensions of a democratic style of government that encourages people to see themselves as individuals and emphasizes self-sufficiency, free choice, consumerism, and individualism. See Ahearn 2001; Wilson 2004.

68. Same-sex marriage has been hotly debated. Some queer scholars accuse gay and lesbian activists and scholars who advocate for same-sex marriage of being assimilationist, of advocating for access into the category of heteronormativity (the "good relationship, marriage, and life"). Using marriage as a platform for "equality" merely reifies "normative" relationships and structures rather than critique the categories on which rights and norms are based. See Brandzel 2005; Somerville 2005.

69. IMBRA (Public Law No. 109-162, Title VIII, Subtitle D, January 5, 2006) was added to the Violence Against Women and Department of Justice Reauthorization Act of 2005 (H.R. 3402).

70. This limit of spousal petitions emerged from high-profile cases in which it was discovered that the U.S. men involved in the murder or abuse of women had petitioned for multiple foreign brides.

71. The petition can be found at the link titled "Freedom to Choose: Freedom to Date" at http://usaimmigrationattorney.com/immigrationtopic-swindow.html. Also see Gary Bala's (2006) discussion of IMBRA.

72. For Cantwell's full statement, see Cantwell 2004.

73. Nicole Constable, in the introduction to her edited book *Cross-Border Marriages* (2005), makes two interventions that are relevant to this discussion. The first is that even though brides move from less developed locations to more developed ones, or from the poorer Global South to the wealthier Global North, the idea that they are marrying "up"—or hypergamy, in anthropological terms—works for spatial logics but not necessarily in understanding the diversity of women, some of whom are from the professional and middle classes (10). The anthology also draws from scholarship on Asian women who desire to migrate to a host of

locales outside the United States, such as Japan, Canada, South Korea, and India (ibid., 7).

74. See the Tahirih Justice Center 2009, 9n. 16, for a discussion of the Tahirih Justice Center's research project (April 2006) that produced statistics on the difference in income between those searching for romance and marriage on Match.com versus IMBs.

75. I found the link to the USCIS document in N. Bernstein 2010a.

76. Gary Bala, visa fraud "profile factors," Planet-Love.com, June 13, 2004.

77. In August 2009, the immigration agency dismissed proof of financial documents submitted by a couple married since 1993, a marriage between a female U.S. national and a man from India, "noting, for example, that the joint account they opened in 1997 showed low balances of $8.11 and $62.15 in two 2008 statements." See N. Bernstein 2010b.

78. Coutin 2003. Also see Coutin 2000.

79. Chapkis 2005.

80. Kapur 2005.

81. Chapkis 2005; Kempadoo 2005.

82. Broad-based support against the trafficking industry has included Evangelical Christian groups and mainstream feminist foundations such as the Feminist Majority. For more on the complicated terrain of sex trafficking, see E. Bernstein 2007a; Boris, Gilmore, and Parreñas 2010; and Schaeffer-Grabiel 2011.

83. In *The Transformation of Intimacy* (1992), Anthony Giddens points out that romantic love as the foundation for marriage is a relatively recent idea that emerged in western Europe in the late eighteenth century with the ideology of individualism that arose from capitalism. According to Lawrence Stone, in his book *The Family, Sex and Marriage in England, 1500–1800* (1977), the combination of the invention of private property, the increased importance of subjectivity, the Romantic movement (which emphasized imagination, emotion, and rebellion against authority), and economic and demographic change enabled the emergence of ideologies of happiness and relations of love within the family.

84. Rebhun 1999, 29–30.

85. Recent studies are beginning to question the separation of love, romance, and emotion from economic concerns. In Amalia Cabezas's study of "monetized sexual-affective relations" between Cuban women and foreign men, she argues that we must locate sexual relations within a tourist context beyond that of a business transaction overdetermined by trade and commodification. Sex with foreigners, she argues, functions as a more complex exchange in which love, spirituality, mutual respect, and money intermingle. See Cabezas 2009, 38. For others, love and sex entail a rational decision. Denise Brennan

argues that Dominican sex workers who hope to marry foreign, mostly European, men both hold out the possibility of love and also perform love. "For Sousúa's sex workers, choosing to 'fall in love' with one man over another is a rational process with serious material consequences. Contrary to the notion of 'falling in love' as a kind of elation that comes with losing control of one's senses or wits, for these women, being in love—or pretending to be in love—requires alertness, savvy, and determination." Brennan 2004, 96. She argues that marriage in this tourist economy (famous for sex tourism) has nothing to do with emotion-driven love or romance but is more driven by strategies of obtaining a visa and greater financial security.

86. Hochschild 2003.

87. Lieba Faier also argues that Filipina entertainment workers who marry Japanese men express love as "a term for claiming selfhood and asserting belonging in a modern, global world." See Faier 2007, 154.

NOTES TO CHAPTER 2

1. Kelsky 2001.

2. Mexican and Latin American feminists have, since the 1990s, made great strides in bringing about more gender equity into the legal spheres that rely on gender differences between men and women and patriarchal codes of marriage. For more on the intersection of gender and the law, see Baitenmann, Chenaut, and Varley 2007; Fries and Matus 1999; Lagarde y de los Ríos 2005.

3. Anthony Giddens theorizes the shift to modern life through the following: (1) the delinking of experience from the tangible, especially as mass media stimulate social relations without direct contact, (2) the predominance of a system of experts (psychologists, doctors, social workers), and (3) the presence of reflexivity and the self. See Giddens 1990.

4. The North American owner cut out his Mexican business partner (who he said was rarely around), raising more concern in Guadalajara over his legitimacy to operate the business as a foreigner. In fact, although a legitimate introduction agency, Mexican Wives was recently closed down, presumably because it owed money in back taxes. The media in Guadalajara, however, spun a different story about the closing down of this company. For a week, media and radio programs incorrectly reported that the agency was involved in the trafficking of prostitutes from Mexico to Russia, in an attempt to ruin its reputation and to prevent women from joining other affiliated agencies in Guadalajara. This company has reopened under a new name.

5. The company slowly phased down its tours to Mexico to one time a year because the Colombia tours were so much more popular and lucrative.

6. It is difficult to say how many women are signed up with these agencies because some are members of more than one agency, and the numbers of women constantly change. Mexican Wives has anywhere from two hundred to five hundred female participants, although the number of active members is much lower. There are also over three hundred Internet companies advertising women from Asia, Russia, the Caribbean, and Latin America.

7. Some agencies decided to charge women to make sure they are serious about the prospects of marriage.

8. The middle to upper classes in Mexico are more likely to hold visas because they can prove their intent to return to Mexico through stable jobs, bank accounts, and the ownership of cars and/or property. For women who are not legally migrating for education or work, they must obtain a fiancée visa. Matchmaking agencies provide detailed information on their websites or at the actual agency and sometimes even sell "immigration kits" with all of the relevant paperwork and information.

9. Salazar 2001, 147.

10. Oliviera 1990.

11. Female work was no longer a temporary state or a rarity but was incorporated into women's lives as a rite of passage through which women could escape isolation in the home. See Hondagneu-Sotelo 1994, 13.

12. Sarah LeVine finds that national fertility rates declined in the 1970s and '80s; the average number of children Mexican women bore lowered from 6.7 in 1970 to 3.46 in 1989. LeVine, in her book *Dolor y alegría* (1993, 197) gathered this information from 1991 UNICEF data.

13. Hondagneu-Sotelo 1994, 221n. 42, citing Cordera Campos and González Tiburcio 1989, 114.

14. During the time I was conducting my research in Guadalajara, even those women with good wages, such as Spanish-language teachers at the University of Guadalajara's foreign-language schools (with foreign-level tuition fees), only make an average of slightly less than $500 a month. The professional class, including doctors and lawyers, are paid more in social prestige than in livable wages.

15. Carrillo 2002.

16. This statistic is from Internet World Stats, "Mexico: Internet Statistics and Telecommunications Reports," http://www.internetworldstats.com/am/mx.htm (accessed January 2009).

17. Sassen 2002.

18. O'Dougherty 2002, 22–23.

19. García Canclini 2001.

20. Hirsch 2003; Hirsch and Wardlow 2006; Padilla et al. 2007.

21. I have changed the names of all of the women interviewed, and unless otherwise specified, the quotations are from face-to-face interviews. All translations from Spanish into English are my own.

22. "Econónmicamente, están más estables que los hombres. . . . Ya tienen su propia casa, su carro, y lujos que muchos hombres no se los pueden dar. Y lo más curioso de aquí que es el coraje que tiene el hombre aquí en México es que la mujer—por eso como que pone más el machismo—que muchas mujeres sobresalgan más que ellos. Pero bueno, lo bueno de otras personas de otros países es que admiran ese tipo de mujer."

23. "Me he tocado ver que los hombres de allá están dispuestos, o sea, a compartir quehaceres y algo que aqui casi, casi no ocurre, o sea, allá este. . . . Pues a me han dicho que 'yo cocino para ti,' no algo que aqui pues: 'Como que me vas a cocinar?' O sea, allá es que los hombres son mas independientes desde mas pequeño, este, yo pienso que saben valorar mas todos los aspectos, no? . . . Y eso es lo que, este, en cierta manera les va a dar un poco mas de madúrese y . . . es libertad que ellos mismos sienten por lo mismo a la mejor tienen menos prejuicios, no, que los de aqui."

24. See Hondagneu-Sotelo 1994. Arlie Hochschild makes a similar argument in her U.S.-based study *The Second Shift* (1994).

25. I thank Renato Rosaldo for pointing this out to me.

26. Interview, November 21, 2001. "La mujer Mexicana del año 2001 está despertando de su cruel realidad. Se está y se le están dando mas opciones de vivir una vida con calidad, llena de realizaciones laborales y personales, de mejorar su ingreso por cápita. Se le está tomando en cuenta dentro de la fuerza de la clase trabajadora, y no solo como máquina de hacer niños. Ni como ama de casa que mas bien es una sirvienta sin sueldo y sin reconocimiento de su propia familia y de las personas que le rodean. La mujer mexicana tiene varios años que está despertando a mejores oportunidades de vida en todos los aspectos y con actitudes, desea que se le reconozca su labor día a día con la misma destreza y capacidad intelectual como la del varón. La mujer de nuestro país, 'Raza de Bronce" está despertando de su largo letargo que duró centurias y ahora está aceptando su propio valor (aunque esto le causó malos tratos, humillaciones, torturas y hasta la muerte. No, no exagero, Felicitas. Es cierto). . . . Lo mas importante, pienso yo, es reconocer su propio valor ante si misma y ante los demás, que se respete como valioso ser humano."

27. See Lagarde y de los Ríos 2010, xxi; and Fregoso and Bejarano 2010.

28. See "Shock Jock" 2003.

29. There are numerous feminist debates on gender and nationalism in the United States that focus on the ways women are marginally positioned

within national agendas: Yuval-Davis 1997; McClintock 1995; Kaplan, Alarcón, and Moallem 1999; and Mayer 2000. The feminist debates on women's sexual role as reproducers of the family and nation are numerous. Some Latin American feminists argue that women's sexual difference, their reproduction of love and kin, has not only reinforced their subordinate position to patriarchal structures of power and the law but also ignited violence between men. Lorena Fries and Verónica Matus argue that women's subordinate sexual position and reproductive role in the family contribute to their diminished rights in relation to the law. See Fries and Matus 1999; Lagarde y de los Ríos 2005. Given the rise of Mexican and U.S. nation-building with modernity, decolonial feminist scholars have critiqued the ways that native women's bodies are equated with premodernity and the past. See Lugones 2010; Pérez 1999; Aldama and Quiñonez 2002.

30. Anzaldúa 1987.

31. Foucault (1978) 1990; McClintock 1995.

32. Wahneema Lubiano describes the "crisis" of modernity as a "'spectacle of men out of control,' arguing that those in dominant positions articulate their sense of destabilization and disequilibrium as they begin to experience gendered and racial constraints themselves." Alarcón, Kaplan, and Moallem 1999, 2, quoting Lubiano 1991, 152.

33. While the Mexican state controls forms of culture embedded within territorial identities—such as archaeological sites, museums, and the promotion of arts and crafts—the audiovisual industry is dominated by foreign films, the majority from the United States. In fact, the Instituto Mexicano de Cinematografía estimates that U.S. cinema accounts for 62 percent of films released in Mexico, and others think this number will soon rise to 80 percent. See García Canclini 1997, 253. In Guadalajara, 48 percent of films come from the United States, 29 percent come from other countries, and 13 percent are from Mexico. U.S. films, however, are shown in 74 percent of all the movie salons. See Sánchez Ruiz 1996, 116–117.

34. Chicana theorists and historians have rewritten the story of La Malinche from Octavio Paz's rendition of her as a traitor to emphasizing her role as a translator, a feminist, and a strong figure who used her limited role to help save as many indigenous people as possible from the violence of conquest. For some of this iconic revisionist work, see Alarcón 1983, 1989; Alcalá 2001; Anzaldúa 1987; Candelaria 1980; Del Castillo 1974; and Pérez 1991. In contrast, Paz harshly views her as a passive figure: "Her passivity is abject: she does not resist violence, but is an inert heap of bones, blood and dust. . . . She is nothingness." See Paz 1961, 85–86.

35. The offspring produced between Cortés and Malintzin was later coined by José Vasconcelos to be the turbulent beginnings of "*la raza cosmica*." See Vasconcelos 1997.

36. See Paz 1961.

37. Traditional gender roles continue to play an important part in Mexican culture but vary between rural and urban areas, between the educated and working classes, and so on. This is especially true of younger men, who are better educated and who learn gender roles through diverse media such as film, music, and stories of life outside Mexico. Luis Leñero Otero's term "machismo *light*" may be a more appropriate way to talk about contemporary forms of machismo. Leñero Otero 1994, quoted in Keijzer 1999, 313. Many men realize that they can no longer exercise the kind of patriarchy carried out by their fathers and grandfathers. Anthropologists such as Matthew Gutmann are careful to contextualize the changing historical, class, and regional meanings of manliness or machismo. In Gutmann's book *The Meanings of Macho* (1996), he also highlights some of the positive qualities of machismo, such as men's sense of caring and duty toward their children and families.

38. The building of empire during the U.S.-Mexico War of 1846–48, when the United States took over one-fifth of Mexico's territory, created what Shelley Streeby calls a "white egalitarian patriotism" built on the backs of negative characterizations of Mexican men. See Streeby 2002, 91. José Limón also discusses the erotics of empire building in the U.S. Southwest in *American Encounters* (1998). Yet, while Mexican men were painted in a negative light, Mexican women were idealized as those who waited for the Anglos to save them from tyranny. For Reginald Horsman (1981), both politicians and poets sought to extinguish and absorb the Mexican race through the union of American men and Mexican women. Mexican women of purer blood, the upper-class Spaniards, were characterized as more naturally fit romantic partners for the purer blood of the "Yankee chivalry." Mexican men, by contrast, were portrayed as dirty, lazy, and downtrodden. Also see Kaplan 2002.

39. Domínguez-Ruvalcaba 2007, 98. In this book, Domínguez-Ruvalcaba analyzes the homoerotic contours of Mexican masculinity and discourses of machismo during the postrevolutionary period as both sensual and violent. He argues that the critique of machismo is an expression of modernizing the nation. Within much of the scholarship critical of machismo since the 1930s, he says, "the masculine image appears, as the revolution had proposed, as an allegory of domination, the colonial condition, and the obstacle for modernization" (ibid.).

40. In Doris Sommer's investigation of Mexican literature, she argues that nation-building depended on naturalizing heterosexual love and romance. She says, "Romantic passion, on my reading, gave a rhetoric

for the hegemonic projects in Gramsci's sense of conquering the antagonistic through mutual interest, or 'love,' rather than through coercion."
Sommer 1991, 6.

41. Anna says, "In these three days, he conquered her with his thoughtfulness. Because he would not leave her alone, he followed her wherever
she went [*laughs*]." ("En esos tres días, él la conquistó con sus detalles.
Porque no la soltaba, la perseguía 'pa donde iba.'")

42. García Canclini 2001.

43. Illouz 1997.

44. Eva Illouz traces the practice of dating, as opposed to calling on a
woman at home, in the United States to the rise in real income during
the first decades of the twentieth century, which quickly "made consumption an inherent element of any romantic encounter" (1997, 54).
Etiquette books reinforced this pattern by defining consumption as
symbolic of the "good treatment" of a woman by her partner.

45. I translated e-mail exchanges for Cody for over a year and followed his
love quests in Mexico, Peru, and Guatemala. He made sure to select
only "high"-class women, most who were educated professionals with
strong family ties.

46. Illouz 1997, 195.

47. Ibid., 30. Theorists of Mexican popular culture, such as Jean Franco,
approach the ways women in Mexico are influenced by media consumption. In Franco's study on romance narratives in Mexican and
U.S. mass media, *Plotting Women* (1989), she discovers that women
are incorporated differently through romantic plots that perpetuate the international division of labor. Lower-class Mexican *novelas*
reproduce women's role as producers through narratives that support a strong work ethic (even if it means prostitution) as the path
to women's liberation from macho men or oppressive family situations. On the other hand, in U.S. Harlequin novels (read mostly by
white, middle-class women), women obtain social power through
their ability to seduce the powerful, a skill that leads to rewards such
as marriage, comfort, and abundance (Franco 1989). These narratives maintain class divisions between the United States and Mexico
through romantic narratives in which women who want to get ahead
in Mexico must work, while white women seduce their way into marriages that increase their social standing. Yet Franco does not talk
about the ways mass-media narratives impact middle- to upper-class
women in Mexico, especially as mass media from the United States
are increasingly circulated into Mexico. In *telenovelas*, romance,
passion, and marriage afford women upward mobility and status in
addition, of course, to high does of drama.

48. Salazar 2001, 185.

49. Jennifer Hirsch, in *A Courtship after Marriage* (2003, 87), finds a similar trend in the ways older Mexican women describe marriage as destiny or divine will, while younger women define it by individual choice, of someone who is both a good provider and a companion.
50. J. Samuel Escobar argues, "By 1916 there were 170,000 Protestants in Latin America and it is estimated that there are 48 million in 1990." Escobar 1994, 27. Protestantism has spread to impoverished Latin American masses who have given up on Liberation Theology and to the middle class, who similarly crave a new "hope" for Latin America that departs from traditional structures of power and privilege. In addition, within this cross-national context, women associated Christianity with Anglo Protestants in the United States, defining religion within a cultural *and* racial context.
51. Escobar, quoting from Kenneth Scott Latourette (*The Great Century*), draws parallels between the current swing to Protestantism and its history of missionary expansion. Protestant missionaries saw the opportunity to spread into Latin America during the crisis and decline of the Catholic Church during the war of independence with Spain in 1810–1824. Ibid., 31.
52. Salazar 2001, 15.
53. Turkle 1995, 26.
54. Carrier 1995.
55. In Michael Hardy's discussion of Internet relationships (2004, 213), he refers to Anthony Giddens's idea of modern intimacy to understand the broader contexts of Internet dating. See Giddens 1992.
56. Ehrenreich and Hochschild 2002b, 3.

NOTES TO CHAPTER 3

1. There are three chat boards available for men seeking brides from Russia, Asia, and Latin America at http://www.Planet-Love.com.
2. For more on how the national discourse of immigration depends on the erasure of the United States' exclusion of otherness, see Behad 2005.
3. I am thinking here of Edward Said's book *Orientalism* (1978).
4. Phone interview with Texan agency owner, December 16, 2000.
5. Interview with Hermosillo agency owner, July 18, 2000.
6. Women thought the photos were for a magazine mailed directly to men.
7. These percentages are an approximation from data I collected about the men while attending three tours in Mexico.
8. In R. W. Connell's definition of hegemonic masculinity (the gender practice which guarantees the dominant position of men and the subordination of women), he borrows from Gramsci's notion of consent to argue that this form of masculinity is not fixed but in constant motion and always contestable. See Connell 1995, 76.

9. The impossibility of separating the virtual from face-to-face encounters is tackled by Lori Kendall in her book *Hanging Out in the Virtual Pub* (2002), in which she presents interviews of participants both on-line and off-line. Contrary to the literature that understands the Internet as a distinct space where identities are fabricated in a much different fashion than in off-line interactions, Kendall conducts an in-depth ethnography of interactions on muds (text-only on-line forums) as well as interviews with participants in their homes. She unravels the mixed results, where "relationships both suffer and benefit from the conditions of online interactions and where participants both disrupt and reproduce power relations and hierarchies existing in offline social contexts" (12). Nicole Constable, in *Romance on a Global Stage* (2003), also situates her methodology as an Internet ethnography that blurs the lines between on-line and face-to-face interactions.

10. He also said that George H. W. Bush believed that "the family is the point of light in a world of darkness." Phone interview, November 18, 2008.

11. Many men backed up these feelings by discussing increasing state surveillance of these marriages and popular media that focuses on male abuse and the need for legal protection of women.

12. See chapter 5 for a discussion of why some women support strict immigration laws.

13. This also happens to be an older advertising slogan for the U.S. on-line dating service One and Only, which is now Match.com.

14. The literature on these topics is vast, but for some sources that document the stress on African American families during slavery, see Morrison 1987; Dunaway 2003; and Miles 2005. The migration literature detailing the separation of families is similarly vast, but some key texts include Parreñas 2001, 2005; and Dreby 2010. On the challenges of interracial marriage historically, see Hodes 1999; Sollors 2000; Moran 2001; and Pascoe 2009. Finally, for a book on the banning of gay marriage and migrants in relation to discourses of terrorism, see Lugo-Lugo and Bloodsworth-Lugo 2009. Also see Luibhéid 2008 for a discussion of the politics of gay marriage in relation to immigration.

15. A chat-room participant responded to the negative portrayal of men who travel to Russia for a bride on the television program *From Russia with Love*, on which members of the National Organization for Women (NOW) were interviewed. He said, "And as far as NOW is concerned. Don't they have anything better to do, like go feed the hungry or something. If they want to save all the women in the world, why not start right at home and educate the women here what they are doing wrong. But they will never admit it's them. It's always us. The big bad men

again. Idiots. I think I'm done. Thanks for letting me voice my opinion."
Posting on Planet-Love.com, February 6, 2000.

16. See www.ilovelatins.com (accessed October 20, 2008).

17. Davidson and Sánchez Taylor 2005, 95.

18. See the website www.amorincali.com/Memorial.htm, which discusses
the agency's "Summer Bachelor Tours."

19. *Time* magazine's article on the future of race, as well as advertising campaigns, suggested that racial morphing was the wave of the
future. The images that accompanied the well-cited "The New Face of
America" article (1993) utilized digital morphing to depict a woman
who is a mixture of racial types. Throughout, the magazine draws on
"melting pot" and assimilation theory and the belief that racial mixing
will dilute the threatening effects of immigrants to U.S. structures of
whiteness. Racial mixing promises to manage and overcome racial
divisions in America.

20. In *Manly States*, Charlotte Hooper uncovers the opportunistic language
used by the *Economist* in its understanding of globalization: "Fears that
low wage economies will eventually pinch many of the rich world's jobs
are overdone. . . . Emerging economies will spend their export revenues
from textiles and consumer electronics on more sophisticated products
from industrial economies" (2001, 159).

21. Interview, March 28, 2005.

22. Interview, September 2001.

23. Clark, posting on Planet-Love.com, February 23, 2001, http://www.
planet-love.com/gclark/gclark02/.

24. In *Stiffed* (1999, 9), Susan Faludi describes the term *feminazis* to refer to
the radical feminists who men fear have gone beyond equal treatment
and are now trying to steal male power and exercise control over them.

25. See Popenoe 1996.

26. Ibid., 197.

27. Kline 2001, 164.

28. This happened to John when the ex-husband of his wife, Monica, cost
him thousands of dollars in bribes before he would sign the necessary
paperwork to allow her son to migrate to the United States.

29. Makow 2000, 12.

30. Hochschild 2002, 26.

31. http://www.latinlifemates.com/faq.stm (accessed June 28, 2001).

32. Laughlin 1997.

33. He went on to say that he likes women my skin color (light brown or
olive toned) or darker. After I told him I am married, he went right on
to ask me out on a date, in front of three other men. We all looked at
him aghast, and before I could respond, they jumped on him for his
lack of respect.

34. Calvo 2001; Inda 2002; Briggs 2002; Chavez 2004; and Gutiérrez 2008.
35. In *Brave New Families* (1990), Judith Stacey describes the modern family as much more open and diverse (including gay family forms, single-headed households, etc.) than the patriarchal nuclear family.
36. Makow 2000, 123.
37. It is noteworthy that they divorced after two years because in 1986, President Reagan signed the Immigration Marriage Fraud Amendment (IMFA) in hopes of decreasing marriage scams by imposing a two-year waiting period for women to obtain permanent residency status.
38. There has been a great deal of feminist scholarship on women's role as missionaries in relation to British imperialism and U.S. empire. See Tyrrell 1991; Chaudhuri and Strobel 1992; and Santiago-Valles 1999; and Newman 1999.
39. For more on the historical whitening of the Polish, Germans, Italians, and Irish, see Jacobson 1998.
40. Interview, September 2001.
41. This quote is from a participant in a film project by Eleanor Ford titled *The Internet Bride* (2004).
42. Most men I interviewed equate feminism with white, upwardly mobile women and assume Latin American women and, to a lesser extent, U.S. women of color to be more feminine and thus not feminist.
43. For some examples of feminist work on the mutability of the body in cyberspace, see Turkle 1995; McRae 1996; A. Stone 1996; Nakamura 2002; and Nguyen 2003.
44. There has been a recent surge of retreats for men to get in touch with their warrior spirits in response to the lack of modern rituals of manhood that tie men to their communities, their fathers, or other men. Churches across the nation are leading young men to tap into their masculinity through a variety of activities, including a pseudo-military battle that translates into men, dressed in army suits, battling out paintball competitions in the wilderness. On the quieter side, support-group sessions encourage men to share their difficult relationships with their absent or distant fathers.
45. Messner 1997, 26.
46. See Katz 1993, 34.
47. Foucault 1990, 61–67.
48. Bly's book *Iron John* (1990) also warned that men grow up in families headed by women where the father is either absent or preoccupied with work. Interestingly enough, however, the absence of father figures is again blamed on feminists for usurping men's dominant place in the family.
49. Messner 1997, 17.
50. Personal e-mail interview, September 13, 2004.

51. Several women told me that Steve found them at this tour and invited them to join his agency.
52. Various scholars have argued that the exchange of women is a critical practice to the making of social relations, especially for the strengthening of (homo)social bonds between men. See Lévi-Strauss 1969; Rubin 1975. Eve Kosofsky Sedgwick's book *Between Men* (1985) argues that the term *homosocial* brings back the broken link between heterosexual male bonding and homosexual desires.
53. Posting on Planet-Love.com, October 12, 2003.
54. Makow 2000, 12.
55. Posting on Planet-Love.com, December 3, 2000.
56. Posting on Planet-Love.com, December 2, 2000.
57. Hondagneu-Sotelo and Messner 1994.
58. Posting on Planet-Love.com, June 24, 1999.
59. Ibid.
60. Tayman 2000, 139.
61. Posting on Planet-Love.com, November 5, 2000.
62. Posting on Planet-Love.com, November 5, 2000.
63. Posting on Planet-Love.com, October 10, 2003.
64. Noble 2002.
65. Posting on Planet-Love.com, April 30, 2000.

NOTES TO CHAPTER 4

1. Women's ages ranged from eighteen to fifty-five, although most were between eighteen and thirty-five.
2. The agency I accompanied offered tours to Cali twice a year.
3. Waxer 2002.
4. Murdock 2008, 7.
5. Alexander 1997; Kempadoo 1999, 2004; Brennan 2004.
6. Harvey 1989. Aihwa Ong, in *Flexible Citizenship* (1999), links the idea of flexibility to how the Chinese business class uses its access to multiple passports to flaunt its global citizenship and to accumulate capital.
7. This move from the ordinary to the spectacular, from individual difference to universal sameness, is a tension others have theorized in the cosmetic surgery industry. See Davis 1995; Haiken 1997; and Blum 2003.
8. They both knew I was a researcher writing a book on the matchmaking marriage industry, and as such, I did not charge for my translating services, although Seth paid for my meal and offered me a tip (which I refused) at the end of a long night.
9. A typical wage in Cali can be as low as $130 a month.
10. Other women I spoke to similarly described the multiple surgery procedures they procured as an investment in their self, their career, and their future.

11. University students from across the Global South have had to make up for low-paying jobs through part-time, vacation-oriented sex work. See Cabezas 2009; Johnson 2007; and Acharya 2006.

12. After I followed Bill to the detective's office, the workers in the office, amused by my research project, shared how common a practice it was for locals and especially those from other countries to hire a private detective to follow women they were dating. The cost was quite cheap, as the whole process cost Bill about $100. When I described to other Colombians this scenario of how a U.S. man hired a detective to find his missing "fiancée," they laughed heartily and explained a popular saying in Colombia that U.S. tourists are *pendejos*, or innocently uninformed. The term is not nearly as strong as its usage in Mexico but comes from the locals' sense that tourists have no idea what people's real lives are like in Colombia, that they are sheltered from the complex and difficult realities that the majority of Colombia's population faces, and that they are unaware of how complicit the U.S. government has been in Colombia's social instability and violence.

13. Wade 1997. For a discussion of blackness and beauty in Brazil, see Hanchard 1994.

14. Rivero 2003, 67.

15. Fusco 1997; Aparicio 1998; Wade 2000; Kempadoo 1999, 2004.

16. Kirk 2003, 72.

17. In the nineteenth century, the Catholic Church bore heavily on definitions of beauty. A woman's beauty was defined by her character, or her internal being, expressed primarily through her actions. During the twentieth century, more external views of beauty dominated, including a more visual depiction of beauty from the body's surface. See Stanfield (manuscript in progress).

18. Waxer 2002, 20.

19. Of the three tours I attended in Mexico, I saw only one engagement, between a couple that had communicated for months over e-mail before the two met in person at the tour.

20. Bérubé 2005.

21. Ibid. This number increased greatly from 1999, when it was estimated that over three million Colombians had migrated, or about 8 percent of the population: Guarnizo, Sánchez, and Roach 1999, 371.

22. A documentary filmed in Colombia, *La Corona* (2008), chronicles beauty pageants that take place in a jail cell. Even in prison, beauty is an important activity for uplifting the spirit of female inmates, for representing lesbian desire, and for offering female inmates a measure of hope and self-respect.

23. For a discussion of sex tourism in Cartagena, see Mayorga and Velásquez 1999.

24. This is an argument made by Michael Stanfield, a professor at the University of San Francisco, in an interview by Juan Forero about his book in progress on Colombian beauty pageants, titled "Beauty and the Beast." See Forero 2001.

25. Wade 1999, 455.

26. Ibid.

27. This is a term that originated by scholars in the context of Brazil. See Twine 1998.

28. Lobo 2005, 66.

29. Sarah Banet-Weiser, in *The Most Beautiful Girl in the World* (1999), has also argued that women who participate in beauty pageants are not victims or dupes of dominant constructions of beauty. Instead, she places interviews with women alongside feminist discourse to analyze them as engaged in cultural truths, both socially constructed and embedded within particular belief systems (16). Ruth Holliday and Jacqueline Sánchez Taylor (2006) take this argument even further to argue that cosmetic alteration, or "false" recourse to beauty, assumes an active negotiation with beauty toward women's own ends.

30. Forero 2001.

31. Transnational media corporations such as Univisión, located in the United States, also provide safer opportunities for Colombian female journalists, who do not have to fear violent backlashes within their local, highly politicized social milieus.

32. Cepeda 2003, 222.

33. This photo is posted on GlobalLatinas' website "Singles Vacation Tours." One might argue that the swimsuits represent the Puerto Rican flag.

34. A shorter version of the "Colombia Is Passion" official website in English can be found at http://www.colombia.travel/en/international-tourist/colombia/colombia-is-passion (accessed July 22, 2010).

35. See the I Love Latins IMB website: http://www.ilovelatins.com/ (accessed December 18, 2010); and the Colombian Connections website: http://colombianconnections.com/why-colombia.php (accessed December 18, 2010).

36. Another series of videos reflecting the remaking of Colombia's image states, "The only risk is wanting to stay." See the official website at http://www.colombia.travel/en/international-tourist/colombia/tourism-campaign (accessed September 23, 2011).

37. "Sin duda alguna, la pasión es la mejor materia prima de nuestros ciudadanos." See the official website at http://190.7.104.29/es/colombia-es-pasion/ipor-que-colombia-es-pasion (accessed July 22, 2010).

38. Ibid.: "el motor que nos impulsa a dar lo mejor de nosotros mismos por el bien del país."

39. A shorter version of the "Colombia Is Passion" official website in English can be found at http://www.colombia.travel/en/international-tourist/colombia/colombia-is-passion (accessed July 22, 2010).

40. Ibid.: "Es tener una identidad, un nombre y una reputación. En la coyuntura actual de globalización, es importante que los países se diferencien de otros, para así poder competir en el mercado internacional."

41. Ibid.: "La marca Colombia es Pasión busca que el mundo conozca un país en plena vía de desarrollo, con una economía estable, una geografía privilegiada, grandes recursos naturales, pero sobre todo gente cálida, amable y apasionada."

42. In the Mexican version of this *telenovela* aired on Telemundo in October 2009, called *Sin senos [breasts] no hay paraíso*, young women are lured from Colombia to Mexico by a member of the Juarez cartel and told they will be more successful if they have breast augmentation. Unknowingly, they are used as "mules," shipped to Mexico with cocaine smuggled into their silicone breasts.

43. Alexander 1997, 83.

44. Ibid., 90.

45. Davidson and Sánchez Taylor 2005, 89. Also see Sánchez Taylor 2000.

46. Ibid., 86.

47. Fusco 1996, 1997.

48. Tenório 2002.

49. *Betty la fea* aired between 1999 and 2002 on the Colombian network RCN. The global popularity of this *telenovela* has led to the production of similar plotlines in over a dozen countries.

50. Not only did about one in five Colombians watch the show, but it gained popularity in places as far away as Hungary, Israel, the Philippines, and many other countries. See Martinez 2001.

51. Rivero 2003, 73.

52. Ibid., 78.

53. Thomas 2001, 268.

54. T. Pratt 2000.

55. Ibid. Colombian *telenovelas* are known for depicting scenarios and social interactions in a more "realistic" manner than their Mexican and Venezuelan counterparts. See López 1995 and Rincón 2000 for a discussion of soap operas in Latin America.

56. Martinez 2005.

57. Kempadoo 2004, 40.

58. Another interesting example of the violence and possibility of gendered uses of the body are black, male boxers in Chicago. Loïc Wacquant separates the outside perception of boxing, as a debasing form of submission to external constraints and material necessity, from boxers' own perceptions. Boxing affords some men a means for "carving

out a margin of autonomy from their oppressive circumstances and for
expressing their ability to seize their own fate and remake it in accor-
dance with their inner wishes." Wacquant 1995, 501. Boxing, akin to the
gendered turn to beauty, full of suffering and exploitation, also infuses
men's lives with "a sense of value, excitement, and accomplishment"
(ibid., 501). Also see Wacquant 2004.

59. Hennessey 2000, 78.
60. Ibid.
61. Haraway 1991.
62. Ong 1999, 40.
63. Wilson 2004, 178.
64. See his stimulating recent book, *Pretty Modern* (2010). Also see Marcia
    Ochoa's *Queen for a Day* (forthcoming) for a discussion of the ways
    beauty mediates transgender Venezuelans' relation to the modern world.
65. Foucault 1988.
66. Kaw 1993; Haiken 1997; Bañales 2005; Gilman 1999.
67. Davis 1995.
68. Davis 2003.
69. I spent over a year translating love letters from women across various
    Latin American countries for Cody. Due to his search for a "high qual-
    ity" woman, he asked me to scrutinize women's letters and language use
    for clues as to their class and education background.
70. Gilman argues this in "Black Bodies, White Bodies" (1985).
71. Negrón-Muntaner 1997, 189, quoting Beauvoir 1989, 159.
72. Negrón-Muntaner makes this argument for the Puerto Rican diaspora
    through a theorization of Jennifer Lopez's behind (1997, 189; and 2003).
73. For a discussion about cosmetic surgery in the barrage of television
    shows such as *Extreme Makeover, The Swan*, and others, see Weber 2005,
    2009.
74. It is not only heterosexual women who turn to cosmetic surgery to
    erotically enhance their bodies. Brazilian prostitutes in Don Kulick's
    book *Travesti* (1998) injected silicone into erotic zones of the body such
    as the hips and buttocks as a means of increasing the return on their
    sexual labor. In Annick Prieur's book *Mema's House* (1998), some of her
    transgender subjects use cosmetic surgery to pass as a woman in order
    to have sex with men.
75. Martin 1998, 79.
76. President George W. Bush's creation of policies and public support to
    increase the power of the individual in fighting terrorism similarly
    speaks to the polyvalent nature of surveillance.
77. Erynn Masi Cassanova found a similar expression evident in Ecuador:
    "No hay mujer fea, sino mal arreglada" (There are no ugly women, just
    poorly groomed ones). Adolescent youth turned to this phrase as a

more inclusive notion of beauty based on hard work rather than nature. See Cassanova 2004, 299.

78. Women from the professional class at the tour also described cosmetic surgery through the narrative of investing in themselves and their futures.

NOTES TO CHAPTER 5

1. For more on gendered forms of citizenship, see Yuval-Davis 1997, 1999; Yuval-Davis and Werbner 1999. Only more recently have scholars turned to intimacy to trace the centrality of the private sphere as a terrain for national belonging and citizenship. See Berlant 1997; Gender and Cultural Citizenship Inter-University Working Group 2009.

2. Various on-line sources claim the divorce rate in the United States is at 49–51 percent. See Dana Hinders, "Divorce Statistics," LoveToKnow Divorce, http://divorce.lovetoknow.com/Divorce_Statistics (accessed December 28, 2010); and the U.S. Census Bureau, "Decennial Census Data on Marriage and Divorce," http://www.census.gov/hhes/socdemo/marriage/data/census/index.html (accessed December 28, 2010).

3. In an on-line discussion of the Planet-Love.com survey results, the administer, Dan, said, "We broadcast emails to more than 200,000 people—we promoted the survey through a Press Release to the mass media—and as you probably recall, we promoted the survey through our outlets here at PL [Planet-Love] and elsewhere." "Re: Survey Results—First Questions," Planet-Love.com, November 5, 2008.

4. Honig 2001, 4.

5. Ibid., 4.

6. Ibid., 74.

7. In Mexico, respectable femininity contrasts with *la puta* (the prostitute), who because of her excessive sexuality is blamed for an array of brutal violences enacted against her body. See Fregoso 2003, 2006; Schmidt Camacho 2005; Wright 2006. In addition, Jasbir Puar (2007) draws from the work of Giorgio Agamben to discuss the boundaries between queers destined for death and those whose exceptional sexual status and normative lives guarantees them for life.

8. In a similar vein, in *Methodology of the Oppressed* (2000, 58), Chela Sandoval uses the term "differential" to trace the ways U.S. feminists of color move "between and among" ideological positions and, like the gears of a car, shift into various tactical modes for intervening with power.

9. A 2006 issue of *Global Network: A Journal of Transnational Affairs* dedicated an entire issue to South Asian transnational marriages that emphasizes the intimate and emotional complexities between partners and their families, especially in light of media- and policy-driven

accounts that highlight the abuse and economic motives behind arranged marriages. See especially the article by Alison Shaw and Katharine Charsley (2006).

10. Their desire to accentuate class similarities may also explain their hope to minimize the stigmas of these kinds of marriages: that she married him for his money or lifestyle in the United States and the popular belief that he wanted a docile wife from Mexico.

11. Posting on LWL, May 5, 1999.

12. Posting on LWL, May 6, 1999.

13. I am using the term "outlaw" in a much different sense than Kate Borstein, whose semiautobiographical book *Gender Outlaw* (1995) understands a gender outlaw as those transvestites, such as herself, who seek to work outside gender dimorphism.

14. It can take a couple of months to two years for a woman to adjust her status so she can be eligible for a work permit. Most men also aid their new spouses by helping with lengthy paperwork applications for Social Security cards, work permits, driving permits, and the paperwork to petition to bring women's children from Latin America. This increases the stress level of women but also of the men juggling the new demands of time, money, and emotional needs.

15. Menjívar 2000.

16. Personal e-mail interview, February 5, 2004.

17. Ibid.

18. Marta E. Savigliano argues in her book *Tango and the Political Economy of Passion* (1995) that Latin American passion fuels the explosion of tango from Buenos Aires to Paris to Tokyo. For more on how the history of Brazil has contributed to its present construction as an erotic culture, see Parker 1991.

19. Constable 2003.

20. For women who do not find these on-line networks, they build friendships with other Latinas at their church, through language classes, or via other foreign-marriage wives from Latin America.

21. Posting on LWL, May 22, 1999.

22. Most of the e-mail exchanges are in Spanish, with an occasional message in English or Portuguese.

23. Other topics include prenuptial agreements, advice on childrearing, how to get over feelings of homesickness, and so on. Women on these lists have organized cyber baby showers and even sent gifts to each other, while also discovering creative ways to meet each other in person.

24. Posting on LWL, June 5, 2002.

25. These cyber-Latina networks are advertised on men's chat rooms such as Planet-Love.com and Latina-Women-List and encouraged by women's husbands.

26. Posting on Latina-Women-List, June 27, 2001.
27. Ibid.
28. Personal interview, April 13, 2008. "Fire and Passion" was also the name of one of the agencies they started in Brazil.
29. For more on the history of race in relation to European immigrants, see Jacobson 1998.
30. Personal interview, April 13, 2008; italics mine.
31. Migrants' claims to love and intense feelings for their husband and the United States distance them from the popular conception that they use the system for their own benefit. Lieba Faier interviewed Filipina hostesses in Japan who describe their motivations for marrying through claims to "love" in order to differentiate those who make pragmatic choices (what women describe as "cold and calculating") from those who marry for "love" (characterized as "loving and decent"). See Faier 2007, 155. In Rhacel Parreñas' book, *Illicit Flirtations* (2011), Filippina entertainers refuse to separate financial concerns from love. Gifts and money augment the intensity of their feelings for their Japanese clients.
32. The Brazilian Constitution of 1988 was amended in 1994 to declare that nationals who acquire another nationality will not lose their Brazilian nationality. See the Constitutional Amendment Review, No. 3, 1994 DOU 09.06.94.
33. Haag 1999, 98.
34. Ibid., 97.
35. Here Haag quotes from Emory Bogardus, a professor of political science who wrote the book *Essentials of Americanization* (1923).
36. Rebhun 1999, 50.
37. Marita translated a long e-mail from another woman: "Si nos necesitan, aprendara valornos como iguales, a no pensar que todas somos malas porque alguna vez tuvieron una mala experiencia. Aprendan a valor el sacrificio que hacemos al dejar a nuestras familias en nuestro pais por venir en buscar de un hombre bueno y un gran amor." The original e-mail from May 13, 2008, was reposted on the LWL e-mail exchange on May 15, 2008.
38. Posting on LWL, May 18, 2008.
39. Ibid.
40. I am drawing from Lauren Berlant's definition of an "intimate public" in *The Female Complaint* (2008). While her formulation draws on the making of female consumers in the nineteenth century, foreign marriage chat rooms resemble the shared sense of history and, I would add, wounded relationship to the nation that makes these spaces a "porous, affective scene of identification among strangers that promises a certain experience of belonging and provides a complex of consolation, confirmation, discipline, and discussion about how to live as an *x*" (viii).
41. Eng and Han 2000.

42. In *The Commercialization of Intimate Life* (2003), Arlie Hochschild argues that gratitude produces economic relations organized not simply on feelings of appreciation but on a structural position of indebtedness (or what she calls an "economy of gratitude"). Hochschild 2003, 105.

43. The hundreds of thousands of people gathered across cities in the United States began in response to proposed legislation known as H.R. 4437, which would raise penalties for illegal immigration and classify unauthorized immigrants and anyone who helped them enter or remain in the United States as felons. As part of the wider immigration debate, most of the protests sought not only an overhaul of this bill but also a path to legalization for those who had entered the United States without proper documents. Some protests fell on May Day, thus creating solidarity with workers regardless of citizenship status.

44. I am thinking here of the formative scholarship in the collection of essays in Eng and Kazanjian 2003; Eng and Han 2000; and Muñoz 1999, 2006.

45. Lowe 1996, 56.

46. The transnational scope of women's family obligations—including the flow of money, gifts, communication, and travel—is often debated, as this model conflicts with and reorders the nuclear basis of U.S. family forms. Since the 1990s, scholarship complicating the linear movement of migration has exploded into a plethora of analyses on transnational migration. While too numerous to document here, many draw from the work of Glick Schiller, Basch, and Blanc-Szanton 1992; Rouse 2004; and Ong 1999.

47. Posting on Planet-Love.com, May 9, 2003.

48. Personal e-mail interview, October 19, 2003.

49. Cabezas 2009; and Parreñas 2011.

50. Scott 1990.

51. E-mail interview, December 10, 2004. For scholarship on the emotional complexities for migrant women (and men) who leave families behind, see Hondagneu-Sotelo and Avila 2007; Dreby 2010; Parreñas 2005; and Yeoh and Lam 2009.

52. E-mail interview, LWL, May 15, 2008. Naomi Wolf similarly argues in her article "The Porn Myth" (2003) that pornography does not, as Andrea Dworkin argued in 1980s, necessarily lead to rape and violence against women but instead deadens men's libido toward "real women." Young women on college campuses similarly have said that they cannot compete with pornographic images of women on the Internet: "For how can a real woman—with pores and her own breasts and even sexual needs of her own . . . possibly compete with a cybervision of perfection, downloadable and extinguishable at will, who comes, so to speak,

utterly submissive and tailored to the consumer's least specification?" Wolf 2003.

53. This statement was made in Spanish by a woman who had a friend translate it for LWL, in relation to negative depictions of Latinas by a man who claimed that his Colombian wife left him for someone else after she realized he was not as rich as she thought he was.

54. I spend time detailing the plot of this film because it recycles a familiar U.S. plotline in the 1990s and into the present, far from ghettoized to one or two films, that exemplifies Latinas as moral bodies necessary for the reproduction of communities and nations. For example, in *A Walk in the Clouds* (1995), Latinas promise to rejuvenate a war-torn nation and the psychologically damaged soldiers who return. In *Fool's Rush In* (1997), the Latino family and Latina spirituality promise to save an Anglo-American culture plagued by capitalist relations of alienation.

Acharya, Arun Kumar. 2006. "International Migration and Trafficking of Mexican Women to the United States." In *Trafficking and the Global Sex Industry*, edited by Karen Beeks and Delila Amir, 21–32. Lanham, MD: Lexington Books.

Agustín, Laura María. 2007. *Sex at the Margins: Migration, Labour Markets and the Rescue Industry*. London: Zed Books.

Ahearn, Laura M. 2001. *Invitations to Love: Literacy, Love Letters, and Social Change in Nepal*. Ann Arbor: University of Michigan Press.

Alarcón, Norma. 1983. "Chicana's Feminist Literature: A Re-vision through Malintzín/or Malintzín: Putting Flesh Back on the Object." In *This Bridge Called My Back: Writings by Radical Women of Color*, edited by Cherríe Moraga and Gloria Anzaldúa, 124–142. New York: Kitchen Table Women of Color Press.

———. 1989. "Traddutora, Traditora: A Paradigmatic Figure of Chicana Feminism." *Cultural Critique* 13: 57–87.

Alarcón, Norma, Caren Kaplan, and Minoo Moallem. 1999. Introduction to *Between Woman and Nation: Nationalisms, Transnational Feminisms, and the State*, edited by Caren Kaplan, Norma Alarcón, and Minoo Moallem, 1–16. Durham: Duke University Press.

Alcalá, Rita Cano. 2001. "From Chingada to Chingona: La Malinche Redefined, or, A Long Line of Hermanas." *Aztlán* 26 (2): 33–61.

Aldama, Arturo J., and Naomi H. Quiñonez, eds. 2002. *Decolonial Voices: Chicana and Chicano Cultural Studies in the 21st Century*. Bloomington: Indiana University Press.

Alexander, M. Jacqui. 1994. "Not Just (Any) Body Can Be a Citizen: The Politics of Law, Sexuality and Postcoloniality in Trinidad and Tobago and the Bahamas." *Feminist Review* 48: 5–23.

———. 1997. "Erotic Autonomy as a Politics of Decolonization: An Anatomy of Feminist and State Practice in the Bahamas Tourist Economy." In *Feminist Genealogies, Colonial Legacies, Democratic Futures*, edited by M. Jacqui Alexander and Chandra Talpade Mohanty, 63–100. New York: Routledge.

———. 2005. *Pedagogies of Crossing: Meditations on Feminism, Sexual Politics, Memory, and the Sacred*. Durham: Duke University Press.

Alexander, M. Jacqui, and Chandra Talpade Mohanty. 1997. *Feminist Genealogies, Colonial Legacies, Democratic Futures*. New York: Routledge.

Allen, Robert C., ed. 1995. *To Be Continued . . . : Soap Operas around the World*. London: Routledge.

Almaguer, Tomás. 1994. *Racial Fault Lines: The Historical Origins of White Supremacy in California*. Berkeley: University of California Press.

Altman, Dennis. 2001. *Global Sex*. Chicago: University of Chicago Press.

Anagnost, Ann. 2000. "Scenes of Misrecognition: Maternal Citizenship in the Age of Transnational Adoption." *Positions* 8 (2): 389–421.

Anderson, Benedict. 1983. *Imagined Communities: Reflections on the Origin and Spread of Nationalism*. London: Verso.

Anderson, Michelle J. 1993. "A License to Abuse: The Impact of Conditional Status on Female Immigrants." *Yale Law Journal* 102 (6): 1401–1430.

Anzaldúa, Gloria. 1987. *Borderlands/La Frontera*. San Francisco: Aunt Lute Books.

Aparicio, Frances. 1998. *Listening to Salsa: Gender, Latin Popular Music, and Puerto Rican Cultures*. Middletown, CT: Wesleyan University Press.

Appadurai, Arjun. 1996. *Modernity at Large: Cultural Dimensions of Globalization*. Minneapolis: University of Minnesota Press.

Arrellano, Gustavo. 2010. "Make a Run for the Altar." *L.A. Weekly*, July 8. http://www.laweekly.com/2010-07-08/news/make-a-run-for-the-altar/.

Baitenmann, Helga, Victoria Chenaut, and Ann Varley, eds. 2007. *Decoding Gender: Law and Practice in Contemporary Mexico*. New Brunswick: Rutgers University Press.

Bala, Gary. 2006. "The Backdoor Law That Sabotages International Romance." Posted by d652v1311 on *BritishExpats.com*, February 5. http://britishexpats.com/forum/showthread.php?t=353168.

Bañales, Victoria M. 2005. "'The Face Value of Dreams': Gender, Race, Class, and the Politics of Cosmetic Surgery." In *Beyond the Frame: Women of Color and Visual Representation*, edited by Angela Davis and Neferti X. M. Tadiar, 131–152. New York: Palgrave Macmillan.

Banet-Weiser, Sarah. 1999. *The Most Beautiful Girl in the World: Beauty Pageants and National Identity*. Berkeley: University of California Press.

Barry Kathleen. 1979. *Female Sexual Slavery*. New York: NYU Press.

———. 1995. *The Prostitution of Sexuality: The Global Exploitation of Women*. New York: NYU Press.

Beauvoir, Simone de. 1989. *The Second Sex*. New York: Vintage Books.

Beck, Ulrich, and Elizabeth Beck-Gernsheim. 1995. *The Normal Chaos of Love*. Translated by Mark Ritter and Jane Wiebel. Cambridge, UK: Polity.

Behad, Ali. 2005. *A Forgetful Nation: On Immigration and Cultural Identity in the United States*. Durham: Duke University Press.

Behar, Ruth, and Deborah A. Gordon. 1995. *Women Writing Culture*. Berkeley: University of California Press.

Bell, David, and Jon Binnie. 2000. *The Sexual Citizen: Queer Politics*. Malden, MA: Blackwell.

Bend It like Beckham. 2002. Directed by Gurinder Chadha. Kintop Pictures. 112 minutes.

Berlant, Lauren. 1997. *The Queen of America Goes to Washington City: Essays on Sex and Citizenship*. Durham: Duke University Press.

———. 2008. *The Female Complaint: The Unfinished Business of Sentimentality in American Culture*. Durham: Duke University Press.

Berlant, Lauren, and Michael Warner. 1998. "Sex in Public." *Critical Inquiry* 24: 547–566.

Bernstein, Elizabeth. 2007a. "The Sexual Politics of the 'New Abolitionism.'" *Differences: A Journal of Feminist Cultural Studies* 18 (3): 128–151.

———. 2007b. *Temporarily Yours: Intimacy, Authenticity, and the Commerce of Sex*. Chicago: University of Chicago Press.

Bernstein, Nina. 2008. "An Agent, a Green Card, and a Demand for Sex." *New York Times*, March 21. http://www.nytimes.com/2008/03/21/nyregion/21immigrant.html?pagewanted=.

———. 2010a. "Do You Take This Immigrant?" *New York Times*, July 11. http://www.nytimes.com/2010/06/13/nyregion/13fraud.html.

———. 2010b. "Wed in 1993, but Stuck in Immigration Limbo." *New York Times*, June 13. http://www.nytimes.com/2010/06/14/nyregion/14marriage.html?ref=nyregion.

Bérubé, Myriam. 2005. "Country Profiles: Colombia: In the Crossfire." Migration Information Source. Nov. http://www.migrationinformation.org/Profiles/display.cfm?ID=344.

Betty la fea. 1999–2001. Fernando Gaitán. Directed by Mario Ribero. Radio Cadena Nacional.

Blum, Virginia. 2003. *Flesh Wounds: The Culture of Cosmetic Surgery*. Berkeley: University of California Press.

Bly, Robert. 1990. *Iron John: A Book about Men*. Reading, MA: Addison-Wesley.

Bogardus, Emory. 1923. *Essentials of Americanization*. Los Angeles: University of Southern California Press.

Boris, Eileen, Stephanie Gilmore, and Rhacel Parreñas. 2010. "Sexual Labors: Interdisciplinary Perspectives toward Sex as Work." *Sexualities* 13 (2): 131–137.

Borstein, Kate. 1995. *Gender Outlaw: On Men, Women, and the Rest of Us*. New York: Vintage Books.

Bourdieu, Pierre. 1984. *Distinction: A Social Critique of the Judgment of Taste*. London: Polity.

Bouvier, Virginia Marie. 2004. *Women and the Conquest of California, 1542–1840: Codes of Silence*. Tucson: University of Arizona Press.

Brandzel, Amy L. 2005. "Queering Citizenship? Same-Sex Marriage and the State." *GLQ* 11 (2): 171–204.

Brennan, Denise. 2004. *What's Love Got to Do with It? Transnational Desires and Sex Tourism in the Dominican Republic*. Durham: Duke University Press.

Briggs, Laura. 2002. *Reproducing Empire: Race, Sex, Science, and U.S. Imperialism in Puerto Rico*. Berkeley: University of California Press.

Cabezas, Amalia. 2009. *Economies of Desire: Sex and Tourism in Cuba and the Dominican Republic*. Philadelphia: Temple University Press.

Calvo, Luz. 2001. "Border Fantasies: Sexual Anxieties and Political Passions in the Mexico-US Borderlands." Ph.D. diss., University of California, Santa Cruz.

Candelaria, Cordelia. 1980. "La Malinche, Feminist Prototypes." *Frontiers* 5 (2): 1–6.

Cantú, Lionel, Jr., with Nancy A. Naples and Salvador Vidal Ortiz. 2009. *The Sexuality of Migration: Border Crossings and Mexican Immigrant Men*. New York: NYU Press.

Cantwell, Maria. 2004. "Proposed Law Would Regulate International Marriage Brokers." Statement of Senator Maria Cantwell, Foreign Relations Committee. July 14. Distributed by the Bureau of International Information Programs, U.S. Department of State. http://usinfo.org/wf-archive/2004/040714/epf307.htm.

Carrier, Joseph. 1995. *De Los Otros: Intimacy and Homosexuality among Mexican Men*. New York: Columbia University Press.

Carrillo, Héctor. 2002. *The Night Is Young: Sexuality in Mexico in the Time of AIDS*. Chicago: University of Chicago Press.

Cassanova, Erynn Masi. 2004. "'No Ugly Women': Concepts of Race and Beauty among Adolescent Women in Ecuador." *Gender and Society* 18 (3): 287–308.

Cepeda, María Elena. 2003. "Shakira as the Idealized Transnational Citizen: A Case Study of Colombianidad in Transition." *Latino Studies* 1: 211–232.

Chain of Love. 2001. Directed by Marije Meerman. Icarus Films. 50 minutes.

Chang, Grace. 2000. *Disposable Domestics: Immigrant Women Workers in the Global Economy*. Cambridge, MA: South End.

Chapkis, Wendy. 1997. *Live Sex Acts: Women Performing Erotic Labor*. New York: Routledge.

———. 2005. "Soft Glove, Punishing Fist: The Trafficking Victims Protection Act of 2000." In *Regulating Sex: The Politics of Intimacy and Identity*, edited by Elizabeth Bernstein and Laurie Schaffner, 51–66. New York: Routledge.

Chaudhuri, Nupur, and Margaret Strobel, eds. 1992. *Western Women and Imperialism: Complicity and Resistance*. Bloomington: Indiana University Press.

Chauncey, George. 2004. *Why Marriage? The History Shaping Today's Debate over Gay Marriage.* New York: Basic Books.

Chavez, Leo R. 2001. *Covering Immigration: Popular Images and the Politics of the Nation.* Berkeley: University of California Press.

———. 2004. "A Glass Half Empty: Latin Reproduction and Public Discourse." *Human Organization* 63 (2): 173–188.

Chávez-García, Miroslava. 2004. *Negotiating Conquest: Gender and Power in California, 1770s to 1880s.* Tucson: University of Arizona Press.

Choy, Catherine Ceniza. 2003. *Empire of Care: Nursing and Migration in Filipino American History.* Durham: Duke University Press.

Clifford, James, and George E. Marcus, eds. 1986. *Writing Culture: The Poetics and Politics of Ethnography.* Berkeley: University of California Press.

Collier, Jane Fishburne. 1997. *From Duty to Desire: Remaking Families in a Spanish Village.* Princeton: Princeton University Press.

"Colombia Is Passion." n.d. Official website. http://www.colombia.travel/en/international-tourist//colombia/colombia-is-passion.

Connell, R. W. 1995. *Masculinities.* Berkeley: University of California Press.

Constable, Nicole. 2003. *Romance on a Global Stage: Pen Pals, Virtual Ethnography, and "Mail Order" Marriages.* Berkeley: University of California Press.

———, ed. 2005. *Cross-Border Marriages: Gender and Mobility in Transnational Asia.* Philadelphia: University of Pennsylvania Press.

Coontz, Stephanie. 1992. *The Way We Never Were: American Families and the Nostalgia Trap.* New York: Basic Books.

———. 2005. *Marriage, a History: From Obedience to Intimacy or How Love Conquered Marriage.* New York: Viking.

Cordera Campos, Rolando, and Enrique González Tiburcio. 1989. "Percances y damnificados de la crisis economica" [Mishaps and Victims of the Economic Crisis]. In *México: El reclamo democratico*, edited by Rolando Cordera Campos et al. México, DF: Siglo Veintiuno Editores.

Cott, Nancy. 1998. "Marriage and Women's Citizenship in the United States, 1830–1934." *American Historical Review* 103 (5): 1440–1474.

———. 2000. *Public Vows: A History of Marriage and the Nation.* Cambridge: Harvard University Press, 2000.

Coutin, Susan Bibler. 2000. *Legalizing Moves: Salvadoran Immigrants' Struggle for U.S. Residency.* Ann Arbor: University of Michigan Press.

———. 2003. "Suspension of Deportation Hearings and Measures of 'Americanness.'" *Journal of Latin American Anthropology* 8 (2): 58–94.

Cowboy del Amor. 2006. Directed by Michèle Ohayon. Documentary. Emerging Pictures. 86 minutes.

Davidson, Julia O'Connell, and Jacqueline Sánchez Taylor. 2005. "Travel and Taboo: Heterosexual Sex Tourism in the Caribbean." In *Regulating Sex: The*

Politics of Intimacy and Identity, edited by Elizabeth Bernstein and Laurie Schaffner, 83–99. New York: Routledge.

Davis, Kathy. 1995. *Reshaping the Female Body: The Dilemma of Cosmetic Surgery*. New York: Routledge.

———. 2003. *Dubious Equalities and Embodied Differences: Cultural Studies on Cosmetic Surgery*. New York: Rowman and Littlefield.

Del Castillo, Adelaida R. 1974. "Malintzín Tenepal: A Preliminary Look into a New Perspective." *Encuentro Femenil* 1 (2): 58–77.

Domínguez-Ruvalcaba, Héctor. 2007. *Modernity and the Nation in Mexican Representations of Masculinity: From Sensuality to Bloodshed*. New York: Palgrave Macmillan.

Dreby, Joanna. 2010. *Divided by Borders: Mexican Migrants and Their Children*. Berkeley: University of California Press.

Dunaway, Wilma. 2003. *The African-American Family in Slavery and Emancipation*. Cambridge: Cambridge University Press.

Edmonds, Alexander. 2010. *Pretty Modern: Beauty, Sex and Plastic Surgery in Brazil*. Durham: Duke University Press.

Ehrenreich, Barbara, and Arlie Russell Hochschild, eds. 2002a. *Global Woman: Nannies, Maids, and Sex Workers in the New Economy*. New York: Metropolitan Books.

———. 2002b. Introduction to *Global Woman: Nannies, Maids, and Sex Workers in the New Economy*, edited by Barbara Ehrenreich and Arlie Russell Hochschild, 1–13. New York: Metropolitan Books.

Eng, David L., and Shinhee Han. 2000. "A Dialogue on Racial Melancholia." *Psychoanalytic Dialogues* 10: 667–700.

Eng, David L., and David Kazanjian, eds. 2003. *Loss: The Politics of Mourning*. Berkeley: University of California Press.

Enloe, Cynthia. 1989. *Bananas, Beaches, and Bases: Making Feminist Sense of International Politics*. Berkeley: University of California Press.

Enss, Chris. 2005. *Hearts West: True Stories of Mail-Order Brides on the Frontier*. Guilford, CT: TwoDot.

Escobar, J. Samuel. 1994. "The Church in Latin America after Five Hundred Years." In *New Face of the Church in Latin America: Between Tradition and Change*, edited by Guillermo Cook, 21–37. New York: Orbis Books.

Espín, Oliva M. 1999. *Women Crossing Boundaries: A Psychology of Immigration and Transformations of Sexuality*. New York: Routledge.

Faier, Lieba. 2007. "Filipina Migrants in Rural Japan and Their Professions of Love." *American Ethnologist* 34 (1): 148–162.

———. 2009. *Intimate Encounters: Filipina Women Remaking Rural Japan*. Berkeley: University of California Press.

Falcón, Sylvanna M. 2007. "Rape as a Weapon of War: Militarized Rape at the U.S.-Mexico Border." In *Women and Migration in the U.S.-Mexico*

Borderlands: A Reader, edited by Denise A. Segura and Patricia Zavella, 203–223. Durham: Duke University Press.

Faludi, Susan. 1999. *Stiffed: The Betrayal of the American Man*. New York: HarperCollins.

Farquhar, Judith. 2002. *Appetites: Food and Sex in Post-Socialist China*. Durham: Duke University Press.

Farrer, James. 2002. *Opening Up: Youth Sex Culture and Market Reform in Shanghai*. Chicago: University of Chicago Press.

Fernandez-Kelly, Maria Patricia. 1983. *For We Are Sold, I and My People: Women and Industry on Mexico's Frontier*. Albany: SUNY Press.

Fools Rush In. 1997. Directed by Andy Tennant. Columbia Pictures. 109 minutes.

Forero, Juan. 2001. "Out There: Colombia; Who's the Fairest of Them All?" *New York Times*, November 4.

Foucault, Michel. (1978) 1990. *The History of Sexuality, Vol. 1: An Introduction*. Translated by Robert Hurley. London: Penguin.

———. 1988. *The History of Sexuality, Vol. 3: The Care of the Self*. London: Penguin.

Fragomen, Austin T., Jr. 1997. "The Illegal Immigration Reform and Immigrant Responsibility Act of 1996: An Overview." *International Migration Review* 31 (2): 438–460.

Franco, Jean. 1989. *Plotting Women: Gender and Representation in Mexico*. New York: Columbia University Press.

Frank, Katherine. 2002. *G-Strings and Sympathy: Strip Club Regulars and Male Desire*. Durham: Duke University Press.

Freeman, Carla. 2007. "Neoliberalism and the Marriage of Reputation and Respectability: Entrepreneurship and the Barbadian Middle Class." In *Love and Globalization: Transformations of Intimacy in the Contemporary World*, edited by Mark B. Padilla, Jennifer Hirsch, Miguel Muñoz-Laboy, Robert E. Seber, and Richard G. Parker, 3–37. Nashville: Vanderbilt University Press.

Fregoso, Rosa-Linda. 2003. *MeXicana Encounters: The Making of Social Identities on the Borderlands*. Berkeley: University of California Press.

———. 2006. "We Want Them Alive! The Politics and Culture of Human Rights." *Social Identities* 12 (2): 109–138.

Fregoso, Rosa-Linda, and Cynthia Bejarano. 2010. *Terrorizing Women: Feminicide in the Americas*. Durham: Duke University Press.

Friedan, Betty. 1963. *The Feminine Mystique*. New York: Norton.

Fries, Lorena, and Verónica Matus. 1999. *El derecho: Trama y conjura patriarcal*. Santiago, Chile: LOM editions / La Morada.

Fusco, Coco. 1996. "Hustling for Dollars." *Ms.*, September–October, 62.

———. 1997. "Adventures in the Skin Trade." *Utne Reader*, July–August, 67–69, 107–109.

García Canclini, Nestor. 1997. "Will There Be Latin American Cinema in the Year 2000? Visual Culture in a Postnational Era." In *Framing Latin American Cinema: Contemporary Critical Approaches*, edited by Ann Marie Stock, 246–258. Minneapolis: University of Minnesota Press.

———. 2001. *Consumers and Citizens: Globalization and Multicultural Conflicts*. Minneapolis: University of Minnesota Press.

Gender and Cultural Citizenship Inter-University Working Group. 2009. "Collectivity and Comparativity: A Feminist Approach to Citizenship." In *Gendered Citizenships: Transnational Perspectives, Knowledge Production, Political Action, and Culture*, edited by Kia Lilly Caldwell, Kathleen Coll, Tracy Fisher, Renya Ramirez, and Lok Siu, 1–18. New York: Palgrave Macmillan.

Giddens, Anthony. 1990. *The Consequences of Modernity*. Stanford: Stanford University Press.

———. 1992. *The Transformation of Intimacy: Sexuality, Love and Eroticism in Modern Societies*. Cambridge, UK: Polity.

Gilman, Sander L. 1985. "Black Bodies, White Bodies: Toward an Iconography of Female Sexuality in Late Nineteenth-Century Art, Medicine, and Literature." *Critical Inquiry* 12 (1): 204–242.

———. 1999. *Making the Body Beautiful: A Cultural History of Aesthetic Surgery*. Princeton: Princeton University Press.

Glenn, Evelyn Nakano. 1986. *Issei, Nisei, War Bride: Three Generations of Japanese American Women in Domestic Service*. Philadelphia: Temple University Press.

Glick Schiller, Nina, Linda Basch, and Cristina Blanc-Szanton, eds. 1992. *Towards a Transnational Perspective on Migration: Race, Class, Ethnicity, and Nationalism Reconsidered*. New York: New York Academy of Sciences.

Glodava, Mila, and Richard Onizuka. 1994. *Mail-Order Brides: Women for Sale*. Fort Collins, CO: Alaken.

González, Deena J. 1999. *Refusing the Favor: The Spanish-Mexican Women of Santa Fe, 1820–1880*. New York: Oxford University Press.

González-López, Gloria. 2005. *Erotic Journeys: Mexican Immigrants and Their Sex Lives*. Berkeley: University of California Press.

Greenblatt, Stephen. 1989. "Towards a Poetics of Culture." In *The New Historicism*, edited by H. Aram Vesser, 1–14. New York: Routledge.

Grewal, Inderpal. 2005. *Transnational America: Feminisms, Diasporas, Neoliberalisms*. Durham: Duke University Press.

Guarnizo, Luis Eduardo, Arturo Ignacio Sánchez, and Elizabeth M. Roach. 1999. "Mistrust, Fragmented Solidarity, and Transnational Migration: Colombians in New York City and Los Angeles." *Ethnic and Racial Studies* 22 (2): 367–396.

Gutiérrez, Elena R. 2008. *Fertile Matters: The Politics of Mexican-Origin Women's Reproduction*. Austin: University of Texas Press.

Gutmann, Matthew C. 1996. *The Meanings of Macho: Being a Man in Mexico City*. Berkeley: University of California Press.

Guy, Donna J. 1991. *Sex and Danger in Buenos Aires: Prostitution, Family, and Nation in Argentina*. Lincoln: University of Nebraska Press.

Haag, Pamela. 1999. *Consent: Sexual Rights and the Transformation of American Liberalism*. Ithaca: Cornell University Press.

Haiken, Elizabeth. 1997. *Venus Envy: A History of Cosmetic Surgery*. Baltimore: Johns Hopkins University Press.

Hanchard, Michael. 1994. "Black Cinderella? Race and the Public Sphere in Brazil." *Public Culture* 7: 165–185.

Haney López, Ian F. 1996. *White by Law: The Legal Constructions of Race*. New York: NYU Press.

Haraway, Donna. 1991. *Simians, Cyborgs, and Women: The Reinvention of Nature*. New York: Routledge.

Hardy, Michael. 2004. "Mediated Relationships: Authenticity and the Possibility of Romance." *Information, Communication, and Society* 7 (2): 207–222.

Harvey, David. 1989. *The Condition of Postmodernity: An Enquiry into the Origins of Cultural Change*. Oxford, UK: Blackwell.

Heilbrun, Carolyn G. 1998. *Writing a Woman's Life*. New York: Norton.

Hennessy, Rosemary. 2000. *Profit and Pleasure: Sexual Identities in Late Capitalism*. New York: Routledge.

Hirsch, Jennifer S. 2003. *A Courtship after Marriage: Sexuality and Love in Mexican Transnational Families*. Berkeley: University of California Press.

Hirsch, Jennifer S., and Holly Wardlow, eds. 2006. *Modern Loves: The Anthropology of Romantic Courtship and Companionate Marriage*. Ann Arbor: University of Michigan Press.

Hochschild, Arlie Russell. 1994. *The Second Shift*. New York: Avon Books.

———. 1997. *The Time Bind: When Work Becomes Home and Home Becomes Work*. New York: Metropolitan Books.

———. 2002. "Love and Gold." In *Global Woman: Nannies, Maids, and Sex Workers in the New Economy*, edited by Barbara Ehrenreich and Arlie Russell Hochschild, 15–30. New York: Metropolitan Books.

———. 2003. *The Commercialization of Intimate Life: Notes from Home and Work*. Berkeley: University of California Press.

Hodes, Martha. 1999. *Sex, Love, Race: Crossing Boundaries in North American History*. New York: NYU Press.

Holliday, Ruth, and Jacqueline Sánchez Taylor. 2006. "Aesthetic Surgery as a False Beauty." *Feminist Theory* 7 (2): 179–195.

Hondagneu-Sotelo, Pierrette. 1994. *Gendered Transitions: Mexican Experiences of Immigration*. Berkeley: University of California Press.

———. 2001. *Doméstica: Immigrant Workers Cleaning and Caring in the Shadows of Affluence*. Berkeley: University of California.

Hondagneu-Sotelo, Pierrette, and Ernestine Avila. 2007. "'I'm Here, but I'm There': The Meanings of Latina Transnational Motherhood." In *Women and Migration in the U.S.-Mexico Borderlands: A Reader*, edited by Denise A. Segura and Patricia Zavella, 388–412. Durham: Duke University Press.

Hondagneu-Sotelo, Pierrette, and Michael A. Messner. 1994. "Gender Displays and Men's Power: The 'New Man' and the Mexican Immigrant Man." In *Theorizing Masculinities*, edited by Harry Brod and Michael Kaufman, 200–218. Thousand Oaks, CA: Sage.

Honig, Bonnie. 2001. *Democracy and the Foreigner*. Princeton: Princeton University Press.

hooks, bell. 2000. *All About Love: New Visions*. New York: William Morrow.

Hooper, Charlotte. 2001. *Manly States: Masculinities, International Relations, and Gender Politics*. New York: Columbia University Press.

Horsman, Reginald. 1981. *Race and Manifest Destiny: The Origins of American Racial Anglo-Saxonism*. Cambridge: Harvard University Press.

Illouz, Eva. 1997. *Consuming the Romantic Utopia: Love and the Cultural Contradictions of Capitalism*. Berkeley: University of California Press.

———. 2007. *Cold Intimacies: The Making of Emotional Capitalism*. Malden, MA: Polity.

Immigration and Naturalization Service, U.S. Department of Justice. 1978–2001. *Statistical Yearbook of the Immigration and Naturalization Service*. Washington, DC: The Service.

Inda, Xavier Jonathan. 2002. "Biopower, Reproduction, and the Migrant Woman's Body." In *Decolonial Voices: Chicana and Chicano Cultural Studies in the 21st Century*, edited by Arturo J. Aldama and Naomi Quiñonez, 98–112. Bloomington: Indiana University Press.

The Internet Bride. 2004. Directed Eleanor Ford. Granada Centre for Visual Anthropology. MA project in Visual Anthropology, University of Manchester, October.

Jacobson, Matthew Frye. 1998. *Whiteness of a Different Color: European Immigrants and the Alchemy of Race*. Cambridge: Harvard University Press.

Johnson, Ericka. 2007. *Dreaming of a Mail-Order Husband: Russian-American Internet Romance*. Durham: Duke University Press.

Johnson, Kevin R., and Kristina L. Burrows. 2003. "Struck by Lighting? Interracial Intimacy and Racial Justice." *Human Rights Quarterly* 25 (2): 528–566.

Kaplan, Amy. 2002. *The Anarchy of Empire in the Making of U.S. Culture*. Cambridge: Harvard University Press.

Kaplan, Caren, Norma Alarcón, and Minoo Moallem, eds. 1999. *Between Woman and Nation: Nationalisms, Transnational Feminisms, and the State*. Durham: Duke University Press.

Kapur, Ratna. 2005. *Erotic Justice: Law and the New Politics of Postcolonialism*. London: Glasshouse.

Katz, Alfred H. 1993. *Self-Help in America: A Social Movement Perspective.* New York: Twayne.

Kaw, Eugenia. 1993. "Medicalization of Racial Features: Asian American Women and Cosmetic Surgery." *Medical Anthropology Quarterly*, New Series, 7 (1): 74–89.

Keijzer, Benno de. 1999. "Los derechos sexuales y reproductivos desde la dimensión de la masculinidad." In *México diverso y desigual: Enfoques socio-demográficos: V Reunión de investigación sociodemográfica en México*, edited by Beatriz Figueroa Campos, 307–318. México, DF: El Colegio de México.

Kelsky, Karen. 2001. *Women on the Verge: Japanese Women, Western Dreams.* Durham: Duke University Press.

Kempadoo, Kamala, ed. 1999. *Sun, Sex, and Gold: Tourism and Sex Work in the Caribbean.* New York: Rowman and Littlefield.

———. 2004. *Sexing the Caribbean: Gender, Race, and Sexual Labor.* New York: Routledge.

———. 2005. "From Moral Panic to Global Justice: Changing Perspectives on Trafficking." In *Trafficking and Prostitution Reconsidered: New Perspectives on Migration, Sex Work, and Human Rights*, edited by Kamala Kempadoo, Jyoti Sanghera, and Bandana Pattanaik, vii–xxxiv. Boulder, CO: Paradigm.

Kempadoo, Kamala, and Jo Doezema, eds. 1998. *Global Sex Workers: Rights, Resistance, and Redefinition.* New York: Routledge.

Kendall, Lori. 2002. *Hanging Out in the Virtual Pub: Masculinities and Relationships Online.* Berkeley: University of California Press.

Kerber, Linda K. 1998. *No Constitutional Right to Be Ladies: Women and the Obligations of Citizenship.* New York: Hill and Wang.

Kirk, Robin. 2003. *More Terrible than Death: Massacres, Drugs, and America's War in Colombia.* New York: Public Affairs.

Kline, Wendy. 2001. *Building a Better Race: Gender, Sexuality, and Eugenics from the Turn of the Century to the Baby Boom.* Berkeley: University of California Press.

Kolodny, Annette. 1984. *The Land before Her: Fantasy and Experience of the American Frontiers, 1630–1860.* Chapel Hill: University of North Carolina Press.

Kulick, Don. 1998. *Travesti: Sex, Gender, and Culture among Brazilian Trans-gendered Prostitutes.* Chicago: University of Chicago Press.

La Corona. 2008. Directed by Amanda Micheli and Isabel Vega. Runaway Films and Vega Films. 40 minutes.

Lagarde y de los Ríos, Marcela. 2005. *Para mis socias de la vida: Claves feministas para el poderío y la autonomía de las mujeres, los liderazgos entrañables y las negociaciones en el amor.* San Cristobal, Argentina: Hora y Horas.

———. 2010. "Preface: Feminist Keys for Understanding Feminicide: Theoretical, Political, and Legal Construction." In *Terrorizing Women: Feminicide in the Américas*, edited by Rosa-Linda Fregoso and Cynthia Bejarano, xi–xxvi. Durham: Duke University Press.

Laughlin, Meg. 1997. "Finding Love in Colombia." *Miami Herald*, November 14.

Leñero Otero, Luis. 1994. "Los varones ante la planificación familiar." In *Maternidad sin riesgos en México*, edited by María del Carmen Elu y Ana Langer. México, DF: Instituto Mexicano de Estudios Sociales.

LeVine, Sarah, in collaboration with Clara Sutherland Correa. 1993. *Dolor y alegría: Women and Social Change in Mexico*. Madison: University of Wisconsin Press.

Lévi-Strauss, Claude. 1969. *The Elementary Structures of Kinship*. Boston: Beacon.

Limón, José E. 1998. *American Encounters: Greater Mexico, the United States, and the Erotics of Culture*. Boston: Beacon.

Lobo, Gregory J. 2005. "Rearticulaciones colombianas: Raza, belleza, hegemonía" [Colombian Rearticulations: Race, Beauty, Hegemony]. In *Pasarela paralela: Scenarios de la estética y el poder en los reinados de belleza* [Parallel Catwalks: Scenes of the Aesthetics and Power in Beauty Pageants], edited by Chloe Rutter-Jensen, 57–67. Bogotá, Colombia: Editorial Pontificia Universidad Javeriana.

Lone Star. 1996. Directed by John Sayles. Columbia Pictures. 135 minutes.

López, Ana. 1995. "Our Welcomed Guests: Telenovelas in Latin America." In *To Be Continued . . . : Soap Operas around the World*, edited by Robert Allen, 256–284. London: Routledge.

Love for Rent. 2006. Directed by Michael Terence. MiamiLA Entertainment. 96 minutes.

Lowe, Lisa. 1996. *Immigrant Acts: On Asian American Cultural Politics*. Durham: Duke University Press.

Lubiano, Wahneema. 1991. "Shuckin' Off the African-American Native Other: What's 'Po-Mo' Got to Do with It?" *Cultural Critique* 18: 149–186.

Lugo-Lugo, Carmen R., and Mary K. Bloodsworth-Lugo, eds. 2009. *A New Kind of Containment: The War on Terror, Race, and Sexuality*. Amsterdam: Rodopi.

Lugones, Maria. 2010. "Toward a Decolonial Feminism." In "Feminist Legacies / Feminist Futures: The 25th Anniversary Issue," special issue, *Hypatia* 25 (4): 742–759.

Lugones, Maria, and Elizabeth V. Spelman. 1983. "Have We Got a Theory for You!" *Women's Studies International Forum* 6 (6): 573–581.

Luhmann, Niklas. 1986. *Love as Passion: The Codification of Intimacy*. Cambridge, UK: Polity.

Luibhéid, Eithne. 2002. *Entry Denied: Controlling Sexuality at the Border*. Minneapolis: University of Minnesota Press.

———. 2005a. "Heteronormativity, Responsibility, and Neo-liberal Governance in U.S. Immigration Control." In *Passing Lines: Sexuality and*

Immigration, edited by Brad Epps, Keja Valens, Bill Johnson González, 69–101. Cambridge: Harvard University Press.

———. 2005b. "Introduction: Queering Migration and Citizenship." In *Queer Migrations: Sexuality, U.S. Citizenship, and Border Crossings*, edited by Eithne Luibhéid and Lionel Cantú, ix–xlvi. Minneapolis: University of Minnesota Press.

———. 2008. "Sexuality, Migration, and the Shifting Line between Legal and Illegal Status." *GLQ* 14 (2–3): 289–315.

Luibhéid, Eithne, and Lionel Cantú, eds. 2005. *Queer Migrations: Sexuality, U.S. Citizenship, and Border Crossings*. Minneapolis: University of Minnesota Press.

MacKinnon, Catharine. 1987. *Feminism Unmodified: Discourses on Life and Law*. Cambridge: Harvard University Press.

Makow, Henry. 2000. *A Long Way to Go for a Date*. Winnipeg, Canada: Silas Green.

Manalansan, Martin F., IV. 2003. *Global Divas: Filipino Gay Men in the Diaspora*. Durham: Duke University Press.

Martin, Emily. 1998. "Fluid Bodies, Managed Nature." In *Remaking Reality: Nature at the Millennium*, edited by Bruce Braun and Noel Castree, 64–83. London: Routledge.

Martinez, Margarita. 2001. "Colombian Soap Opera with Ugly Duckling Heroine Winding Down." Associated Press. *LubbockOnline*, April 24. http://lubbockonline.com/stories/042401/ent_042401021.shtml.

———. 2005. "Colombians under Spell of TV Ugly Duckling." *Daily Camera*, November 5. http://www.thedailycamera.com/entertainment/television/a257252a.html.

Massumi, Brian. 2002. *Parables for the Virtual: Movement, Affect, Sensation*. Durham: Duke University Press.

Mayer, Tamar. 2000. *Gender Ironies of Nationalism: Sexing the Nation*. London: Routledge.

Mayorga, Laura, and Pilar Velásquez. 1999. "Bleak Pasts, Bleak Futures: Life Paths of Thirteen Young Prostitutes in Cartagena, Colombia." In *Sun, Sex, and Gold: Tourism and Sex Work in the Caribbean*, edited by Kamala Kempadoo, 157–182. New York: Rowman and Littlefield.

McClintock, Anne. 1995. *Imperial Leather: Race, Gender, and Sexuality in the Colonial Contest*. New York: Routledge.

McRae, Shannon. 1996. "Coming Apart at the Seams: Sex, Text, and the Virtual Body." In *Wired Women: Gender and New Realities in Cyberspace*, edited by Lynn Cherny and Elizabeth Reba Weise, 242–264. Seattle: Seal.

Menjívar, Cecilia. 2000. *Fragmented Ties: Salvadoran Immigrant Networks in America*. Berkeley: University of California Press.

Messner, Michael A. 1997. *Politics of Masculinities: Men in Movements*. Thousand Oaks, CA: Sage.

Miles, Tiya. 2005. *Ties That Bind: The Story of an Afro-Cherokee Family in Slavery and Freedom*. Berkeley: University of California Press.

Modleski, Tania. 1982. *Loving with a Vengeance: Mass-Produced Fantasies for Women*. Hamden, CT: Archon Books.

Mohanty, Chandra Talpade. 1991. "Under Western Eyes: Western Scholarship and Colonial Discourses." In *Third World Women and the Politics of Feminism*, edited by Chandra Talpade Mohanty, Ann Russo, and Lourdes Torres, 51–80. Bloomington: Indiana University Press.

———. 2003. *Feminism without Borders: Decolonizing Theory, Practicing Solidarity*. Durham: Duke University Press.

Moore, Henrietta. 1994. *A Passion for Difference: Essays in Anthropology and Gender*. Bloomington: Indiana University Press.

Moran, Rachel F. 2001. *Interracial Intimacy: The Regulation of Race and Romance*. Chicago: University of Chicago Press.

Morrison, Toni. 1987. *Beloved: A Novel*. New York: Knopf.

Muñoz, Jose Esteban. 1999. *Disidentifications: Queers of Color and the Performance of Politics*. Minneapolis: University of Minnesota Press.

———. 2006. "Feeling Brown, Feeling Down: Latina Affect, the Performativity of Race, and the Depressive Position." *Signs: Journal of Women in Culture and Society* 31 (3): 675–688.

Murdock, Donna. 2008. *When Women Have Wings: Feminism and Development in Medellín, Colombia*. Ann Arbor: University of Michigan Press.

Nakamura, Lisa. 2002. *Cybertypes: Race, Ethnicity, and Identity on the Internet*. New York: Routledge.

Nathan, Debbie. 1999. "Work, Sex, and Danger in Ciudad Juárez." *NACLA* 33 (3): 24–30.

Negrón-Muntaner, Frances. 1997. "Jennifer's Butt." *Aztlán: A Journal of Chicano Studies* 22 (2): 181–195.

———. 2003. "Jennifer's Butt." In *Perspectives on Las Américas: A Reader in Culture, History, and Representation*, edited by Matthew C. Gutmann, Félix V. Matos Rodríguez, Lynn Stephen, and Patricia Zavella, 297–298. Malden, MA: Blackwell.

"The New Face of America: How Immigrants Are Reshaping America." 1993. *Time*, November 18. http://www.time.com/magazine/0,9263,7601931118,00.html.

Newman, Louise. 1999. *White Women's Rights: The Racial Origins of Feminism in the United States*. New York: Oxford University Press.

Nguyen, Mimi. 2003. "Queer Cyborgs and New Mutants: Race, Sex, and Technology in Asian American Cultural Productions." In *AsiaAmerica.Net: Ethnicity, Nationalism, and Cyberspace*, edited by Rachael C. Lee and Sau-Ling Cynthia Wong, 281–305. New York: Routledge.

Noble, David W. 2002. *Death of a Nation: American Culture and the End of Exceptionalism*. Minneapolis: University of Minnesota Press.

Ochoa, Marcia. *Queen for a Day: Transformistas, Misses, and Mass Media in Venezuela*. Durham: Duke University Press, forthcoming.

O'Dougherty, Maureen. 2002. *Consumption Intensified: The Politics of Middle-Class Daily Life in Brazil*. Durham: Duke University Press.

Oliviera, Orlandina de. 1990. "Empleo feminino en México en tiempos de recesión económica: Tendencia recientes." In *Mujer y crisis: Respuestas ante la recessión*, edited by Neuma Aguiar, Lourdes Arizpe S., et al. Caracas, Venezuela: Editorial Nueva Sociedad.

Ong, Aihwa. 1999. *Flexible Citizenship: The Cultural Logics of Transnationality*. Durham: Duke University Press.

———. 2006. *Neoliberalism as Exception: Mutations in Citizenship and Sovereignty*. Durham: Duke University Press.

Padilla, Mark B., Jennifer S. Hirsch, Miguel Muñoz-Laboy, Robert E. Sember, and Richard G. Parker. 2007. "Introduction: Cross-Cultural Reflections on an Intimate Intersection." In *Love and Globalization: Transformations of Intimacy in the Contemporary World*, edited by Mark B. Padilla, Jennifer S. Hirsch, Miguel Muñoz-Laboy, Robert E. Sember, and Richard G. Parker. Nashville: Vanderbilt University Press.

Paper Dolls / Bubot Nayer. 2006. Directed by Tomer Heymann. Heymann Brother Films. 80 minutes.

Parker, Richard G. 1991. *Bodies, Pleasures, and Passions: Sexual Culture in Contemporary Brazil*. Boston: Beacon.

Parreñas, Rhacel Salazar. 2001. *Servants of Globalization: Women, Migration, and Domestic Work*. Stanford: Stanford University Press.

———. 2005. *Children of Global Migration: Transnational Families and Gendered Woes*. Stanford: Stanford University.

———. 2011. *Illicit Flirtations: Labor, Migration, and Sex Trafficking in Tokyo*. Stanford: Stanford University Press.

Pascoe, Peggy. 2009. *What Comes Naturally: Miscegenation Law and the Making of Race in America*. Oxford: Oxford University Press.

Paz, Octavio. 1961. *The Labyrinth of Solitude: Life and Thought in Mexico*. Translated by Lysander Kemp. New York: Grove.

Pérez, Emma. 1991. "Sexuality and Discourse: Notes from a Chicana Survivor." In *Chicana Lesbians: The Girls Our Mothers Warned Us About*, edited by Carla Trujillo, 159–184. Berkeley, CA: Third Woman.

———. 1999. *The Decolonial Imaginary: Writing Chicanas into History*. Bloomington: Indiana University Press.

Pew Research Center (in association with *Time* magazine). 2010. "The Decline of Marriage and Rise of New Families." November 18. http://www.pewsocialtrends.org/2010/11/18/the-decline-of-marriage-and-rise-of-new-families/ (accessed April 30, 2012).

Popenoe, David. 1996. *Life without Father: Compelling New Evidence That Fatherhood and Marriage Are Indispensable for the Good of Children and Society.* Cambridge: Harvard University Press.

Povinelli, Elizabeth. 2006. *The Empire of Love: Toward a Theory of Intimacy, Genealogy, and Carnality.* Durham: Duke University Press.

Pratt, Timothy. 2000. "An Ugly Duckling Steals Colombians' Hearts." *Christian Science Monitor,* January 25. http://csmonitor.com/cgi-bin/durable-Redirect.pl?/durable/2000/01/25/ p7s1.html.

Prieur, Annick. 1998. *Mema's House, Mexico City: On Transvestites, Queens, and Machos.* Chicago: University of Chicago Press.

Pruitt, Deborah, and Suzanne LaFont. 1995. "For Love or Money: Romance Tourism in Jamaica." *Annals of Tourism Research* 22 (2): 422–440.

Puar, Jasbir. 2007. *Terrorist Assemblages: Homonationalism in Queer Times.* Durham: Duke University Press.

Radway, Janice A. 1984. *Reading the Romance: Women, Patriarchy, and Popular Culture.* Chapel Hill: University of North Carolina Press.

Rae, Karen L. 1988. "Alienating Sham Marriages for Tougher Immigration Penalties: Congress Enacts the Marriage Fraud Act." *Pepperdine Law Review* 15 (1): 181–205.

Rafael, Vincent. 2000. *White Love and Other Events in Filipino History.* Durham: Duke University Press.

———. 2005. *The Promise of the Foreign: Nationalism and the Technics of Translation in the Spanish Philippines.* Durham: Duke University Press.

Rebhun, L. A. 1999. *The Heart Is Unknown Country: Love in the Changing Economy of Northeast Brazil.* Stanford: Stanford University Press.

Reddy, Chandan. 2005. "Asian Diasporas, Neoliberalism, and Family: Reviewing the Case for Homosexual Asylum in the Context of Family Rights." *Social Text* 23 (3–4): 101–119.

Rincón, Omar. 2000. "Alabadas sean las ellas de pantalla." *Gaceta* 47: 14–19.

Rivero, Yeidy M. 2003. "The Performance and Reception of Televisual 'Ugliness' in *Yo soy Betty la fea.*" *Feminist Media Studies* 3 (1): 65–81.

Rofel, Lisa. 2007. *Desiring China: Experiments in Neoliberalism, Sexuality, and Public Culture.* Durham: Duke University Press.

Rosaldo, Renato. 1994. "Cultural Citizenship and Educational Democracy." *Cultural Anthropology* 9 (3): 402–411.

Rouse, Roger. 2004. "Mexican Migration and the Social Space of Postmodernism." In *Transnational Spaces,* edited by Peter Jackson, Philip Crang, and Claire Dwyer, 24–39. London: Routledge.

Rubin, Gayle. 1975. "The Traffic in Women: Notes on the 'Political Economy' of Sex." In *Toward an Anthropology of Women,* edited by Rayna R. Reiter, 157–210. New York: Monthly Review Press.

Said, Edward. 1978. *Orientalism.* New York: Pantheon Books.

———. 1994. *Culture and Imperialism.* New York: Vintage Books.

Salazar, Tania Rodríguez. 2001. *Las razones del matrimonio: Representaciones, relatos de vida y sociedad.* Guadalajara: Universidad de Guadalajara.

Sánchez Ruiz, Enrique E. 1996. "Los medios de difusión masiva: La internacionalización y las identidades en el occidente de México." In *Globalización y regionalización: El occidente de México,* edited by Humberto González Chávez and Jesús Arroyo Alejandre, 97–128. Guadalajara: Universidad de Guadalajara.

Sánchez Taylor, Jacqueline. 2000. "Tourism and 'Embodied' Commodities: Sex Tourism in the Caribbean." In *Tourism and Sex: Culture, Commerce and Coercion,* edited by Stephen Clift and Simon Carter, 41–53. London: Pinter.

Sandoval, Chela. 2000. *Methodology of the Oppressed.* Minneapolis: University of Minnesota Press.

Santa Ana, Otto. 2002. *Brown Tide Rising: Metaphors of Latinos in Contemporary American Public Discourse.* Austin: University of Texas Press.

Santiago-Valles, Kelvin. 1999. "'Higher Womanhood' among the 'Lower Races': Julia McNair Henry in Puerto Rico and the 'Burdens' of 1898." *Radical History Review* 73: 47–73.

Sassen, Saskia. 2002. "Global Cities and Survival Circuits." In *Global Woman: Nannies, Maids, and Sex Workers in the New Global Economy,* edited by Barbara Ehrenreich and Arlie Russell Hochschild, 254–274. New York: Metropolitan Books.

Savigliano, Marta E. 1995. *Tango and the Political Economy of Passion.* Boulder, CO: Westview.

Schaeffer-Grabiel, Felicity. 2006a. "Flexible Technologies of Subjectivity and Mobility across the Americas." In "Rewiring the 'Nation': The Place of Technology in American Studies," special issue, *American Quarterly* 58 (3): 891–914.

———. 2006b. "Planet-Love.com: Cyberbrides in the Americas and the Transnational Routes of U.S. Masculinity." *Signs: Journal of Women in Culture and Society* 31 (2) (Winter): 331–356.

———. 2011. "Transnational Media Wars over Sex Trafficking: Abolishing the 'New Slave Trade' or the New Nativism?" *Circuits of Visibility: Gender and Transnational Media Cultures,* edited by Radha S. Hegde, 103–123. New York: NYU Press.

Schmidt Camacho, Alicia R. 2005. "Ciudadano X." *New Centennial Review* 5 (1): 255–292.

Scott, James C. 1990. *Domination and the Arts of Resistance: Hidden Transcripts.* New Haven: Yale University Press.

Sedgwick, Eve Kosofsky. 1985. *Between Men: English Literature and Male Homosocial Desire.* New York: Columbia University Press.

Seminara, David. 2008. "Hello, I Love You, Won't You Tell Me Your Name: Inside the Green Card Marriage Phenomenon." *Backgrounder* (Center for Immigration Studies), November. http://www.cis.org/marriagefraud.

Shaw, Alison, and Katharine Charsley. 2006. "Rishtas: Adding Emotion to Strategy in Understanding British Pakistani Transnational Marriages." *Global Networks: A Journal of Transnational Affairs* 6 (4): 405–421.

Shimizu, Celine Parreñas. 2007. *The Hypersexuality of Race: Performing Asian/American Women on Screen and Scene*. Durham: Duke University Press.

"Shock Jock Rails against Mexico's Modern Women." 2003. *Christian Science Monitor*, Feb. 18. http://www.csmonitor.com/2003/0218/p01s03-woam.html.

Shorter, Edward. 1975. *The Making of the Modern Family*. New York: Basic Books.

Simons, Lisa Anne. 2001. "Marriage, Migration, and Markets: International Matchmaking and International Feminism." Ph.D. diss., University of Denver. http://usaimmigrationattorney.com/images/MarriageMigration-Markets.pdf.

Sin senos no hay paraíso. 2008–2009. Created by Gustavo Bolivar. Directed by Miguel Vaoni and Ramiro Meneses. Telemundo Studios and RTI Colombia. June 16, 2008–June 22, 2009 (U.S.).

Sin tetas no hay paraíso. 2006. Created by Gustavo Bolívar Moreno. Directed by Luis Alberto Restrepo. Caracol TV.

Smith, Anna Marie. 2001. "The Politicization of Marriage in Contemporary American Public Policy: The Defense of Marriage Act and the Personal Responsibility Act." *Citizenship Studies* 5 (3): 303–320.

Sollors, Werner. 2000. *Interracialism: Black-White Intermarriage in American History, Literature, and Law*. Oxford: Oxford University Press.

Somerville, Siobhan B. 2005. "Queer Loving." *GLQ* 11 (3): 335–370.

Sommer, Doris. 1991. *Foundational Fictions: The National Romances of Latin America*. Berkeley: University of California Press.

Spivak, Gayatri Chakravorty. 1988. "Can the Subaltern Speak?" In *Marxism and the Interpretation of Culture*, edited by Cary Nelson and Lawrence Grossberg, 271–313. London: Macmillan.

Stacey, Judith. 1990. *Brave New Families: Stories of Domestic Upheaval in Late-Twentieth-Century America*. Berkeley: University of California Press.

Stanfield, Michael. *Beauty and the Beast: Modernity, Identity, and Beauty in Colombia, 1845–1985*. Manuscript in progress.

Stern, Alexandra Minha. 2005. *Eugenic Nation: Faults and Frontiers of Better Breeding in Modern America*. Berkeley: University of California Press.

Stone, Allucquére Rosanne. 1996. *The War of Desire and Technology at the Close of the Mechanical Age*. Cambridge: MIT Press.

Stone, Lawrence. 1977. *The Family, Sex and Marriage in England, 1500–1800*. New York: Harper Colophon Books.

Streeby, Shelley. 2002. *American Sensations: Class, Empire, and the Production of Popular Culture*. Berkeley: University of California Press.

Suzuki, Nobue. 2000. "Between Two Shores: Transnational Projects and Filipina Wives in/from Japan." *Women's Studies International Forum* 23 (4): 431–444.

Tadiar, Neferti Xina M. 2004. *Fantasy Production: Sexual Economies and Other Philippine Consequences for the New World Order.* Hong Kong: Hong Kong University Press.

Tahirih Justice Center. 2009. "Frequently Asked Questions: International Marriage Broker Regulation Act of 2005 (IMBRA)." http://www.tahirih.org/site/wp-content/uploads/2009/03/FAQs-IMBRA-11.08.10.pdf.

Tayman, John. 2000. "Project Wife." *Men's Journal*, December, 136–142.

Tenório, Maria Cristina. 2002. *Las mujeres no nacen, se hacen: Modelos culturales de mujer entre adolescentes de sectores populares.* Cali, Colombia: Universidad del Valle, COLCIENCIAS.

Thai, Hung Cam. 2008. *For Better or for Worse: Vietnamese International Marriages in the New Global Economy.* New Brunswick: Rutgers University Press.

Thomas, Florence. 2001. *La mujer tiene la palabra.* Bogotá, Colombia: Aguilar.

Turkle, Sherry. 1995. *Life on the Screen: Identity in the Age of the Internet.* New York: Simon and Schuster.

Twine, France Winddance. 1998. *Racism in a Racial Democracy: The Maintenance of White Supremacy in Brazil.* New Brunswick: Rutgers University Press.

Tyrrell, Ian. 1991. *Woman's World/Woman's Empire: The Women's Christian Temperance Union in International Perspective, 1880–1930.* Chapel Hill: University of North Carolina Press.

U.S. Senate, Subcommittee on Immigration and Refugee Policy. 1986. *Hearing on Fraudulent Marriage and Fiance Arrangements to Obtain Permanent Resident Immigration Status before the Subcommittee on Immigration and Refugee Policy of the Committee on the Judiciary.* 99th Cong., 1st sess. (July 26, 1985).

Vasconcelos, José. 1997. *The Cosmic Race / La raza cósmica.* Translated by Didier T. Jaén. Baltimore: John Hopkins University Press.

Villipando, Venny. 1989. "The Business of Selling Mail-Order Brides." In *Making Waves: An Anthology of Writings by and about Asian American Women,* edited by Asian Women United of California, 318–326. Boston: Beacon.

Visweswaran, Kamala. 1994. *Fictions of Feminist Ethnography.* Minneapolis: University of Minnesota Press.

Wacquant, Loïc. 1995. "The Pugilistic Point of View: How Boxers Think and Feel about Their Trade." *Theory and Society* 24: 489–535.

———. 2004. *Body and Soul: Notebooks of an Apprentice Boxer.* Oxford: Oxford University Press.

Wade, Peter. 1997. *Race and Ethnicity in Latin America.* London: Pluto.

———. 1999. "Making Cultural Identities in Cali, Colombia." *Current Anthropology* 40 (4): 449–471.

———. 2000. *Music, Race, and Nation: Música Tropical in Colombia*. Chicago: University of Chicago Press.

A Walk in the Clouds. 1995. Directed by Alfonso Arau. Twentieth Century-Fox. 102 minutes.

Waxer, Lise. 2002. *The City of Musical Memory: Salsa, Record Grooves, and Popular Culture in Cali, Colombia*. Middletown, CT: Wesleyan University Press.

Weber, Brenda R. 2005. "Beauty, Desire, and Anxiety: The Economy of Sameness in ABC's *Extreme Makeover*." *Genders* 41. http://www.genders.org/g41/ g41_weber.html.

———. 2009. *Makeover TV: Selfhood, Citizenship, and Celebrity*. Durham: Duke University Press.

Which Way Home. 2009. Directed by Rebecca Cammisa. Documentrass Films. 90 minutes.

"Wife Jailed for Sham Marriage." 2004. *CBC News*, October 1. http://www.cbc. ca/news/story/2004/10/01/shamwedding_041001.html.

Wilson, Ara. 2004. *The Intimate Economies of Bangkok: Tomboys, Tycoons, and the Avon Ladies in the Global City*. Berkeley: University of California Press.

Wolf, Naomi. 2003. "The Porn Myth." *New York*. http://nymag.com/nymetro/ news/trends/n_9437/.

Wright, Melissa W. 2006. *Disposable Women and Other Myths about Global Capitalism*. New York: Routledge.

Writing Desire. 2000. Directed by Ursula Biemann. VHS. New York: Women Make Movies. 23 minutes.

Yang, Wen-Shan, and Melody Chia-Wen Lu, eds. 2010. *Asian Cross-Border Marriage Migration: Demographic Patterns and Social Issues*. Amsterdam: Amsterdam University Press.

Yeoh, Brenda S. A., and Theodora Lam. 2009. "The Costs of (Im)mobility: Children Left Behind and Children Who Migrate with a Parent." In *Perspectives on Gender and Migration*, 120–148. New York: United Nations.

Young, Robert J. C. 1995. *Colonial Desire: Hybridity in Theory, Culture and Race*. London: Routledge.

Yuh, Ji-Yeon. 2002. *Beyond the Shadow of Camptown: Korean Military Brides in America*. New York: NYU Press.

Yuval-Davis, Nira. 1997. *Gender and Nation*. London: Sage.

———. 1999. "The 'Multi-Layered Citizen': Citizenship in the Age of Globalization." *International Feminist Journal of Politics* 1 (1): 119–136.

Yuval-Davis, Nira, and Pnina Werbner, eds. 1999. *Women, Citizenship and Difference*. London: Zed Books.

Zaldivar, R. A. 1985. "Fake Marriage to Enter U.S. Called Epidemic." *Miami Herald*, July 24, 1A.

Zavella, Patricia. 1993. "Feminist Insider Dilemmas: Constructing Ethnic Identity with 'Chicana' Informants." *Frontiers: A Journal of Women's Studies* 13 (3): 53–76.

———. 1997. "'Playing with Fire': The Gendered Construction of Chicana/ Mexicana Sexuality." In *The Gender/Sexuality Reader: Culture, History, Political Economy*, edited by Roger N. Lancaster and Micaela di Leonardo, 402–418. New York: Routledge.

———. 2003. *"Talkin' Sex*: Chicanas and Mexicanas Theorize about Silences and Sexual Pleasures." In *Chicana Feminisms: A Critical Reader*, edited by Gabriela Arredondo, Aída Hurtado, Norma Klahn, Olga Nájera Ramírez and Patricia Zavella, 228–253. Durham: Duke University Press.

Zelizer, Viviana A. 2005. *The Purchase of Intimacy*. Princeton: Princeton University Press.

Limón, José, 180n38

Lone Star (film), 46

Love and intimacy: aspiration and, 6; authenticity of, 3, 17–19, 21–22, 28, 35, 81, 137, 142; barriers to, 7; commercialization of, 2–3, 9–10, 176n87; conquest through, 67–68, 80, 180n40; courtship and, 5; economics of, 6, 9, 12, 16; expressions of, 22; feminists and, 55, 176n2; in film, 46–47, 65, 67, 179n33, 180n38; goals for, 9; as heterosexual, 2, 9–10, 16, 22, 25, 27, 35, 167n62; migration for, 8, 35, 37; mobility and, 52–53, 135; as myth, 139; nationalism and, 67, 154; as obligation, 21, 161; opportunity for, 15, 139; outlaw and, 138, 141–42, 161; politics of, 22; pornography as opposed to, 156, 158–59, 194n52; reciprocity in, 157; as romantic, 1, 6–8, 21, 35, 37, 52, 166nn41–42, 175n83, 175n85; sacrifice for, 151, 157, 193n37; self-realization for, 7; subjectivity of, 47; transformation through, 160; trust and, 32, 141, 157; in U.S., 32, 168n2; as virtual, 6, 72. *See also* Capitalism; Choice, freedom of; Citizenship; Commercialization; Consumption; Cybermarriage; Democracy; Femininity; Imperialism, U.S.; Patriotism; Sexuality

Love for Rent (film), 159–61, 195n54

Loving v. Virginia, 42–43, 171n34

Lugones, Maria C., 165n35

Luibhéid, Eithne, 25, 37, 40, 170n16

Lutwak v. United States, 170n11

LWL. *See* Latin-Women-List

Machismo, 60–64, 67, 76, 80, 178n23, 178n26, 180n37, 180n39

Mail-order brides: from Asia and Russia, 4; cybermarriage for, 54; exploitation and, 17, 48, 144, 160–61; legislation for, 137; stereotypes for, 79; visibility of, 39

La Malinche, 65, 179n34

Malinchista, 65, 67, 71, 180n35

Malintzin. *See* La Malinche

Maria Full of Grace (film), 50

Marketing: of body, 131, 190n74; capitalism and, 2; of Latinas, 1–2, 9–10, 12, 20, 23, 92–93, 94, 131, 164n22. *See also* "Colombia Is Passion"; Cybermarriage; International Marriage Broker; International marriage broker; Sexuality; *specific brokers*

Martin, Emily, 131

Masculinity. *See* Latin men; Western men

Match.com, 49, 183n13

Media: on cybermarriage, 17; familiarity with U.S. culture through, 54; from Mexico, 16, 181n47. See also *Telenovelas*

Men. *See* Latin men; Western men

Meritocracy, individualism and, 16, 70, 96, 144, 150

Messner, Michael A., 103

Messner, Michael M., 99

Methodology of the Oppressed (Sandoval), 191n8

Mexican Wives, 56–57, 176n4, 177n6

Mexico: attitudes of, 55–56; as conservative, 71; corruption and violence in, 10–11, 55; courtship in, 73–74, 187n19; cybermarriage industry in, 3, 10, 54–55; family reunification immigration from, 40, 172n39, 172n41; fertility rates in, 58, 177n12; gay marriage and adoption in, 63; image of, 65; laws in, 63; NAFTA and, 3, 59, 153, 164n24; Operation Gatekeeper and, 163n3; peso crisis in, 58, 177n11; remittances to, 58; technology industries in, 59, 71, 77; tourism in, 77; U.S. films in, 65, 179n33; values of, 58. *See also* Catholicism; Class system; Consumption; Femininity; Gender; Internet; *Machismo*; Media; North American Free Trade Agreement; Prostitution; Protestantism; Trafficking; Vacation Romance Tour, in Guadalajara, Mexico

Migration: chain of love and, 23–24, 167nn53–54; family reunification for, 34, 38, 40, 86, 172n39, 172n41,

ABOUT THE AUTHOR

Felicity Amaya Schaeffer is Associate Professor in the Feminist Studies Department and is affiliated with the Latin American and Latino Studies Department at the University of California, Santa Cruz.